THE JOHN HARVARD LIBRARY

Bernard Bailyn
Editor-in-Chief

VIEWS AND REVIEWS
IN AMERICAN LITERATURE
HISTORY AND FICTION

FIRST SERIES

By

WILLIAM GILMORE SIMMS

Edited by C. Hugh Holman

THE BELKNAP PRESS OF
HARVARD UNIVERSITY PRESS

Cambridge, Massachusetts

1962

Distributed in Great Britain by Oxford University Press, London

Library of Congress Catalog Card Number 62-17226

Printed in the United States of America

CONTENTS

VIEWS AND REVIEWS
IN AMERICAN LITERATURE
HISTORY AND FICTION

FIRST SERIES

INTRODUCTION

William Gilmore Simms was the most prolific, the most versatile, and the most successful Southern antebellum man of letters. Although he lacked the genius of Poe and his works have suffered from the corrosion of time more seriously than have John Pendleton Kennedy's and Henry Timrod's, Simms was from the early 1830's to the Civil War the outstanding Southern literary figure and as close to being a representative writer as the Old South produced. In his long career as poet, novelist, critic, historian, biographer, essayist, and dramatist, a stream of words flowed from his busy pen; and as an editor on at least ten Southern periodicals, he encouraged and directed the flow of words from other pens than his own.

In his own day Simms's fame rested on his novels and to a very limited extent on his poetry; in ours it rests almost exclusively on two or three novels. Yet in total output Simms probably produced more literary criticism than he did any other form of writing. He steadily directed reviews, notices, literary comments, and critical essays to virtually every Southern literary journal from 1825, when he began writing for the short-lived and amateurish *Album*, until his death in 1870, at which time he was conducting a literary section in the Charleston *Courier* and contributing articles to a number of other journals. His last published work was *The Sense of the Beautiful*, an address on aesthetics published as a pamphlet in Charleston in 1870.[1] Most of this prodigious quantity of critical writing remains buried in the yellowing files of the journals in which it appeared, much of it is unsigned, and in many cases the problem of accurate attribution is virtually insolu-

---

[1] *The Sense of the Beautiful. An Address* (Charleston, 1870).

ble; and all copies of many issues of the journals themselves seem to have crumbled away to dust. Thus Simms is less known as a critic than he is in any other role.[2]

The bulk of this criticism shows seriousness about literature, a desire to be honest, a reasonably firm adherence to standards, and adequacy without brilliance. Simms's views of art and life were seldom original; he borrows freely from the general Romantic tenets of his age and at the same time demonstrates clearly that he has gone to school to the British quarterlies and the Scottish "common sense" critics.[3] Typical of his time, he has debts to Coleridge and Carlyle that defy measure and analysis. Professor Parks, who has explored a large amount of Simms's uncollected critical writing, concludes that "he was a good but not a great critic." [4] Thus it is not surprising that Simms has not found a significant place in the history of American criticism. Furthermore, he collected his criticism only once, for Wiley and Putnam's Library of American Books, as *Views and Reviews in American Literature, History and Fiction*, First Series and Second Series.[5]

[2] Edd Winfield Parks, *William Gilmore Simms As Literary Critic* (University of Georgia Monographs, No. 7, Athens, 1961) is the only extended study in print of Simms's criticism. Raymond C. Palmer's dissertation, "The Prose Fiction Theories of William Gilmore Simms" (Indiana University, 1946); C. Hugh Holman's dissertation, "William Gilmore Simms's Theory and Practice of Historical Fiction" (University of North Carolina, 1949); and Edward T. Herbert's dissertation, "William Gilmore Simms As Editor and Literary Critic" (University of Wisconsin, 1957) are all unpublished. Bernard Smith, in *Forces in American Criticism* (New York, 1939), pp. 125–131, is one of the few historians of American criticism to take Simms seriously.

[3] See H. H. Clark, "Changing Attitudes in Early American Criticism," *The Development of American Literary Criticism*, ed. Floyd Stovall (Chapel Hill, 1955), pp. 15–74. Simms reflected, apparently often unconsciously, most of the critical issues and movements of literary criticism in America before 1850.

[4] Parks, *Simms As Critic*, p. 110.

[5] The title-page of each carries the date 1845, although the First Series volume appeared in 1846 and the Second Series volume in 1847. These were paperbound books; they were also offered for sale bound together in cloth in one volume in 1847.

These collections are not truly representative of Simms's total criticism,[6] for they were assembled for special purposes
and as a part of a heated literary controversy over nationalism.

Views and Reviews, First Series, is the best known and the
best of the volumes. Publication of the Second Series was de-
layed, and when it did appear the volume was greatly shortened from Simms's original plans. The First Series assembles
a group of Simms's critical writings which were selected, he
said, to be "illustrative of our history, our materials of art, the
moral of our aims, and the true development of our genius."[7]
It is united by common themes and beliefs: the need for a native literature, the belief that such a native literature should
find its subjects in the American past, an adherence to Jeffer-
sonian-Jacksonian agrarianism with an attendant distrust of
cities, industry, and capitalism, and a commitment to the idea
that literature flourishes best in an egalitarian and not an aristocratic society. *Views and Reviews* was also a virtual manifesto
in the Young America literary wars of the 1840's. Thus it is
an important document in American literary and cultural history, whatever its weaknesses as criticism may be.

Views and Reviews, First Series, consisted of eleven essays,
all originally published in Southern literary journals in the
1840's. Five of the essays are examples of the nineteenth-
century review article, owing obvious debts in form and manner to the British quarterlies. These essays employ books as
the bases for extended comments on the subjects of the books.
The other six essays are the parts of a series of lectures on
American history as a subject for fictional and artistic treatment.

The first essay, "Americanism in Literature," struck the

[6] Parks, in *Simms As Critic*, p. 112, states that these volumes gained "a certain unity but at the expense of a fair representation of Simms' critical
views."

[7] See "Advertisement" below, p. 5.

keynote for the volume. It argues for a distinctively American subject matter and manner in literature and vigorously asks for freedom from both British models and British critical standards, on the grounds that a democratic society can and must produce a native and democratic art.

In the six connected essays that make up "The Epochs and Events of American History as Suited to the Purposes of Art in Fiction," Simms first discusses the kind of truth which the new "scientific" history seeks. As opposed to this high and exclusive concentration on fact, he urges that the artist seek truth to human motives, to human aspirations, to the appreciation of virtue and the admiration of heroes and present this truth as the core and meaning of a nation's history. He then takes up the story of Benedict Arnold as material for historical drama and asks that the dramatic poet rather than attempt a literal record seek out a moment of action in which the "ideal of a hero" can be presented. In converting Arnold into the subject matter of such a drama, Simms takes liberties with history that often appear ludicrous; yet, as John Paul Pritchard has pointed out, "Simms's argument anticipates recent theory about artistic process. It derives from Coleridge's concept of the secondary imagination at work together with the fancy, and adds to it the New Critic's emphasis upon the relation between artist and image." [8] Simms next discusses as subjects for art the four periods of American history — the period of exploration from the voyage of Cabot to the settlement of Jamestown, the period from Jamestown to the accession of George the Third, the period of the Revolution and the early Federal era, and the period from the beginning of the nineteenth century to 1845. He then examines Hernando de Soto and the French settlements of Gaspard de Coligny as subjects for romance, and concludes his exploration of American history as a subject for a vital and native art with speculations on

[8] *Criticism in America* (Norman, Okla., 1956), p. 96.

the kinds of paintings that would represent the essence of the Pocahontas story. The six essays taken together form a passionate assertion that there is no paucity of American materials for romance and make an implicit plea that American writers and artists begin more vigorously to employ them.

In the article "Literature and Art Among the American Aborigines," ostensibly a review of two works by Henry R. Schoolcraft, Simms continues his efforts to demonstrate the artistic use of American materials. He sees in the American Indian all the materials of primitive epic art, plus a freedom from the bondage of historical record and fact, a freedom that allows the artist a full use of his imagination.

The essay on "Daniel Boon" is a review of Boone's autobiography. In it Simms elevates the historical figure of Boone to the proportions of a mythic image and sees in him all the virtues of a natural and primitive paradise. In many respects this essay is a biographical sketch but one that seeks the significant meaning in Boone's life and is close in method and tone to Thomas Carlyle's essays in *On Heroes, Hero-Worship, and the Heroic in History*.

This debt to Carlyle becomes very obvious in "Cortes and the Conquest of Mexico," a long review essay based on Prescott's history and *The Dispatches of Hernando Cortes*. Here Simms sketches in detail Cortes's conquest of Mexico, emphasizing the attributes that made the Spanish commander an archetypal military hero.

The concluding essay on "The Writings of James Fenimore Cooper" is a careful analysis of Cooper's method in his novels, a piece of technical criticism which demonstrates what Bernard Smith meant when he said that Simms "had a decided interest in the mechanics of composition — plot, invention — a greater interest by far than the famous critics of New England." [9] William Cullen Bryant praised this essay as the

[9] *Forces in American Criticism*, p. 126.

best and most judicious treatment of Cooper's novels.[10] In it Simms also defends Cooper from his Whig attackers and pays tribute to his contributions to the making of a national literature.

None of the themes and ideas in *Views and Reviews* were new in the 1840's either to American writers or to Simms. One of the principal values of the volume lies in how well it sums up many aspects of Simms's own career and how well it brings together many of the aspects of the movement toward a native and self-consciously national literature in America in the first half of the nineteenth century. It can best be understood in the light of certain events and recurring ideas in Simms's life and in his cultural environment.

One of the basic attitudes in *Views and Reviews* is, surprisingly, a liberal democratic egalitarianism that expresses itself in passionate adherence to Jacksonian democracy and in opposition to the conservative Whig view of the national and artistic life. With Simms that Jacksonianism was an intellectual faith and an emotional commitment.

Gilmore Simms was the son of an Irish immigrant, who failed in a small mercantile business in Charleston, South Carolina, left his two-year-old son in the care of the boy's maternal grandmother, and went west, first to Tennessee and later to Mississippi.[11] In Tennessee the elder Simms became an officer of undetermined rank in the Tennessee Volunteers under

[10] "Simms," *Homes of American Authors* (New York, 1853), p. 262.

[11] There is no adequate biographical study of Simms. The only book-length biography, by William P. Trent (Boston, 1892), although incomplete, sometimes in error in fact, and often poor in historical and critical judgment, is still the most nearly reliable treatment. A. S. Salley's biographical sketch in *The Letters of William Gilmore Simms*, ed. Mary C. S. Oliphant, A. T. Odell, and T. C. D. Eaves (5 vols.; Columbia, S. C., 1952–1956), I, lix–lxxxix, contains much new information but is not always accurate and should be used with care. *The Letters* and their extensive annotation form an invaluable repository of information on Simms's life between 1832 and 1870. The biographical data in the Introduction and Chronology of the present edition are drawn primarily from these sources.

General Andrew Jackson, was active in Jackson's campaigns against the Creek and the Seminole Indians, and fought in the Western Army against the invaders of New Orleans.[12] After the Peace in 1815 he settled in Mississippi, and there his city-bred son visited at least twice, traveling over wide ranges of the Indian country and delighting in the rough frontier life he found there. The image of his stalwart father remained in Gilmore Simms's mind throughout his life.[13] Thus one of his early and strong emotional ties was to "Old Hickory," and never did he break it, or even desire to.

But the Irish immigrant's son had himself chosen the literary life, after a brief experience with the law, and in the late 1820's he found himself in a proud, aristocratic city, struggling for status against a virtual caste system. In 1848 he was to declare:

> Our manners, moulded with the nicest art,
> Fit for the court, but foreign to the mart;
> Our pride, that points to ancestors of worth,
> Whose deeds, perchance, were nobler than their birth,

and a little further along in the poem to say:

> The generous youth, in mind and soul erect,
> Is on the threshold of performance check'd;
> Let him refuse to bend as they demand,
> And he becomes a stranger in the land.[14]

In 1852 he wrote of a Charleston lady as one "denuded of vigour by the successive intermarriages of cousins for an hundred years." [15] The egalitarian distrust of the aristocracy was being strengthened by observation. In 1829, after editing the *Southern Literary Gazette* (1828–1829) and publishing a verse pamphlet and three volumes of poetry, Simms invested his small

---

[12] *Letters*, I, 160; *Southern Bivouac*, I (October, 1885), 261; *International Magazine*, V (1852), 433.

[13] Trent, *Simms*, pp. 12–13. Trent is paraphrasing a manuscript "Personal Memorabilia" by Simms.

[14] *Charleston and Her Satirists; A Scribblement* (Charleston, 1848), pp. 6, 11.

[15] *The Golden Christmas* (Charleston, 1852), p. 20.

maternal inheritance in a daily newspaper, the Charleston *City Gazette*. Founded in 1787 and edited at one time by Peter Freneau, brother of the poet, it was an avowed party journal, a voice of the party of Jefferson. It was, therefore, also the spokesman for President Jackson and the cause of Union in the Nullification Controversy which arose as a result of South Carolina's attempt to nullify the Tariff of 1828. As a party editor supporting "Old Hickory," Simms proved to be vigorous, direct, and tactless, often arguing intemperately and sometimes unpleasantly *ad hominem*. He was a committed Jacksonian and a consistent Jeffersonian. He even supported Daniel Webster in his debate with Robert Y. Hayne and praised his "able and unanswerable defense of the Constitution." [16] He asserted his faith in the good intentions of his fellowmen to the North and was willing to join James Blair when he pled with Congress for relief from the "tariff of abominations." [17] He called Secretary of the Treasury McLane's proposed tariff in 1832 a compromise to which neither party could in reason object,[18] and his support of the Adams tariff bill, which passed with the South Carolina Unionists voting for it, brought upon him the charge that he had sold out to Northern manufacturers and capitalists, a charge which he repeatedly and angrily refuted. On one occasion he narrowly escaped being attacked by an angry mob of nullifiers.[19] As the nullification sentiment grew, the number of subscribers to the *City Gazette* decreased, and its revenue dropped dangerously. On June 7, 1832, Simms sorrowfully sold the newspaper, assuming its large debts himself, and the period of his greatest political involvement was at an end. He was abandoning, he later wrote, "the profession of the patriot and politician." [20] This painful struggle had annealed his Jeffersonian spirit although

---

[16] The Charleston *City Gazette*, March 9, 1830.
[17] *Ibid.*, March 7, 1832.
[18] *Ibid.*, May 8, 1832.
[19] Trent, *Simms*, pp. 62–65.
[20] *Guy Rivers* (New York, 1855), p. 9.

it had not calmed his always intemperate emotions.[21] Simms
was to be an ardent supporter of Andrew Jackson, Martin
Van Buren, and their party until he deflected to General
Zachary Taylor over the slavery issue in 1848.[22]

It was natural, too, for so intense a Jacksonian democrat to
be concerned with an egalitarian literature that had its roots
in American soil and had shrugged off the forms of art and
life which aristocratic societies, and particularly that of England, had developed. Almost from the beginning of his career,
the contrast of American culture to that of England had been
of concern to Simms. One of his very first publications when
he turned Northward after the debacle of the *Gazette* in 1832
was a long review of Mrs. Francis Milton Trollope's *Domestic Manners of the Americans* in the *American Quarterly Review*.[23] Throughout his life he remained keenly aware of the
conflict of attitudes about art between British and American
critics, often alluding to it in his correspondence and in essays
such as his articles on "Southern Literature" in the *Magnolia*.[24]
As the essays in *Views and Reviews* demonstrate, Simms
carried the issue back to Thomas Jefferson's patriotic claims
in his *Notes on the State of Virginia* in 1787:

So far the Count de Buffon has carried this new theory of the
tendency of nature to belittle her productions on this side of the Atlantic. Its application to the race of whites, transplanted from Europe

[21] On November 25, 1832, in a letter to James Lawson, he called South
Carolina "this, once high, but now damnably defiled scene of brutal prosti-
tution and tyranny" and expressed the belief that "her name and star place
[should be] blotted out, and her territory divided among the contiguous &
more loyal states," *Letters*, I, 47.

[22] On Charleston and Jeffersonianism, see the excellent brief discussion by
Henry Adams, *History of the United States of America during the First
Administration of Thomas Jefferson* (New York, 1889), I, Chap. v. On the
nullification controversy, see C. S. Boucher, *The Nullification Controversy
in South Carolina* (Chicago, 1916) and Frederic Bancroft, *Calhoun and the
South Carolina Nullification Movement* (Baltimore, 1928).

[23] "Mrs. Trollope and the Americans," *American Quarterly Review*, XII
(September, 1832), 109-133; reprinted in modified form in *Views and Reviews*, Second Series, pp. 1-56.

[24] *Magnolia*, III (January, February, 1841), 1-6, 69-74.

remained for the Abbé Raynal. "One must be astonished (he says) that America has not yet produced one good poet, one able mathematician, one man of genius in a single art or a single science." "America has not yet produced one good poet." When we shall have existed as a people as long as the Greeks did before they produced a Homer, the Romans a Virgil, the French a Racine and Voltaire, the English a Shakespeare and Milton, should this reproach be still true, we will enquire from what unfriendly causes it has proceeded, that the other countries of Europe and quarters of the earth shall not have inscribed any name in the roll of poets. . . . As in philosophy and war, so in government, in oratory, in painting, in the plastic art, we might shew that America, though but a child of yesterday, has already given hopeful proofs of genius, as well of the nobler kinds, which arouse the best feelings of man, which call him into action, which substantiate his freedom, and conduct him to happiness, as of the subordinate, which serve to amuse him only. We therefore suppose, that this reproach is as unjust as it is unkind; and that, of the geniuses which adorn the present age, America contributes its full share.[25]

To these remarks the British *Monthly Review* had promptly replied:

It is but a very few years since the Americans set up for themselves as an independent people, and these *children of yesterday*, with the usual presumption of youth, affect to consider themselves as the most enlightened race existing; and hold the contemporary descendants of their ancestors very cheap! . . .

As to the articles of genius and learning, the Americans do not require our antiquity before they produce a '*Shakespeare or a Milton*'; they had not to undergo the progressive drudgery of emerging from barbarism, for they carried over with them all the knowledge of the age which produced these poets, and have enjoyed regular importations from thence down to the present day. Rural scenery is favourable to poetic inspiration; so that amid the wild novelty which the Americans have for near two centuries enjoyed '*should this reproach be still true*' some other cause must be assigned, for the Muses not having accompanied British freedom when they crossed the Atlantic.[26]

This controversy continued, fed by the heightened feelings of the War of 1812 and its aftermath, revived by the ungenerous remarks of British travelers in America, and intensified from

---

[25] Ed. William Peden (Chapel Hill, 1954), pp. 64-65.
[26] *Monthly Review*, LXXVIII (1788), 377, 459.

time to time by the lingering sense of colonialism and inferiority in America.[27] The publication in England and America in 1840 of Henry Reeve's translation of Part II of Alexis de Tocqueville's *Democracy in America*, with its discussion of the "Influence of Democracy on the Action of Intellect in the United States," revived and intensified these issues.[28] But in the 1840's an influential group of American writers, critics, and poets were supporting the British position, notable among them being Henry Wadsworth Longfellow.[29]

Thus when Simms embarked upon a defense of American writing in the essays in *Views and Reviews* he was engaging in a conflict of long standing, one in which his emotional and political affiliations had already determined his stance. The vigor with which he defended the richness of American materials for romance was also dictated in part by an active career as novelist, dramatist, and narrative poet in which he had dealt extensively with indigenous material. But a large factor was also the persistence in American letters of a tendency to deplore the absence in American life of those elements out of which art of the highest order could be fashioned.

James Fenimore Cooper, who, as Simms pointed out in *Views and Reviews*, did as much as any single writer to demonstrate the usability of American materials for romance, also lamented the absence of such materials. In 1828, in *Notions of the Americans*, he had written:

The second obstacle [the first was competition with unprotected British books] against which American literature has to contend, is in the poverty of materials. There is scarcely an ore which contributes

[27] See William B. Cairns, *British Criticism of American Writings, 1783–1815* (University of Wisconsin Studies in Language and Literature, No. 1, Madison, 1918) and *British Criticism of American Writings, 1815–1833* (*ibid.*, No. 14, Madison, 1922).

[28] Alexis de Tocqueville, *Democracy in America*, trans. Henry Reeve, ed. Phillips Bradley (New York, 1957), II, 411–436, 505–506.

[29] Longfellow's clearest statement on the subject is in chapter xx of his novel, *Kavanagh* (1849).

to the wealth of the author, that is found, here, in veins as rich as in Europe. There are no annals for the historian; no follies (beyond the most vulgar and commonplace) for the satirist; no manners for the dramatist; no obscure fictions for the writer of romance; no gross and hardy offences against decorum for the moralist; nor any of the rich artificial auxiliaries of poetry. The weakest hand can extract a spark from the flint, but it would baffle the strength of a giant to attempt kindling a flame from a pudding-stone. . . . I have never seen a nation so much alike in my life, as the people of the United States, and what is more, they are not only like each other, but they are remarkably like that which common sense tells them they ought to resemble. . . .

. . . All the attempts to blend history with romance in America have been comparatively failures, (and perhaps fortunately,) since the subjects are too familiar to be treated with the freedom that the imagination absolutely requires.[30]

Such an attitude was common in America; for example, E. W. Johnston in 1831 asked, "Without fable—without associations—without manners to paint—how can there be imagination?" [31] Hawthorne was to assert it as late as 1860:

No author, without a trial, can conceive of the difficulty of writing a romance about a country where there is no shadow, no antiquity, no mystery, no picturesque and gloomy wrong, nor anything but a commonplace prosperity, in broad and simple daylight, as is happily the case with my dear native land. It will be very long, I trust, before romance-writers may find congenial and easily handled themes, either in the annals of our stalwart republic, or in any characteristic and probable events of our individual lives. Romance and poetry, ivy, lichens, and wallflowers, need ruin to make them grow.[32]

To Simms, who was convinced that a fresh and different material for romantic treatment existed in America, such statements needed refutation, particularly when they came from the lips of the admired Cooper, who had himself "convinced the people not only that there was gold in the land, but that

---

[30] *Notions of the Americans* (Philadelphia, 1828), Letter XXIII. The similarity of Cooper's sentiments to those of Alexis de Tocqueville in Part II, Book I, chapter xii of *Democracy in America* is notable.

[31] "American Literature," *Southern Review*, VII (August, 1831), 443.

[32] "The Preface," *The Marble Faun* (Boston, 1883), p. 15.

the gold of the land was good," [33] and from such revered local sources as Hugh Swinton Legaré's *Southern Review*.[34]

A further reason for his defending the adequacy of American materials for fictional purposes was that Simms's reputation rested primarily on his work as an historical novelist, and his career fluctuated with the vicissitudes of the public attitude toward the historical romance and the market for native fiction.

Simms began his novelistic career in 1833 with a crime novelette, *Martin Faber*, which owed debts of style, subject, and social attitude to William Godwin. The following year he published *Guy Rivers*, the first of his novels of the Southwestern border, this one laid in the gold fields of Georgia in the 1820's. This romance was the first of the "Border Romances," novels dealing with the fourth of his periods of American history, that covering "the progress of interior discovery and settlement." [35] In 1835 he reached what was perhaps his peak as a novelist with *The Yemassee*, a romance of Indian warfare against the white settlements in South Carolina in 1715, and *The Partisan*, the first of his seven romances of the American Revolution, concerned with the guerrilla warfare of General Francis Marion. The second of the romances of the American Revolution, *Mellichampe*, appeared the following year. In 1838 he published another "Border Romance," *Richard Hurdis*, a tale of outlaw gangs in Alabama, and *Pelayo*, a romance laid in eighth century Spain. In 1839 appeared *The Damsel of Darien*, a romance of the Spanish conquest of Peru. The next year came a sequel to *Richard Hurdis*, *Border Beagles*, based on the John A. Murrell gang in Mississippi. The third of the romances of the American Revolution, *The Kinsmen* (in later editions called *The Scout*), was published in

---

[33] Simms, "The Writings of James Fenimore Cooper," below, p. 267.

[34] See Benjamin T. Spencer, *The Quest for Nationality* (Syracuse, 1957) for an extended treatment of these movements in American literary history.

[35] Simms, "The Four Periods of American History," below, pp. 75–86.

1841 and was followed the same year by *Confession*, a God-winian tale of crime. With the publication in 1842 of *Beauchampe* (in later editions published as two books, *Charlemont* and *Beauchampe*), a novel based on the Beauchampe-Sharpe murder case in Kentucky, Simms's publication of full-length novels came to a stop until 1851.[36] In these ten most fruitful years of Simms's novelistic career he had concentrated most of his attention on his "four periods of American history," and he had not neglected any of them. That the stream of romances grounded in American materials ceased in 1842 was the result of no wavering in Simms's faith in his material, but was the consequence of major changes in the financial structure of the nation and in the methods of book publishing.

The Panic of 1837 was a major financial collapse that continued until it reached its low point in February, 1843, and then began a gradual recovery that lasted for four years.[37] One result of this depression was a badly deflated book market. In 1838 books were selling slowly; by 1841 they were selling hardly at all. Furthermore, new and rapid printing methods and a new process for manufacturing paper made the production of "cheap books" practical, particularly in the absence of copyright protection for foreign writers. In 1838 the *Great Western* and the *Sirius* crossed the Atlantic by steam. This new and rapid link between England and America quickly resulted in a host of "mammoth weeklies," which reprinted in atrocious form the most popular English writers and offered them for sale at prices sometimes as low as six cents. N. P. Willis's *Corsair*, Park Benjamin's *Brother Jonathan*, Jonas Winchester's *New World*, and George Roberts's

[36] *Count Julian* was published in 1845, but it was written in 1837–1838 as a sequel to *Pelayo* and was lost in transit for five years.

[37] Commodity prices, based on the Warren-Pearson wholesale price index for all commodities, New York, 1910–1914, equal to 100, fell from 110 in 1838 to 75 in 1843, and then rose to 82 in 1848. (Richard B. Morris, *Encyclopedia of American History* [New York, 1953], pp. 508–509.)

Boston Notion, which advertised "104 square feet of reading matter," were exploiting the rich popularity of the English novel of the late 1830's and the 1840's.[38] Traditional publishing procedures began to undergo drastic change.

The successors to the illustrious House of Mathew Carey told the story with grave succinctness:

The system of cheap publications . . . between 1839 and 1843, rendered general literature less attractive [than before]. It was impossible to sell a work of fiction except in paper, and large stocks of Cooper's novels, bound in cloth and utterly unsalable, had to be stripped of their covers and be done up in paper to find a market. The house [of Lea and Blanchard, at this time] gradually withdrew from enterprises like these; it ceased to publish for Irving, it sold the stereotype plates of Cooper's novels.[39]

In 1841 Simms said:

The publishers are very costive — the sales are terribly diminished within the last few years. You will perceive that Irving now writes almost wholly for magazines and Cooper & myself are almost the only persons whose novels are printed — certainly, we are almost the only persons who hope to get anything for them. . . . In this country an Edition now instead of 4 or 5,000 copies, is scarce 2,000. My Damsel of Darien was 3,000. My Kinsmen not more than 2,000.[40]

In 1847 he wrote: ". . . my income from Literature which in 1835 was $6000 per annum, is scarce $1500 now, owing to the operation of cheap reprints which pay publishers & printers profits only & yield the author little or nothing." [41] The situation was made unmistakably plain in a letter which Simms received from his publishers, Lea and Blanchard, in December, 1841:

[38] Frank Luther Mott, *A History of American Magazines, 1741–1850* (Cambridge, Mass., 1938), pp. 354–363.

[39] Anon., *One Hundred and Fifty Years of Publishing 1785–1935* [Lea and Febiger] (Philadelphia, 1935), pp. 25–26.

[40] Letter to James Henry Hammond, August 16, 1841, *Letters,* I, 271.

[41] Letter to James Henry Hammond, December 24, 1847, *Letters,* II, 385.

"Confession" is a total failure, "The Kinsmen" will do better. We do not see much hope in the future for the American writer in light literature — as a matter of profit it might be abandoned.

The channel seems to be glutted with periodical literature particularly the mammoth Weeklies — besides which we go into the market for $1.50 a copy agt English reprints at 90¢.[42]

So Simms turned in the 1840's to biography, criticism, novelettes for the "cheap book" market, and tales for the annuals and gift books.

Early in the decade he became closely affiliated with the Young America group of writers and critics, and this affiliation was to prove to be of major importance. From 1832 on Simms had been closely associated with the Knickerbocker writers and so nearly a part of their "inner circle" that in his own time he was often thought of as in the New York group. The chief among these friends were the poet and editor, William Cullen Bryant; the minor poet, John Lawson; and the actor, Edwin Forrest. For a while in the 1830's he was a contributor to the powerful *Knickerbocker Magazine*, edited by Lewis Gaylord Clark.

But in the 1840's he became active with a group of new writers and critics who were liberal and radical democrats in politics, ardent nationalists in literature, and committed foes of conservatism in Whig politics and Anglophile criticism. This group, known as the Young America group, had grown out of the Tetractys Club, formed in the middle 1830's in New York City by Evert A. Duyckinck, William A. Jones, J. B. Auld, and Russell Trevett. Cornelius Mathews was soon added as a regular member; George Duyckinck was frequently present at the meetings, and others — notably Herman Melville in the late 1840's — met with the group from time to time. These young men were Loco-foco Democrats, optimistic celebrators of America, believers in its "manifest des-

[42] Earl L. Bradsher, *Mathew Carey: Editor, Author, and Publisher* (New York, 1912), p. 93.

tiny," [43] and intense nationalists about art and literature. They wanted a national literature and were willing to see it develop from local and sectional roots; they were willing for their humor to smack rudely of the frontier; and they were committed heart and soul, under the leadership of Mathews, to work for the establishment of an international copyright law. Furthermore, they viewed the revolution in publishing as an opportunity to present good books inexpensively to a growing mass audience.[44]

Their first corporate enterprise was a monthly magazine, *Arcturus*, published from December, 1840, to May, 1842, with Evert Duyckinck and Mathews as joint editors. They were also active in the *Democratic Review*, Duyckinck serving in several editorial capacities on it from time to time.

To Lewis Gaylord Clark and the *Knickerbocker Magazine* circle the Young America group was anathema. Clark's circle consisted of conservative Whigs, Anglophiles and internationalists, and passionate foes of a copyright law. Clark looked upon the *Democratic Review* and the Young America writers as divinely ordained targets for his scorn and vitriolic attack. Cornelius Mathews, the author of *The Career of Puffer Hopkins* and *Big Abel and the Little Manhattan*, he blasted with malicious glee from the beginning. Simms, although a former contributor,[45] became an object of attack when he began expressing Young America ideas in 1842. Edgar Allan Poe became the object of some of the most telling and poisonous

[43] The phrase was coined by John L. O'Sullivan in the *Democratic Review*, an "official" organ of the Young America group. (Arthur M. Schlesinger, Jr., *The Age of Jackson* [Boston, 1946], p. 427.)

[44] Detailed studies of the Young America group and its literary wars in the 1840's may be found in John Stafford, *The Literary Criticism of "Young America": A Study in the Relationship of Politics and Literature, 1837–1850* (Berkeley and Los Angeles, 1952) and Perry Miller, *The Raven and the Whale: The War of Words and Wits in the Era of Poe and Melville* (New York, 1956).

[45] *Knickerbocker Magazine*, VII (February, 1836), 169; VII (January, 1836), 37; XII (November, 1838), 416.

attacks in American literary history after the publication of his "Marginalia" in the *Democratic Review* and his charge in the January 13, 1845, issue of the *Broadway Journal* that Longfellow, the archetypal poet of the Whig critics, was a plagiarist.

At one time Clark had viewed Simms as an important writer and had praised his work.[46] By 1841, however, Simms was publishing in the *Magnolia* a series of articles on "Southern Literature"[47] in which he was arguing vigorously for a national literature on native subjects, attacking Washington Irving as not being truly an American writer, accusing the editors of "the numerous *Soi-disant* literary Journals" of servile, pro-British criticism, and attacking business communities as foes of the arts —"merely trading communities have little or no moral influence," he declared.[48] Clark's recognition of these Young America sentiments was immediate; in the November issue of the *Knickerbocker* he took Southern journals to task for "prating" of a sectional literature. "Our remote contemporaries must avoid one thing," he declared. "They must not ask favor for and claim a ready acceptance of, articles which may be ill-written or otherwise objectionable, merely because they are local manufacture."[49] In April Simms replied; then with its June issue he assumed the editorship of the *Magnolia*, a post he held until June, 1843. Throughout Simms's editorship of the *Magnolia*, he and Clark fired away at each other with increasing anger and sharpness. In August, 1842, Clark, as was his custom, descended to personal abuse: "Least of all, we may add, do we recognize in *him* [Simms] a competent *arbiter literarum*; his 'lots' of labored romances—upon which Time and the silent indifference of the public, more potential than a

---

[46] See, for example, the *Knickerbocker* reviews of *The Yemassee* (V [April, 1835], 341–343) and of *The Partisan* (VI [December, 1835], 577).

[47] *Magnolia*, III (January, February, 1841), 1–6, 69–74.

[48] *Ibid.* (February, 1841), 72.

[49] *Knickerbocker*, XVIII (November, 1841), 462.

thousand censorial voices, are already doing their work—to the contrary notwithstanding . . ." [50]

Simms was abundantly ready for an alliance with the Young America group when, in March, 1843, Cornelius Mathews began with him a correspondence that grew into a friendship always rendered precarious by Simms's inability to dissimulate about Mathews's works, most of which he found less than totally satisfactory. That summer he met and liked Evert A. Duyckinck, the true leader of the Young America writers, and became a full-fledged member of the group. By the end of 1843 he had produced four long and serious articles on "International Copyright Law," the chief point of agitation for the Young America group at the time, and arranged for their publication in the *Southern Literary Messenger*.[51] His object in the series was, he wrote Fenimore Cooper, "to show . . . that great benefit enures to ourselves [from such a law], and that the chief good of the measure will be to emancipate us from the dictation of British mind." [52] He circulated a Memorial on Copyright to the Senate and the House of Representatives and enlisted the able support of his fellow South Carolinian, Dr. Edwin DeLeon, who contributed an article, "Cheap Literature: Its Character and Tendencies," to the *Southern Literary Messenger*.[53]

In 1844 some of Simms's friends in the Barnwell District, where his residence was located some seventy miles inland from Charleston, requested his permission to put him in nomination for the South Carolina Legislature. He permitted his

[50] *Ibid.*, XX (August, 1842), 200. Earlier exchanges may be found in *ibid.*, XIX (May, 1842), 496, and *Magnolia*, Vol. IV (June, 1842).

[51] *Southern Literary Messenger*, X (January, March, June, August, 1844), 7–17, 137–151, 340–349, 449–469. The March and June articles are two parts of one long letter. Benjamin T. Spencer, in *The Quest for Nationality*, p. 145, calls this series of articles "one of the most cogent arguments for copyright before the Civil War."

[52] Letter to James Fenimore Cooper, April 10, 1844, *Letters*, V, 380.

[53] In X (January, 1844), 33–39.

nomination but warned his neighbors that he was not a candidate, would "neither treat nor speechify — [would] not in short cross the road for their suffrage." [54] Although he did campaign a little during the summer, he went to New York on August 13 to attend to his literary affairs and did not return until October 28, after the election in which he had won. At the same time he was offered the editorship of a new monthly literary journal, the *Southern and Western Magazine*, commonly known as *Simms's Magazine*, which he accepted with alacrity, seeing it as a means toward the establishment of "a manly and proper organ of literature and criticism in the South." [55]

Simms not only made the *Southern and Western Magazine* virtually the Southern voice of the Young America group, but he also made it one of the most distinguished Southern journals. He published Young America writers like Duyckinck, Mathews, and J. T. Headley, and argued the cause of literary nationalism in its pages, and he made it a journal of which Edgar Allan Poe could say, "It is as ably edited as any journal of its species in America — if not more ably edited." [56] In the 135 pages of painfully small type that the "Editorial Bureau" occupied in the twelve issues of the magazine, Simms staunchly maintained the position of the Young America group, praising Poe, questioning Longfellow's originality, liking "bold and manly" Whittier for his "energy and life," preferring Hawthorne to other American writers of prose, expecting great things of Emerson "in spite of his Carlyleisms," and liking Catherine Maria Sedgwick even in the face of her attacks on slavery in *Home*. But the magazine needed a circulation of 3,000 to break even, [57] only half of which it had

---

[54] Letter to James Lawson, March 26, 1844, *Letters*, I, 410.
[55] Letter to George F. Holmes, November 18, 1844, *Letters*, I, 442.
[56] *Broadway Journal*, II (August 30, 1845), 121.
[57] John C. Guilds, "William Gilmore Simms as Magazine Editor to 1845" (unpublished dissertation, Duke University, 1954), p. 236.

attained by its second issue,[58] and it reached the end of volume two still at least a thousand short of its needs. Before its demise after twelve numbers, in December, 1845, Simms had made arrangements with Evert A. Duyckinck for the publication of a collection of his essays, including all the long articles which he had written for the *Southern and Western.*

Duyckinck, as editor of Wiley and Putnam, Publishers, was demanding an American literature and urging the utilization of modern publishing methods to reach a large audience with inexpensive books; and he was also, through "The Library of American Books," attempting to publish that literature in an adequate form. The series, a portion of the larger "Library of Choice Reading," presented material from American writers in well-printed books of 100 to 250 pages, bound in paper, and offered for sale at prices varying from 25 cents to 50 cents a copy. In many instances two of these paper bound volumes were bound together in cloth for sale at $1.00. The first volume in "The Library of American Books" was Nathaniel Hawthorne's edition of *A Journal of an African Cruiser,* by Horatio Bridge, published in mid-summer, 1845. Seven more books in the Library actually appeared in 1845: *Tales,* by Edgar A. Poe; *Letters from Italy,* by J. T. Headley; *The Wigwam and the Cabin,* First Part, a collection of short stories by W. G. Simms; *Big Abel and the Little Manhattan,* by Cornelius Mathews; *Wanderings of a Pilgrim under the Shadow of Mont Blanc,* by G. B. Cheever; *Western Clearings,* by Mary Clavers [Mrs. Caroline Kirkland]; and *The Raven and Other Poems,* by Edgar A. Poe. Among the 1846 publications in the Library were: Herman Melville's *Typee,* Hawthorne's *Mosses from an Old Manse,* J. Ross Browne's *Etchings of a Whaling Cruise;* and J. T. Headley's *The Alps and the Rhine.*[59] This list of titles indicates plainly that the short-lived

[58] Letter to Evert A. Duyckinck, February 11, 1845, *Letters,* II, 29.
[59] See Stafford, *Literary Criticism of "Young America,"* pp. 23–24; Miller,

Library was, indeed, serving the cause of American letters well.

Some time during the summer, Duyckinck apparently proposed to Simms a collection of his essays,[60] and on August 7, 1845, Simms accepted the commission, agreeing to prepare "one or two 50 cent vol. of Literary Miscellanies for the American Series." [61] He immediately set to work selecting essays and working toward two fifty-cent volumes to be bound together as the finished book. The first volume was ready and the second under way by October.[62] Then a series of delays began. When Poe's *The Raven* appeared on November 19, 1845, it carried an advertisement stating that Simms's *Views and Reviews* was "just ready." The *Broadway Journal* for November 19, 1845, announcing the publication of *The Raven* and *Western Clearings*, listed *Views and Reviews* for "publication in November." On December 4, the *Broadway Journal* listed *Views and Reviews* for "publication in December." [63] Simms expected the book in November or December, as his letters to Duyckinck show, and by February, 1846, he had grown visibly impatient at its long delay.[64] The cause of the delays is unknown, but it was May 1, 1846, before *Views and*

The Raven and the Whale, pp. 135–167; Randall Stewart, "Hawthorne's Contributions to *The Salem Advertiser*," *American Literature*, V (January, 1934), 328–329. A surprising amount of information on this series is to be found in T. O. Mabbott's Introduction to the Facsimile Text Society edition of *The Raven and Other Poems*, by Edgar A. Poe (New York, 1942), pp. vi–xviii. See also *The First One Hundred and Fifty Years: A History of John Wiley and Sons* (New York, 1957) pp. 16–19.

[60] Miller suggests that Duyckinck's motive was to give Simms's essay on "Americanism in Literature" wider circulation (*The Raven and the Whale*, p. 154).

[61] Letter to Evert A. Duyckinck, August 7, 1845, *Letters*, II, 95.

[62] Letter to Evert A. Duyckinck, October 19, 1845, *Letters*, II, 106; Letter to Evert A. Duyckinck, October 28, 1845, *Letters*, II, 110.

[63] Mabbott, Introduction to *The Raven*, pp. xi, xiv.

[64] Letter to Evert A. Duyckinck, November 13, 1845, *Letters*, II, 118; Letter to Evert A. Duyckinck, December 12, 1845, *ibid.*, II, 123; Letter to Evert A. Duyckinck, February 9, 1846, *ibid.*, II, 142.

Reviews, First Series, appeared, bound in paper to be sold for fifty cents.[65]

Views and Reviews, Second Series, fared even worse. Simms had made plans to include in it a number of his essays from a variety of journals, both Northern and Southern, as the "Advertisement" to the First Series indicates. Yet the end of June, 1846, came without copy having gone to press. Simms, evidently in response to a letter stating Wiley's intention to drop the Second Series from the Library, wrote Duyckinck, threatening suit unless the agreement was carried out; he said, "I cannot suffer my credit to be injured by a failure to publish the sequel of the work begun, and should regard it as certain ruin to the book if the second vol. were not put forth. It will not be sold till complete." And he added ruefully, "[N]ever was vol. put forth with (seemingly) so little disposition on the part of the publisher to bring it properly to the view of the public." [66] The compromise agreement immediately reached was to publish a much smaller volume than Simms had projected. Still the delays continued, for it was July, 1847, before the promised volume appeared,[67] paperbound for sale at fifty cents. It contained "The Domestic Manners of the Americans by Mrs. Trollope," "The American Sagas of the Northmen," "The Case of Major André," "Weems, the Biographer and Historian," and "The Humorous in American and British Literature." In all it had 184 pages and was only three-quarters the size of the first volume. It was also a much more heterogeneous book than the First Series, and it did not contain a single essay of the general distinction of the First Series, despite Whitman's liking for "The Humorous in American and British Literature." [68]

---

[65] *Letters*, II, 142n.

[66] Letter to Evert A. Duyckinck, June 29, 1846, *Letters*, II, 170.

[67] *Letters*, II, 265n. The book bore the date 1845 on its title-page, however.

[68] Whitman clipped this essay when it first appeared as a review of the

Before the second volume of *Views and Reviews* appeared, Duyckinck was no longer editor for Wiley and Putnam; the struggle of the Young America group and the *Knickerbocker* circle had degenerated into invective, innuendo, and insult; Melville and Poe were the centers around which the storm was revolving; and Simms was beginning to turn his eyes homeward, inward, and from the Loco-focos toward Zachary Taylor. If he had felt that the first volume was published with "little disposition on the part of the publisher to bring it properly to the view of the public," he must have felt that the second volume was released surreptitiously. Thus it was the First Series that attracted most of the critical attention which the work received.

The Whigs immediately recognized *Views and Reviews* as a belligerent action by the Young America group. The mighty *North American Review*, usually aloof from these battles, struck the heaviest blow for the internationalists. Cornelius C. Felton, Eliot Professor of Greek Literature at Harvard, in the October, 1846, issue, reviewed the Wiley and Putnam Library of American Books. Mathews's *Big Abel* is bad imitation Dickens, he said; Poe's *Tales* belong to the "forcible-feeble and the shallow-profound" school; Simms's fiction shows no originality. But it was *Views and Reviews* on which Felton centered his scorn: its chauvinism is "without the faintest shadow of sense"; its articles contain "but little valuable criticism; they unfold no principle of beauty, and illustrate no point in the philosophy of literature and art. They breathe an extravagant nationality, equally at war with good taste and generous progress in liberal culture." [69] The next month the *Knickerbocker* quoted this article with delight.[70] The young America group

work of Cornelius Mathews in the *Southern Quarterly Review*, VI (October, 1844), 307–342, wrote on its margin "Very Fine," and kept it. (Spencer, *The Quest for Nationalism*, p. 220.)

[69] *North American Review*, LXIII (October, 1846), 357–381.

[70] "Editor's Table," *Knickerbocker*, XXVIII (November, 1846), 450–454.

countered such attacks in journals like Mathews's *Yankee Doodle*[71] and Duyckinck's *Literary World*, where the patriotic note was struck hard: "Mr. Simms is truly American. The subjects of this collection, from Americanism, the first paper, to the last, are purely American."[72] The few notices of the Second Series and the clothbound volume were very similar in tone. In November, 1847, the *Knickerbocker* magazine quoted the Boston *Morning Post* with obvious relish:

If we understand Mr. Simms and his colleagues, it is necessary that our writers should choose American subjects, in order that their productions, however good, should constitute a real 'American literature'; and that they should fill their books with a certain mysterious 'American spirit,' very difficult to describe and exceedingly hard to imagine. . . . It is a pity that some one of these gentlemen should not *produce a work* which would serve to show what this singular 'American literature' really is. . . .[73]

Clearly Simms was caught up in the Young America group's strident demand for a national literature to accompany an expanding egalitarian society, and *Views and Reviews* was a calculated voice in that demand. As Benjamin T. Spencer has asserted, "The period between 1837 and 1855 . . . witnesses a strong movement toward nationality in American literature, deriving much of its impulse from the buoyancy attendant upon the democratic expansion of the time and characterized by its emphasis on the democratic ideal in letters."[74]

But *Views and Reviews* was not only a polemic in a literary war; it was also a piece of literary criticism, subject to judgment in those terms; and its most perceptive and telling criticism came, not from the *Knickerbocker* circle nor in the pages of Duyckinck's *Literary World*, but from a fellow affiliate of the Young America writers, a fellow Loco-foco Demo-

---

[71] *Yankee Doodle*, I (October 24, 1846), 33.
[72] *Literary World*, II (October 23, 1847), 282.
[73] *Knickerbocker*, XXX (December, 1847), 556.
[74] "A National Literature, 1837–1855," *American Literature*, VIII (May, 1936), 158.

crat, and a fellow author in the Library of American Books — Nathaniel Hawthorne. He reviewed the book in the *Salem Advertiser* of May 2, 1846:

This work . . . is made up of able review-articles, chiefly on historical subjects, and a series of picturesque and highly ornamented lectures on 'American History, as suited to the purposes of Art.' — These are all creditable to the author, and scarcely inferior, in our judgment, to the best of such productions, whether on this or the other side of the Atlantic. Mr. Simms is a man of vigorous and cultivated mind — a writer of well-trained ability — but not, as we feel most sensibly in his best passages, a man of genius. This is especially discernible in the series of lectures above alluded to; they abound in brilliant paragraphs, and appear to bring out, as by a skilfully applied varnish, all the lights and shades that lie upon the surface of our history; but yet, we cannot help feeling that the real treasures of his subject have escaped the author's notice. The themes suggested by him, viewed as he views them, would produce nothing but historical novels, cast in the same worn out mould that has been in use these thirty years, and which it is time to break up and fling away. To be the prophet of Art requires almost as high a gift as to be a fulfiller of the prophecy. Mr. Simms has not this gift; he possesses nothing of the magic touch that should cause new intellectual and moral shapes to spring up in the reader's mind, peopling with varied life what had hitherto been a barren waste. He can merely elaborate what is already familiar. His style, we think, is one which, in a higher or lower degree of finish, is proper to men of his literary stamp. It is composed of very good words, exceedingly well put together; but, instead of being imbued and identified with his subject, it spreads itself over it like an incrustation.[75]

Hawthorne points accurately to both the nature and the weaknesses of *Views and Reviews*, and hence he indicates an important aspect of its significance both in Simms's career and in literary history.

That significance is that *Views and Reviews* is a reasonably detailed statement of the purpose, materials, and method of

[75] Stewart, "Hawthorne's Contributions to *The Salem Advertiser*," pp. 331–332. This review would have been even more unfavorable if Hawthorne had been as frank in it as he was in a letter of April 30, 1846, to Duyckinck, accompanying the manuscript of the review: "I know well enough what I like, but am always at a loss to render a reason. Mr. Simms I do not like at all." (*American Literature*, V, 330.)

the historical novel as it was practiced in America from Cooper's *The Spy* in 1821 until the hiatus in the publication of book-length fiction in the 1840's. On such a subject Simms could speak with an authority surpassed only by that of James Fenimore Cooper, for his literary reputation was founded on the historical romances he had written while the genre was at the pinnacle of its popularity in America.

Before 1840 the historical novel had attracted the interest of the best fictional talents in the nation. In the 1830's the fictional successes were by Cooper, Simms, Robert Montgomery Bird, James K. Paulding, and similar followers of the school of Scott.[76] Only Charles Brockden Brown of the significant novelists before 1840 did not use the historical romance as an artistically challenging form, and his career had ended before Scott established the genre and, in his numerous introductions, letters dedicatory, and prefaces to his Waverley novels, produced what still remains the largest body of critical and technical comment on the form.[77] Sir Walter was for Simms in this, as he was in most things, a master and a mentor.[78] Although he echoes Scott's formulas and strictures again and again, he adds nothing new to them; his contribution to the subject is his effort to demonstrate that American history and the American frontier are rich as subject matter for the historical romancer and form, therefore, an adequate material for artistic treatment. In this Simms was contributing to what ultimately proved to be the fruitless efforts of Americans. During this first half-century of the American novel the search for the materials and methods of a viable American romance had

[76] Frank Luther Mott, *Golden Multitudes* (New York, 1947), pp. 306–308.

[77] Perhaps the best summary of Scott's theories of the historical novel is still that by George Saintsbury, in "The Historical Novel," *Essays in English Literature, 1780–1860*, Second Series (London, 1895), pp. 303–383; however, there is no real substitute for Scott's prefaces and his "General Introduction to the Waverley Novels" in the revised edition of *Waverley*.

[78] C. Hugh Holman, "The Influence of Scott and Cooper on Simms," *American Literature*, XXIII (May, 1951), 203–218.

been pursued. Simms in 1835 in his "Advertisement" to *The Yemassee* had tried to distinguish between the novel and the romance, declaring, "Modern romance is the substitute which the people of to-day offer for the ancient epic," and asserting boldly, "The Yemassee is proposed as an American romance." [79] For him and others of his age, as Benjamin T. Spencer suggests, "the genius of European romanticism furnished the imaginative ends; the problem for the American writer was to discover distinctive and appropriate instruments and agencies in the New World toward these ends." [80] Before a truly American romance was to come into existence the imaginative ends supplied by European writers had to give way to fresh and native ends and, as Hawthorne expressed it about *Views and Reviews*, "the same worn out mould that has been in use these thirty years" had to be broken up and flung away.

Between 1840 and 1850 American romance reached its maturity of theme and method, so that it could speak in the 1850's with an authority, a seriousness, and a passionate skill foreign to its earlier modes. The type of romance which *Views and Reviews* attempted to define was, in fact, dead as an artistic form for truly serious writing; and it was calamitous for Simms's career that he did not recognize the fact. In 1850 his romance of the Revolution, *Katharine Walton*, was published serially in *Godey's Lady's Book*.[81] That same year Nathaniel Hawthorne published *The Scarlet Letter*.

After 1847 Simms's attention turned increasingly toward the South and away from the nation. At the center of the issue was slavery; but other factors also contributed. The publication in 1847 of Lorenzo Sabine's *The American Loyalist*,

[79] *The Yemassee* (New York, 1835), I, vi, vii. Parks, in *Simms As Literary Critic*, p. 110, finds this distinction between novel and romance to be Simms's only contribution to critical theory.

[80] Spencer, *The Quest for Nationalism*, p. 96.

[81] In XL (February–June, 1850), 107–118, 161–169, 243–251, 320–326, 397–411; XLI (July–December, 1850), 13–27, 89–100, 162–179, 205–219, 286–298, 332–352.

a serious historical study of Loyalist sentiment and activity during the American Revolution, led many Northerners to question the part the South had played in the winning of American independence. On this issue Simms was increasingly sensitive. In two articles in the *Southern Quarterly Review*, entitled "South Carolina in the Revolutionary War," [82] he defended his state against Sabine's view of it. In 1852 he greeted a revised edition of Kennedy's novel *Horse-Shoe Robinson* — a book he had praised in 1835 — with a long review taking strong exception to its picture of Loyalist sentiment in South Carolina.[83] These increasingly local and defensive attitudes were in part responsible for his return to the fictional treatment of the Revolution, and he produced in rapid succession four romances emphasizing South Carolina's major role in the winning of the Revolution: *Katharine Walton* (book publication, 1851), *The Sword and the Distaff* (later called *Woodcraft*, 1852), *The Forayers* (1855), and *Eutaw* (1856). He published in book form only two other novels: *Vasconselos* (1853), a Spanish romance of de Soto in America, which he had written much of in the 1830's, and *The Cassique of Kiawah* (1859), a romance of Indian warfare in Carolina in 1685. In all of these books he was still working in the Scott mould.

Thus, in the decade when the American novel had its first great flowering, Simms's critical and artistic eyes remained closed to the revolution that was occurring, and he failed to see that the trappings of the historical past, the posturing of the cloud-topping hero, and the picturesque scenery of the decaying castle had to be abandoned if the American writer was to make epic and romance out of the common man and his average life in a democratic nation. Apparently he read his fellow-Young America writer's *Moby-Dick*, but he did not understand Melville's startling effort to dramatize the romance

---

[82] In XIV (July, 1848), 37–77; (October, 1848), 261–337.
[83] *Southern Quarterly Review*, XXII (July, 1852), 203–220.

of the soul through symbol and to define it in wild rhetoric, and he concluded that Ahab's "ravings, and the ravings of Mr. Melville himself . . . are such as would justify a writ *de lunatico* against all parties." [84] Young America's literary revolution had passed Simms by, and he remained caught in the "worn out mould" through which he expressed his steadily narrowing sectionalism.

The standard view of Simms is that he was an ultra-sectionalist, steeped in "southern provincialism," a Fire-Eater of "the Calhoun School," and a blind worshiper of an aristocratic political and social order.[85] Such a view takes the Simms of the 1850's and 1860's and assigns his attitudes at this time to his entire career. Certainly Simms fell victim to the "intellectual blockade" which the defensive South threw around itself,[86] certainly his defense of slavery as an institution was consistent throughout his career,[87] but the intense sectionalism and the political conservatism of his late years were not characteristic of his whole career. Indeed, the pattern of Simms's changing social and political thought was strikingly like that of James Fenimore Cooper; for Cooper shifted from the democratic Jacksonianism of *A Letter to His Countrymen* (1834) to the aristocratic conservatism of his last years.[88]

[84] *Southern Quarterly Review*, n.s., V (January, 1852), 262. The attribution to Simms is uncertain, although he wrote virtually all the brief notices in the *Southern Quarterly Review* at this time.

[85] Trent, *Simms, passim;* Smith, *Forces in American Criticism*, pp. 125–131; Vernon L. Parrington, *Main Currents in American Thought* (New York, 1927), II, 125–136.

[86] Clement Eaton, *Freedom of Thought in the Old South* (Durham, 1940) traces in detail the development of this defensive attitude in the ante bellum South.

[87] His most infamous statement on the subject is his long essay in *The Pro-Slavery Argument* (Charleston, 1852, and Philadelphia, 1853), pp. 175–285. This essay was, in fact, a review of Harriet Martineau's *Society in America*, which was published in 1837 as "The Morals of Slavery" (*Southern Literary Messenger*, III [November 1837], 641–657), and reprinted in pamphlet form in Richmond in 1838 as *Slavery in America*.

[88] Schlesinger, *Age of Jackson*, pp. 375–380.

In 1842, however, Simms could write with complete accuracy and candor, "I am an ultra-American, a born Southron, and a resolute loco-foco." [89] For in the 1840's he was a part of the first major radical democratic movement in American letters, and he did yeoman service in its wars. His *Views and Reviews* remains today an important document in the Young America war, a vigorous expression of the egalitarian ideal in a native literature, and a summary of the ideals of a past literary genre. If in the dark days of the 1860's Simms ever turned its pages, it must have seemed to him to belong to a remote world. But a hundred years later it is still a significant reminder that Gilmore Simms once marched bravely and fought intemperately in the cause of radical democracy.

[89] Letter to George F. Holmes, August 15, 1842, *Letters,* I, 319.

A NOTE ON THE TEXT

The text reprinted here is that of the 1845 edition of *Views and Reviews in American Literature, History and Fiction*, First Series. I have silently corrected a few obvious typographical errors, but I have not changed Simms's eccentricities of punctuation, diction, and sentence structure. I have attempted to indicate in my notes the relationship between passages in Simms's text and events in its literary and cultural milieu. I have also attempted to identify persons and places mentioned in the text, when their identity will not be immediately obvious to the average reader. Simms's habit of quoting snippets of verse and prose, often from a faulty memory, has presented me with some serious problems of identification, some of which I was not able to solve. For the sake of clarity, I have kept my footnotes and the relatively few that Simms used in a single numerical order, indicating Simms's notes at the beginning with the notation [*Simms's note*] and placing any editorial comment in brackets. All notes not bearing at their beginning the words [*Simms's note*] are mine.

C. Hugh Holman

Chapel Hill, North Carolina
February, 1962

CHRONOLOGY OF
THE LIFE OF WILLIAM GILMORE SIMMS

1806 Born in Charleston, S. C., April 17, the son of an Irish immigrant and small mercantile dealer.

1808 Mother died; father, in deep despair with business near bankruptcy, went to the Southwest, leaving him in the care of Mrs. Jacob Gates, his maternal grandmother.

1812–1818 Received all his formal schooling, in public and private schools that he later said were "worthless and scoundrelly."

1818 Was apprentice to an apothecary, as training for a career as a physician.

1824–1825 Visited his father in the Southwest; saw Indian life and frontier conditions in Mississippi, Alabama, and Louisiana.

1825 Began reading law; was one of a "Society of Young Gentlemen" who edited and wrote, *The Album*, a literary weekly, from June to December. The "Society" was probably led by William Timrod, bookbinder. Simms published pamphlet poem, *Monody on the Death of Gen. Charles Cotesworth Pinckney.*

1826 October 19, married Anna Malcolm Giles, childhood sweetheart, who was already ill with tuberculosis.

1827 Admitted to the bar; appointed city magistrate; published *Lyrical and Other Poems* and *Early Lays.*

1828–1829 Founded and edited, with James L. Simmons, the short-lived *Southern Literary Gazette.*

1829 Published *The Vision of Cortes, Cain, and Other Poems.*

1830 Purchased (with a partner, E. S. Duryea) and began editing a daily newspaper, the Charleston *City Gazette*, in which he supported the Union in the Nullification Controversy. Almost attacked by mob for this stand. Father died in Mississippi. Published *The Tri-Color*, a poem.

1831 Active in the Union and States' Rights Party. Visited Southwest, probably to settle father's estate.

1832 February 19, wife died. June 7, sold *Gazette*, which was losing subscribers because of Simms's Union stand, and himself assumed its large debts. Went to Philadelphia, New York, and Connecticut. Published *Atalantis*, his best long poem.

1833 Published *Martin Faber*, novelette of crime; *The Book of My Lady*, collected tales and sketches; and *Memoir of Maynard Davis Richardson*.

1834 Published *Guy Rivers*, his first border romance, which established him as novelist. Edited *The Cosmopolitan*, which contained some of his stories, intended as Charleston annual.

1835 Published *The Yemassee*, a colonial historical novel, his most popular work of fiction, and *The Partisan*, his first romance of the American Revolution.

1836 Published *Mellichampe*, a Revolutionary romance. November 15, married Chevillette Roach; moved to her father's plantation "Woodlands," in the Barnwell District, 70 miles inland from Charleston. For the remainder of his life Simms made "Woodlands" and the Barnwell District his home, spending his winters there and his summers in Northern publishing centers.

1837 Published *Martin Faber and Other Tales*.

1838 Published *Richard Hurdis*, a border romance; *Pelayo*, a romance of Spanish history; and *Carl Werner and Other Tales*, a collection of crime stories.

1839 Published *The Damsel of Darien*, a romance of the Spanish in Peru; and *Southern Passages and Pictures*, poems.

1840 Published *Border Beagles*, a border romance; and *The History of South Carolina*, a school text.

1841 Published *The Kinsmen,* a Revolutionary romance later renamed *The Scout;* and *Confession,* a crime novel.

1842 Published *Beauchampe,* a novel based on the Beauchampe-Sharpe murder case (its first volume was later renamed *Charlemont*); abandoned writing full-length novels for eight years because of national economy, "mammoth weeklies," and "cheap books."

1842–1843 Editor of the *Magnolia* magazine; became active in the Young America-*Knickerbocker* literary war, supporting the Young America side; he remained in the Young America camp until 1848.

1843 Published *Donna Florida,* a narrative poem; *The Geography of South Carolina,* a school text.

1844 Elected a representative from Barnwell District to the South Carolina legislature for 1844–1846 term; during his term of office actively opposed the "Charleston" group. Published *Castle Dismal* and *The Prima Donna,* "cheap book" novelettes, and *The Life of Francis Marion,* his most successful book.

1845 Edited *The Southern and Western Magazine* (12 monthly numbers). Published *Count Julian,* a romance of Spanish history, written in 1838; *The Wigwam and the Cabin,* collected stories; *Helen Halsey,* a novelette; and *Grouped Thoughts and Scattered Fancies,* poems.

1846 Published *Areytos; or, Songs of the South,* poems; *The Life of Captain John Smith; Views and Reviews,* First Series (dated 1845), critical essays.

1847 Published *The Life of Chevalier Bayard,* and *Views and Reviews,* Second Series (dated 1845).

1848 Broke with Young America Loco-foco Democrats to support Zachary Taylor for President. Published *A Supplement to the Plays of William Shakspeare,* a collection of Shakespeare apocrypha; *Charleston and Her Satirists,* and *Lays of the Palmetto,* poems.

1849–1855 Edited the *Southern Quarterly Review*.

1849 Published *The Life of Nathanael Greene; Father Abbot*, sketches; and *Sabbath Lyrics* and *The Cassique of Accabee*, poems.

1850 Published *The Lily and the Totem*, a history of the Huguenots in Florida; *Flirtation at the Moultrie House*, a novelette; and *The City of the Silent*, poems.

1851 Published *Norman Maurice*, blank verse drama; *Katharine Walton*, a Revolutionary romance, serialized in 1850.

1852 Published *Michael Bonham*, a blank verse drama; *The Sword and the Distaff* (renamed *Woodcraft*), a Revoultionary romance; and *The Golden Christmas* and *As Good As a Comedy*, novelettes.

1853 Uniform Edition of his *Works*, illustrated by F. O. C. Darley, begun. Published *Poems*, two volumes; *Vasconselos*, a romance of the Spanish exploration of America, largely written in the late 1830's; *Egeria*, a collection of epigrams; and *Marie de Berniere*, a novelette.

1854 Published *Southward, Ho!*, a collection of short stories.

1855 Published *The Forayers*, a Revolutionary romance.

1856 Published *Eutaw*, a sequel to *The Forayers*. Lectured in defense of slavery in New York City.

1857–1860 Active in the conduct of *Russell's Magazine*, which was edited by Paul H. Hayne.

1859 Published *The Cassique of Kiawah*, a colonial Indian romance, his last novel to appear in book form.

1860 Vigorously supported the idea of secession from the Union.

1862 "Woodlands" partially burned and rebuilt.

1863 September 10, wife died.

1865 "Woodlands" burned again. Simms edited *The Columbia Phoenix*, a newspaper; published *The Sack and Destruction of the City of Columbia, S. C.*

1865–1866 Edited *The Daily South Carolinian,* a Columbia, S. C., newspaper.

1866 Made trip to the North in unsuccessful effort to re-establish his publishing contacts. Published *Joscelyn,* a Revolutionary romance, serially in the *Old Guard* magazine.

1867 Edited *The War Poetry of the South;* published *A Succinct Memoir of the Life and Public Career of Colonel John Laurens.*

1869 Published *The Cub of the Panther,* a border romance, serially in the *Old Guard* magazine; and *Voltmeier,* a romance of the North Carolina mountains, serially in *The Western World* magazine.

1870 Published *The Sense of the Beautiful.* Died June 11, probably of cancer.

VIEWS AND REVIEWS

IN

AMERICAN LITERATURE,

HISTORY AND FICTION.

BY THE AUTHOR OF
"THE YEMASSEE," "LIFE OF MARION," "HISTORY OF SOUTH CAROLINA,"
"RICHARD HURDIS," &C., &C.

FIRST SERIES

NEW YORK:
WILEY AND PUTNAM, 161 BROADWAY.

1845.

[Transcript of the original title page]

TO

PROFESSOR E. GEDDINGS,[1]

OF THE MEDICAL COLLEGE OF SOUTH CAROLINA.

I HAD placed your name, my dear Geddings, in one of the first pages of a favourite study in fiction which I have in hand — the scene of which, on our own Ashley,[2] is very dear to us both; — but it may be some time before this task is finished, and I prefer not to lose the present opportunity of saying to you, how very much, and how faithfully, I am your friend,

THE AUTHOR.

New York, Oct. 1, 1845.

[1] Dr. Eli Geddings (1799–1878) was the family physician of the Simmses. He was professor of anatomy at the Medical School of the University of Maryland from 1831 to 1837. He was professor of anatomy at the Medical College of South Carolina in Charleston from 1837–1858.

[2] No work of fiction by Simms after 1845 is dedicated to Dr. Geddings. The work to which he probably refers here is *The Sword and the Distaff* (Charleston, 1852) later called *Woodcraft*. This work, which is laid on the Ashley, is dedicated to Joseph Johnson, M. D.

ADVERTISEMENT

THE papers contained in the two volumes, of which the present is the first instalment, are drawn from numerous contributions which have been made to the periodical literature of the country in the last fifteen years. They are taken from the pages of the Southern and American Quarterly Reviews; from the American Monthly and the Knickerbocker Magazines; from the Magnolia, Orion, Southern and Western Review, and from other publications of like character.[1] I have detached them, with a single eye to their national objects and characteristics. They constitute a class, in themselves, illustrative of our history, our materials of art, the moral of our aims, and the true development of our genius. They appeal to the utilitarian, not less than to the person of taste. They aim at showing what may be done among us, and insist upon what we should do, in regard to the essential in our progress. I flatter myself that, dealing little in the commonplaces of these themes, I have ample authority in my own experience — which has been that of self-training throughout — for all that I declare and urge, however new or startling it may seem to those whose standards are in stereotypes which no revolutions of the world may disturb or decompose.

[1] This "Advertisement" is intended to introduce both the First and Second Series when they are bound together, but it was written in 1845 for the First Series. When the Second Series appeared Simms's plans for it had been greatly changed. The result is that essays from only the *Southern and Western Magazine*, the *Magnolia*, the *Southern Quarterly Review*, and the *American Review* are used in the two Series.

ARTICLE I

AMERICANISM IN LITERATURE[1]

Americanism in Literature: An Oration before the Phi Kappa and De-
mosthenean Societies of the University of Georgia, at Athens, Au-
gust 8, 1844. By Alexander B. Meek, of Alabama. Charleston: Bur-
ges & James. 1844.[2]

THIS is the right title. It indicates the becoming object of
our aim. Americanism in our Literature is scarcely implied by
the usual phraseology. American Literature seems to be a
thing, certainly, — but it is not the thing exactly. To put
Americanism in our letters, is to do a something much more
important. The phrase has a peculiar signification which is
worth our consideration. By a liberal extension of the cour-
tesies of criticism, we are already in possession of a due
amount of American authorship; but of such as is individual,
and properly peculiar to ourselves, we cannot be said to enjoy
much. Our writers are numerous — quite as many, perhaps, in
proportion to our years, our circumstances and necessities, as
might be looked for among any people. But, with very few
exceptions, their writings might as well be European. They are
European. The writers think after European models, draw
their stimulus and provocation from European books, fashion
themselves to European tastes, and look chiefly to the awards
of European criticism. This is to denationalize the American
mind. This is to enslave the national heart — to place ourselves
at the mercy of the foreigner, and to yield all that is individual,

---

[1] Originally published in the *Southern and Western Magazine*, I (January,
1845), 1–14. Simms's addition of the two long notes is the principal change
between the two versions.

[2] A 39-page pamphlet. Alexander B. Meek (1814–1865) was a politician,
poet, and historian, author of *The Southwest* (1840), *Romantic Passages in
Southwestern History* (1857), and *Songs and Poems of the South* (1857).

in our character and hope, to the paralyzing influence of his will, and frequently hostile purposes.

There is a season, perhaps, when such a condition of dependence is natural enough in the history of every youthful nation. It is in the national infancy that such must be the case. The early labours of a newly established people, in all the intellectual arts, must necessarily be imitative. They advance, by regular steps, from the necessary to the intellectual — from the satisfaction of vulgar cravings, to a desire for the gratification of moral and spiritual tastes; — and, in this progress, they can only advance through the assistance of other nations. This condition is inevitable in the history of a people wanting in homogeneousness at first, and but recently segregated from their several patriarchal trees. Time must be allowed to such a people — time to combine — to exchange thoughts and sympathies — and to learn the difficult, but absolutely necessary duty, of working together, as a community, in harmonious and mutually relying action. Generations must pass away, and other generations take their places, before they shall utterly lose the impressions made upon their plastic infancy by arbitrary models — before they shall begin to look around them, and within themselves, for those characteristics which are peculiar to their condition, and which distinguish the country of their present fortunes. It is idle to say, as has been urged by the British Reviewers in their reply to Mr. Jefferson,[3] that the Anglo-Americans were of full age at the very birth of their

[3] Thomas Jefferson's argument that America was "but a child of yesterday" and had not yet existed long enough to rival Greece, Rome, France, or England in the arts is in "Query VI" of his *Notes on the State of Virginia*, ed. William Peden (Chapel Hill, 1955), pp. 64–65. In the stream of attacks on America and American arts, which reached its height between 1814 and 1825, the *Quarterly Review*, the *Edinburgh Review*, and *Blackwood's Magazine* joined in asserting the artistic inferiority of America. The publication in 1840 of Part II of Alexis de Tocqueville's *Democracy in America* revived the old arguments in the *Edinburgh* and the *Quarterly Reviews*. See [Gilbert Chinard], "The American Dream," *Literary History of the United States*, ed. R. E. Spiller, *et al* (New York, 1948), I, 212.

country. This is scarcely true, even in physical respects. They did not represent the intellect of the nation which they left, though they did its moral and its temperament. They represented neither its tastes, nor its acquisitions, nor its luxuries. The eminence upon which the superior characteristics of the British nation stood, had never been reached by the footsteps of the Pilgrims. They were in possession of the Anglo-Norman genius, no doubt — upon this it will be the duty of the Americans to insist; — but its great attainments — its cherished acquisitions — its tastes, its refinements, its polish, were not theirs. In all these essentials, the founders of the Anglo-American States were in their infancy. And so they were kept for a century, by the novel necessities, the trying hardships, the perilous wars which followed upon their new condition. The conquest of a savage empire — the conflict with barbarian enemies, — kept them back from the natural acquisitions, which were due to their origin and genius. Great Britain herself is fairly chargeable, by her tyrannous exactions and the bloody wars with which she sought us out in the new homes so perilously won in the wilderness, with having withstood our people in their progress to the attainment of those objects the lack of which she this day makes our reproach.

But these excuses can be urged no longer, nor is it necessary that they should. Europe must cease to taunt us because of our prolonged servility to the imperious genius of the Old World. We must set ourselves free from the tyranny of this genius, and the time has come when we must do so. We have our own national mission to perform — a mission commensurate to the extent of our country, — its resources and possessions, — and the numerous nations, foreign and inferior, all about us, over whom we are required to extend our sway and guardianship. We are now equal to this sway and guardianship. The inferior necessities of our condition have been overcome. The national mind is now free to rise to the consideration of its superior wants and more elevated aims; and individuals, here and there, are starting out from the ranks of the multitude, ready and able to lead out, from the bondage of foreign guidance, the genius which, hitherto, because of its timidity, knew nothing of its own resources for flight and conquest.

If the time for this movement has not yet arrived, it is certainly very near at hand. This conviction grows out of the fact that we now daily taunt ourselves with our protracted servility to the European. We feel that we are still too humbly imitative, wanting in the courage to strike out boldly, hewing out from our own forests the paths which should lead us to their treasures, and from the giant masses around us the characteristic forms and aspects of native art. This reproach has been hitherto but too much deserved, qualified only by a reference to the circumstances in our condition at which we have been able to glance only for a moment. We have done little that may properly be called our own; and this failure, due to influences which still, in some degree, continue, is one which nothing but a high and stimulating sense of nationality will enable us to remedy. It is so easy, speaking the English language, to draw our inspiration from the mother country, and to seek our audience in her halls and temples, that, but for the passionate appeals of patriotic censure, it may be yet long years before we throw off the patient servility of our dependence. With a daily influx of thousands from foreign shores, seeking to share our political securities and the blessings of the generous skies and rich soil which we possess, Europe sends us her thoughts, her fashions, and her tastes. These have their influence in keeping us in bondage, and we shall require all the activity of our native mind to resist the influence which she thus exercises upon our national institutions and education. Besides, our very wealth of territory, and the ease with which we live, are obstacles in the way of our improvement. The temptations of our vast interior keep our society in a constant state of transition. The social disruptions occasioned by the wandering habits of the citizen, result invariably in moral loss to the whole. Standards of judgment fluctuate, sensibilities become blunted, principles impaired, with increasing insecurity at each additional remove; and this obstacle in the way of our literary progress must continue, until the great interior shall react, because of its own overflow, upon the Atlantic cities.

There is nothing really to distress us in this survey, unless, — either because of a supineness of character which is not our reproach in merely every-day pursuits, or because of an intrinsic deficiency of the higher intellectual resources, — we continue to yield ourselves to our European teachers. Our literature, so far, has been English in its character. We have briefly striven to show why. Glad are we that we can make some exceptions to this admission — that we can point, here and there throughout the country, to some individuals, and say, here stands a true scion of young America, — this is a plant of our own raising — true to the spirit of the country, — to its genuine heart — a man to represent and speak for the nature which we acknowledge, and of which time shall make us proud. In these instances we find our hope. It is thus that we feel ourselves encouraged to say to our people, and to the workers in the mind of Europe, that we too are making a beginning in a purely individual progress — evolving, however slowly, a national aim and idea, out of the fulness and overflow of the national heart. We are rejoiced to behold symptoms of this independent intellectual working, simultaneously, in remote regions of the country; and flatter ourselves with the vision of a generous growth in art and letters, of which tokens begin to make themselves felt from the Aroostook to the Rio Brave. This evidence needs but sympathy and encouragement to grow powerful, and to challenge a living rank among the great spirits of other lands and periods. As yet, perhaps, the shows are faint and feeble. Few of the hurrying multitude have leisure to behold

them, — our progress declaring itself, as it now does, rather by
its anxieties and cravings, — its discontents with itself, and its
feverish impatience at the advance of other communities —
than by its own proper performances. But such a condition of
the popular mind is the precursor of performance. The wish
to do, is the forerunner of the way. Let us only take something
for granted. Let the nation but yield a day's faith to its own
genius, and that day will suffice for triumph. We do not yet
believe in ourselves, — unless in the meaner respects which
prove our capacity for acquisition only in concerns the most
inferior — in the mechanical arts, — in pursuits regarded as
simply useful, — in selfish desires, and such as are necessary to
our physical condition merely. This scepticism is the great
barrier to be overcome. Our development depends upon our
faith in what we are, and in our independence of foreign judgment. A resolute will, a bold aim, and a spirit that coura-
geously looks within for its encouragements and standards, —
these are our securities for intellectual independence. To these
acquisitions our labours must be addressed. To the want of
these, and the necessity for them, the attention of our people
must be drawn. The popular mind scarcely yet seems to perceive that there is a vast and vital difference between the *self-
speaking* among our people, and that numerous herd, which,
though born, living and walking in our midst, speak never *for*
our hearts, and seldom *from* their own — whose thoughts, no
less than language, are wholly English, and who, in all general
characteristics — so far as the native progress and development
are effected — might as well have been born, dwelling and
dilating in Middlesex or London. It is but to see these things as
we should — to understand the world-wide difference between
writing *for*, and writing *from* one's people. This difference is
the whole, — but *what* a difference! To write *from* a people,
is to *write* a people — to make them live — to endow them
with a life and a name — to preserve them with a history for-

ever. Whether the poet shall frame his song according to custom, or according to the peculiar nature and the need of those for whom it is made, is, in other words, to ask whether he shall be a poet at all or not. It was by properly understanding this difference in ancient days that he grew into the stature of the poet, and won his reputation; and it was through the proper comprehension of this *difference* and this *duty*, on the part of the Poet, that the genius and the history of the great nations have survived all the political disasters which have bowed their pillars in the dust.

Up to the present day — the signs whereof encourage us with better hopes — the question might properly have been asked, how should objects, such as these, be to us of any consideration? — we who live not for the morrow but the day — whose plans are conceived for temporary not eternal refuge — who hurry forward as if we had no children, and who rear them as if we loved them not! Such is the profligacy of every people who show themselves indifferent to the developments of native art. It is by the exhibition of the constructive faculty that the intellectual nature of a people is distinguished. In proportion to the possession and exercise of this faculty, which embodies all the elements of the imagination, will be the moral rank of the nation. We have been very heedless of this matter. Our people have taken too little interest in the productions of the American mind, considered purely as American, whether in art or letters. In all that relates to the higher aims of the social and spiritual nature, England, and what she is pleased to give us, sufficiently satisfies our moral cravings. Yet we have an idea of independence in some respects which tends to show how wretchedly limited has been our ambition. Parties are formed among us to compel the manufacture of our own pots and kettles, our woollens and window glass; parties ready to revolutionize the country, and make all chaos again, if these things be not of our own making:

— made too, — such is the peculiar excellence of the jest, at our own heavy cost and pecuniary injury; — but never a word is said, whether by good sense or patriotism, touching the grievous imposition upon us of foreign opinion and foreign laws, foreign tastes and foreign appetites, taught us through the medium of a foreign, and perhaps hostile and insulting teacher. These, say these profound haberdashers in the wares of patriotism, are really matters of slight concern. Thoughts are common, say the paper manufacturers, and though we insist upon supplying the paper from domestic mills, upon which such thoughts are to be printed, yet these are quite as properly brought from abroad, as conceived and put in proper utterance at home. The European may as well do our thinking. The matter is not worth a struggle. English literature is good enough for us for many hundred years to come.[4] So, for that matter, are English woollens.

But this will not suffice. The question is one which concerns equally our duties and our pride. Are we to aim and arrive at all the essentials of nationality — to rise into first rank and position as a people — to lift our heads, unabashed, among the great communities of Europe — plant ourselves on the perfect eminence of a proud national will, and show ourselves not degenerate from the powerful and noble stocks from which we take our origin? This is a question not to be answered by the

---

[4] [*Simms's note*] This language was actually employed by one of the American reviews of highest rank. Yet these reviews, themselves are anticipated by foreign criticism, as, in most cases, they expend their analysis, upon foreign publications. I have heard an American author speak with wholesale scorn of all American art, and an American painter, of superior distinction, declare that he never allowed himself to read an American book. Neither of these unfortunate persons seemed to perceive, that, in thus disparaging the native genius, they were effectually sealing their own condemnation. [E. W. Johnson, in "The Progress and Disorganization," *American Whig Review*, II (July, 1845), 90–99, attacked American letters in terms such as Simms here indicates. In this article he said: ". . . there are no causes, external to literature, which acting upon it, can, unless very slowly, displace that which we inherit and give us a new one."]

selfishness of the individual nature, unless it be in that generous sort of selfishness which is moved only by the highest promptings of ambition. It is an argument addressed to all that is hopeful and proud in the hearts of an ardent and growing people. It is not addressed to the tradesman but to the man. We take it for granted, that we are not — in the scornful language of the European press, — a mere nation of shop-keepers: [5] — that we have qualities of soul and genius, which if not yet developed in our moral constitution, are struggling to make themselves heard and felt; — that we have a pride of character, — growing stronger (as we trust) with the progress of each succeeding day, — which makes us anxious to realize for ourselves that position of independence, in all other departments, which we have secured by arms and in politics. Mere political security — the fact that we drink freely of the air around us, and at our own choosing partake of the fruits of the earth — is not enough, — constitutes but a small portion of the triumphs, and the objects of a rational nature. Nay, even political security is temporary, always inferior if not wholly uncertain, unless it be firmly based upon the certain and constant vigilance of the intellectual moral. A nation, properly to boast itself and to take and maintain its position with other States, must prove itself in possession of self-evolving attributes. Its character must be as individual as that of the noblest citizen that dwells within its limits. It must do its own thinking as well as its own fighting, for, as truly as all history has shown that the people who rely for their defence in battle upon foreign mercenaries inevitably become

[5] [*Simms's note*] This language, originally applied by Napoleon to the English nation, at the very time when his highest ambition was to transfer to France a portion of that commerce upon which the great distinction and power of the rival country was built up, — has been transferred, by the latter, in a sense still more scornful, to our own. It is, perhaps, no bad sign of our successful progress as a nation, that our national enemy shows herself more angry with us than ever.

their prey, so the nation falls a victim to that genius of another, to which she passively defers. She must make, and not
borrow or beg, her laws. Her institutions must grow out of
her own condition and necessities, and not be arbitrarily
framed upon those of other countries. Her poets and artists,
to feel her wants, her hopes, her triumphs, must be born of
the soil, and ardently devoted to its claims. To live, in fact,
and secure the freedom of her children, a nation must live
through them, in them, and by them, — by the strength of
their arms, the purity of their morals, the vigour of their industry, and the wisdom of their minds. These are the essentials of a great nation, and no one of these qualities is perfectly
available without the co-operation of the rest. And, as we
adapt our warfare to the peculiarities of the country, and our
industry to our climate, our resources and our soil, so the
operations of the national mind must be suited to our characteristics. The genius of our people is required to declare itself after a fashion of its own — must be influenced by its skies,
and by those natural objects which familiarly address themselves to the senses from boyhood, and colour the fancies, and
urge the thoughts, and shape the growing affections of the
child to a something kindred with the things which he beholds. His whole soul must be imbued with sympathies caught
from surrounding aspects within his infant horizon. The heart
must be moulded to an intense appreciation of our woods and
streams, our dense forests and deep swamps, our vast immeasurable mountains, our voluminous and tumbling waters.
It must receive its higher moral tone from the exigencies of
society, its traditions and its histories. Tutored at the knee of
the grand-dame, the boy must grasp, as subjects of familiar
and frequent consideration, the broken chronicles of senility,
and shape them, as he grows older, into coherence and effect.
He must learn to dwell often upon the narratives of the brave
fathers who first broke ground in the wilderness, who fought

or treated with the red men, and who, finally, girded themselves up for the great conflict with the imperious mother who had sent them forth. These histories, making vivid impressions upon the pliant fancies of childhood, are the source of those vigorous shoots, of thought and imagination, which make a nation proud of its sons in turn, and which save her from becoming a by-word and reproach to other nations. In this, and from such impressions, the simplest records of a domestic history, expand into the most ravishing treasures of romance. But upon this subject let us hearken to the writer of the eloquent discourse before us.

Literature, in its essence, is a spiritual immortality; no more than religion a creation of man; but, like the human soul, while enduring the mystery of its incarnation, is subject to the action of the elements, is the slave of circumstance. In the sense in which we would now view it, it is the expression of the spiritual part of our nature, in its intellectual action, whether taking form in philosophy, history, poetry, eloquence, or some other branch of thought. The sum of all this, in any nation, is what constitutes her literature, and it is always modified and coloured by the peculiarities about it. As the river, sliding under the sunset, imbibes for the time, the hues of the heavens, so the stream of literature receives, from the people through which it passes, not only the images and shadows of their condition, but the very force and direction of its current. Every literature, Greek or Roman, Arabic or English, French, Persian or German, acquired its qualities and impression from the circumstances of the time and people. The philosophic eye can readily detect the key, cause and secret of each, and expose the seminal principle from which they grew into their particular shape and fashion. The same scrutinizing analysis will enable us to determine the influences among ourselves, which are to operate in the formation of our literature; as well as to decide whether it will comport with those high spiritual requisitions which I have already avowed, should be demanded from it. Let us then attempt to see how Americanism will develop itself in Literature." pp. 11, 12.

There is something equally thoughtful and fanciful in the passage which follows. It betrays a mind as sensible to the picturesque, as it is searching and speculative. The writer proceeds to illustrate his proposition by glimpses of the physical material which our own country affords for the uses of the native poet.

The physical atributes of our country are all partial to the loftiest manifestations of mind. Nature here presents her loveliest, sublimest aspects. For vastness of extent, grandeur of scenery, genial diversities of climate, and all that can minister to the comforts and tastes of man, this heritage of ours is without a parallel. In its mountains of stone and iron, its gigantic and far-reaching rivers, its inland seas, its forests of all woods, its picturesque and undulating prairies, in all its properties and proportions, it might well be considered, in comparison with the eastern hemisphere, the work of a more perfect and beneficent artist. To the eyes of the Genoese mariner, the wildest dreams of Diodorus and Plato were more than realized. Seneca sang,—

> ———— Venient annis
> Sæcula series, quibus oceanus
> Vincula rerum laxet, et ingens
> Pateat tellus, Typhisque novos
> Detegat orbes: [6]

Yet, not even in the mirror of his prophetic fancy were these more than Elysian fields glossed with all their beauty and sublimity. Even the bilious British satirist, who could see no good in all our institutions, was compelled to confess that here

> ———— Nature showed
> The last ascending footsteps of the God! [7]

Well nigh all this vast expanse of fruitfulness and beauty, too, has been subject to the control of civilized man. Our country has extended her

[6] A quotation, apparently from memory, of Seneca's *Medea*, lines 375–378:

> Venient annis sæcula seris,
> Quibus Oceanus vincula rerum
> Laxet, et ingens pateat tellus,
> Tethysque novos detegat orbes.

Watson Bradshaw's translation, in *The Ten Tragedies of Seneca* (London, 1902), pp. 428–429, reads: "The times will arrive later on, as the years roll onwards, in which the ocean will remove the impediments which now retard human affairs, and a new earth will be opened up to mankind, and the votaries of Tiphys will discover fresh worlds."

[7] Although the source of this quotation has not been located, "the bilious British satirist, who could see no good in all our institutions" may be George Crabbe (1754–1832), author of *The Village, The Parish Registry,* and *Tales of the Hall.*

jurisdiction over the fairest and most fertile regions. The rich bounty is poured into her lap, and breathes its influence upon her population. Their capacities are not pent and thwarted by the narrow limits which restrict the citizens of other countries. No speculative theorist, a Malthus, Stultz or Liceto, has cause here to apprehend the dangers of over-population. Room, bountiful room, is all about us, for humanity to breathe freely in, and to go on expanding in a long future. Do these things afford no promise of intellectual improvement? Are they no incitements to a lofty and expanded literature? Do they furnish no *matériel* for active, generous, elevated thought? Is there no voice coming out from all this fragrance and beauty and sublimity, appealing to the heart and fancy of man, for sympathy, utterance, embodiment? Why, it was once said, that the sky of Attica would make a Bœotian a poet; and we have seen even 'the red old hills of Georgia' draw inspiring melody from the heart of patriotic genius. Physical causes have always operated in the formation and fashioning of literature. In all the higher productions of mind, ancient and modern, we can easily recognize the influence of the climate and natural objects among which they were developed. The sunsets of Italy coloured the songs of Tasso and Petrarch; the vine-embowered fields of beautiful France are visible in all the pictures of Rousseau and La Martine; you may hear the solemn rustling of the Hartz forest, and the shrill horn of the wild huntsman throughout the creations of Schiller and Goethe; the sweet streamlets and sunny lakes of England smile upon you from the graceful verses of Spenser and Wordsworth; and the mist-robed hills of Scotland loom out in magnificence through the pages of Ossian, and the loftier visions of Marmion and Waverly.

Our country, then, must receive much of the character of her literature from her physical properties. If our minds are only original; if they be not base copyists, and servile echoes of foreign masters; if we can assert an intellectual as well as political independence; if we dare to think for ourselves, and faithfully picture forth, in our own styles of utterance, the impressions our minds shall receive from this great, fresh continent of beauty and sublimity; we can render to the world the most vigorous and picturesque literature it has ever beheld. Never had imagination nobler stimulants; never did nature look more encouragingly upon her genuine children. In poetry, romance, history and eloquence, what glorious objects, sights and sounds, for illustration and ornament! I have stood, down in Florida, beneath the overarching groves of magnolia, orange and myrtle, blending their fair flowers and voluptuous fragrance, and opening long vistas between their slender shafts, to where the green waters of the Mexican Gulf lapsed upon the silver-sanded beach, flinging up their light spray into the crimson beams of the declining sun, and I have thought that, for poetic beauty, for delicate inspiration, the scene was as sweet as ever wooed the eyes of a Grecian minstrel on the slopes of Parnassus, or around the fountains of Castaly.

Again: I have stood upon a lofty summit of the Alleghanies, among the splintered crags and vast gorges, where the eagle and the thunder make their home; and looked down upon an empire spread out in the long distance below. Far as the eye could reach, the broad forests swept away over territories of unexampled productiveness and beauty. At intervals, through the wide champaign, the domes and steeples of some fair town, which had sprung up with magical suddenness among the trees, would come out to the eye, giving evidence of the presence of a busy, thriving population. Winding away through the centre too, like a great artery of life to the scene, I could behold a noble branch of the Ohio, bearing upon its bosom the already active commerce of the region, and linking that spot with a thousand others, similar in their condition and character. As I thus stood, and thought of all that was being enacted in this glorious land of ours, and saw, in imagination, the stately centuries as they passed across the scene, diffusing wealth, prosperity and refinement, I could not but believe that it presented a nobler theatre, with sublimer accompaniments and inspirations, than ever rose upon the eye of a gazer from the summits of the Alps or the Appenines.

Such are some of the physical aspects of our country, and such the influence they are destined to have upon our national mind. Very evidently they constitute noble sources of inspiration, illustration and description. For all that part of literature which is drawn from the phases of nature, from the varying moods and phenomena of the outward world, the elements and the seasons, they will be more valuable than all the beauties of the Troad or Campania Felix. Rightly used, they would bring a freshness and spirit into the domain of high thought, which would revive it like a spring-time return, and we might take up, in a better hope, the exultation of Virgil, —

> Jam ultima ætas Cumali carmidis venit,
> Magnus ordo sæclorum nascitur abintegro,
> Et jam virgo redit Saturnia regna redeunt! [8] pp. 12–17.

[8] A paraphrase, apparently from memory, of these lines from Virgil's "Fourth Eclogue" (the "Messianic" eclogue):

> Ultima Cumaei venit iam carminis aetas;
> magnus ab integro sæclorum nascitur ordo.
> iam redit et Virgo, redeunt Saturnia regna.

The translation by H. Rushton Fairclough, in *Virgil* (Loeb Library, Cambridge, Mass., 1947), p. 28, reads: "Now is come the last age of the song of Cumae; the great line of the centuries begins anew. Now the Virgin returns, the reign of Saturn returns."

This is a long extract, but we have no apologies to make for it. Its pictures will interest, its grace, glow and eloquence, delight the reader, until he forgets its length. No one can question the fact that the scenery of a country has always entered largely into the inspiration of the native genius. The heart of the poet is apt to dwell frequently and fondly upon the regions on which the eyes of his youth first opened, with a rare acuteness of delight, even though these were wholly wanting in natural beauty and grossly barren of all the accessories of art. What then must be the effect upon the young genius where the scenery is beautiful or imposing in itself — distinguished by sweetness, grace and loveliness, or stirring deeper and sublimer sentiments by its wild and awe-compelling attributes. That our scenery has not yet found its painter on canvas or in fiction, is due to other than its own deficiencies. It must be our care to prove that it is not because the genius itself is not among us.

One remark may be offered here. In all probability, the merely descriptive poet will be among the latest productions of our land. Britain herself has not produced many poets of this order, nor do they rank, with the single exception of Thomson, among the very noble of her train. Bloomfield was a driveller, and the rank of Somerville is low.[9] The genius of the Anglo-Saxon would seem to be too earnest, too intensely moral in its objects, for the consideration of still life except as subordinate to the action. He puts it in his story, as the painter upon his canvas, as a sort of back-ground, and he usually hurries from this sort of painting to that which better tasks his more exacting powers. In this characteristic the genius of the American is naturally like, — with this difference, that the circumstances of his career tends still more to increase his love of action and his disregard of mere adjuncts and dependencies.

9 Simms is referring to James Thomson (1700–1748), author of *The Seasons;* Robert Bloomfield (1766–1823), author of *The Farmer's Boy;* and William Somerville (1675–1742), author of *The Chase* and *Field Sports.*

He has an aim, and, eager in its attainment, he pauses not to
see how lovely is the lake and valley — how vast the mountain
— how wild the gorge, how impetuous the foaming rush of the
unbridled waters. If he sees or feels, it is but for an instant, —
and he is driven forward, even as the cataract beneath his gaze,
by a power of which he is himself unconscious, and in a direction, the goal of which he is not permitted to behold. Our
orator has already, adequately and sufficiently, instanced the
various charms of scenery which our country possesses. These
will make themselves felt in due season, when the national
mind is permitted to pause in its career of conflict — for such
is the nature of its progress now — for a survey of its conquests and itself. We pass, with him, to other considerations
of still more importance, as essential to Americanism in our
Letters. The extract which we make is brief:

These pleasant anticipations are also justified in part, by the excellent
and diversified character of the population of our country. Herein will
reside one of the strong modifying influences of Americanism upon
literature. Though our population is composed principally of the several varieties of the Anglo-Saxon stock, yet every other race of Europe, and some from the other continents, have contributed to swell
the motley and singular combination. Coming from every quarter of
the globe, they have brought with them their diverse manners, feelings, sentiments, and modes of thought, and fused them in the great
American alembic. The stern, clear-headed, faith-abiding Puritan, the
frank, chivalrous, imaginative Huguenot, the patient, deep-thoughted,
contemplative German, — pilgrims from every clime, creed, and literature — are to be found in contact and intercourse here. They interact
upon each other to fashion all the manifestations of society, in thought
or deed. The contrasts and coincidences, they present under our institutions, afford new and graceful themes for the poet, the novelist
and the philosopher; and the historian will have to give us pictures of
life and humanity here, such as are found not elsewhere. I need but
allude, in this connection, to the existence of three distinct races of
men upon our continent, with their strongly marked peculiarities of
condition, colour and history. The immense rapidity with which our
numbers are increasing — well nigh doubling in every fifteen years! —
will produce an unexampled demand for knowledge, and act as a
powerful impetus to its elevation. Already has the great and fluctuat-

ing intermixture of our population had an influence upon the English language. In no part of the world is our mother tongue spoken with such general purity of pronunciation as in our country. The constant tide of internal emigration tends to rectify the provincialisms into which stationary communities so frequently fall. Otherwise is it even in England. The whole kingdom is broken up into dialects as numerous as her counties; and the respective inhabitants are almost as unintelligible to each other, as if they spoke languages radically distinct. Is it Utopian to expect the proudest results, when one common language shall be employed by the many millions who are to occupy this almost illimitable republic? — But it is in the strong, industrious and wholesome character of our population, that the best hope for our national mind depends. Their habits of life will generate a *muscularity* of intellect, becoming their position and destiny. No effeminacy of thought or feeling will be tolerated among a people, composed of the choicest varieties of every race, stimulating each other to mental exertion, and accumulating wealth and power with almost miraculous rapidity and extent. Such a people, if they should have no powerful impediments, are better fitted than any other to render the world an intellectual illumination, and to bring round in reality the poetic vision of the golden age. pp. 17-19.

But the most imposing considerations arrayed by our author in this discussion, as indicative of the future resources of Americanism in our Literature, are to be found in those passages in which he considers the influence of our political institutions upon the mind of the country. It would afford us great pleasure did our limits suffice to give these passages, but we must content ourselves with a bare glance at their prominent suggestions. Mr. Meek justly draws our attention to the fact, that, of all the ancient tyrannies, but very few of them have contributed to the advancement of letters. He exhibits the baldness in literature of Chaldea, Babylon, Assyria and Phœnicia, and hurriedly compares their performances with the more glorious showings of the free states of the past. And he argues justly that this result is in the very nature of things; — that, as liberty of opinion is favourable to thought and provocative of discussion, so almost must it favour the general development of intellect in all departments. The deduction is absolutely inevitable. Tyranny, on the other hand, always trembling for its sceptre, and jealous of every antagonist influence, watches with sleepless solicitude to impose every fetter upon the free speech of orator and poet. It would seem almost impertinent to insist upon these points, were it not that there really exists among thinking men a considerable difference of opinion upon them, and this difference of opinion is the natural fruit of a too hasty glance only at the surfaces. The friends of aristocracy, lingering fondly over those bright but unfrequent pages in literary history, as associated with a despotism, which are adorned by the works of genius, hurriedly conclude that they are the issues of that despotism itself.[10] They point with confidence to such periods as those of Augustus Cæsar and Leo the Tenth. The courtly sway of the one, and the magnificent ambition of the other, are sufficient to delude the imagination, and hurry the reason aside from a consideration of the true analysis. They overlook the important fact that, in all these cases, it has so happened that men of literary tastes were themselves the despots. It was not that the despotism was itself favourable to such persons, but that the despotism, wielded by a particular hand, was not unwilling to smile with indulgence upon the obsequious poet, and the flattering painter. It so happened that an absolute tyrant was yet possessed of some of the higher sensibilities of the intellectual nature, and had almost as strong a passion for letters and the arts, as for political dominion. Thus feeling, he rendered the one passion in some degree subservient to the other. If it could be shown that his tastes were transmitted with his robes, to his successor, there might be some reason in the faith which we are required to have in the benignant literary influences of

[10] For a classic statement of the position that Simms here discusses, see Alexis de Tocqueville, *Democracy in America*, Part II, Book I, chapter xiii, "Literary Characteristics of Democracy." The Henry Reeve translation of this portion of *Democracy in America* was published in New York in 1840.

such a government; but the sufficient fact that, in the histories of despotism, these brief and beautiful periods shine out alone, and rest like green spots, at remote stages, through a long and lamentable wilderness, would seem to conclude the question.

It was the wealth and taste of the despot that made him a patron, and not because he held the reins of government with a rigorous or easy hand. The peculiar sort of rule in Rome and Italy had no part in making the poet or historian; and, for the patronage itself, accorded by the despot, let the reader turn to the histories of denied and defrauded genius, and see what a scorned and wretched beggar it has ever been in the courts of Aristocracy. Let him look to the history of Tasso for example — let him turn to that curious book of Benvenuto Cellini,[11] — if he would see what sort of countenance is that which mere power is apt to bestow upon the labours of the man of letters or of art. Great wealth, — that of private persons — has done for them much more in every nation. Spenser owed much more to Sydney, and Shakspeare to Southhampton,[12] than either of them ever owed to Elizabeth. We need not multiply examples. The man of genius, in all departments, has achieved his triumphs rather in despite and defiance of despotism than because of its benign and genial atmosphere. The true patron of letters is the lover of them, and where are these persons likely to be more numerous, than in regions where the great body of the people are lifted by the political institutions of the country into a responsibility which tasks the intellect, and requires a certain amount of knowledge in every department. The despotism is apt to absorb in itself all the taste and intellect where it governs. Democracy naturally diffuses them.

[11] *Autobiography of Benvenuto Cellini.* Cellini (1500–1571), Florentine sculptor and goldsmith, wrote his *Autobiography* between 1558 and 1562. It was first published in 1730.
[12] Henry Wriothesley, Third Earl of Southampton (1573-1624), was Shakespeare's friend and patron.

At first, the diffusion would seem to lessen the amount of the whole, — to subtract from its spirit — reduce its volume, and, by too minute division of its parts, to render it feeble and inert for active purposes. But the constant attrition of rival minds in a country where the great body of the people are forced into consideration, strengthens and informs, with a peculiar and quickening vigour, each several share of that capacity with which the genius of the nation was at first endowed. The genius of the nation does not the less act together, because it acts through many rather than through one; and, by insensible transitions, the whole multitude rise to the same elevated platform, upon which, at the beginning, we may have beheld but one leading mind, and that, possibly, borrowed from a rival nation. It is a wondrous impulse to the individual, to his hope, his exertions and his final success, to be taught that there is nothing in his way, in the nature of the society in which he lives; — that he is not to be denied because of his birth or poverty, because of his wealth or his family; — that he stands fair with his comrades, on the same great arena, — with no social if no natural impediments, — and that the prize is always certain for the fleetest in the race.

This must be the natural influence of the democratic principle upon the minds of a people by whose political institutions its supremacy is recognized. Let no man deceive himself by a glance confined only to the actual condition of things around him. No doubt that, in the beginning of a democracy, in that first wild transition state, which follows upon the overthrow of favourite and long acknowledged authorities, art and literature, alarmed at the coil and clamour, will shroud themselves in their cells, venturing abroad only in those dim hours of dusk and twilight, in which a comparative silence promises comparative security. But this is also the history of nearly all of the arts of peace. Commerce and trade, mechanical and mercantile adventure, show themselves nearly equally timid.

True, they are the first to recover from their panic, but this is solely because they belong to the more servile and earthly necessities of our nature. They are followed by the gradual steps of art and science, and these in turn by the lovelier and gentler offspring of united grace and muse. It is the error of persons of taste that, shrinking themselves from the uproar of this transition period, they regard its effects as likely to continue, as being not temporary only, and as destined to perpetuate the commotion which, in our notion, is nothing more than that natural outbreak of elements in the moral, which, in the natural world, almost always harbingers a clear sky and pure, salubrious and settled weather. Such, when the time comes, —when the first rude necessities of a new condition are pacified, and the machine begins to turn evenly and smoothly upon its axis, — such will be the working of democracy. This is not less our faith than our hope. The natural conclusions of reason led us directly to this confidence, even if the history of the past did not afford us sufficient guaranties for the future.

Our orator next instances, with effect, the wholesome influences in our government of the "let alone" principle. This, by the way, is an important matter to be understood. Democracy goes into society, with scarcely any farther desire than that men should be protected from one another — left free to the pursuit of happiness, each in the form and manner most agreeable to himself, so long as he does not trespass upon a solitary right of his neighbour. This is the principle. We do not tolerate any interference of government with those employments of its citizens which violate none of the rights of others, and which do not offend against the sense of a Christian country. To protect or to disparage that occupation of the individual or the community, which, in itself, is regarded as legitimate, is a power which, according to our construction of the social contract in America, is wholly unwarranted by our laws. Something is due certainly to the necessities of the whole; but, for the "general welfare" principle, we insist that the "general necessity and exigency" is the true standard by which we impose restraints, or hold out encouragements. Mr. Meek properly insists upon the value of this "let alone" practice, on the part of government, as vastly promotive of the interests of literature; and particularly dwells upon the advantages, in this regard, which grow out of our system of confederated sovereignties. The very inequalities of things in moral respects, in employments, in climate, soil and circumstance, which we find in these severalties, is at once calculated to provoke the mind in each to exertion, and to endow it with originality. There is none of that even tenor of aspect, in the genius of the country, which somewhat monotonously distinguishes an empire the whole energies of which spring from centralization. A natural rivalry and emulation are the consequence of a form of political independence, which, in all domestic subjects, leaves us utterly free to our own pursuits. We watch the progress of our neighbour, and strive rather to surpass than to follow. There is none of that servile, blind adhesion to a superior, which, in Europe, invariably brings the popular intellect, even in the most remote dependencies of the nation, to the beaten tracks which conduct them to the centre. The very divergencies of our paths are favourable to the boldness, the freedom and the flights of the national intellect. We make our own paths — we trace out our own progress — and, just in due degree as we turn aside from the dictation of those great cities, which, among us, are more immediately allied with the marts of Europe, so do we discover marks of the most certain freshness and originality, though coupled with rudeness and irregularity — a harshness which offends and a wilderness which, we are encouraged to believe, it is not beyond the power of time and training to subdue to equable and noble exercises. To any one who looks into the character of our people, — who passes below the surface, and sees in what way the great popular heart beats in the several States of the confederacy, — with what calm, consistent resolve in some — with what impatient heat in others — how cold but how clear in this region, — how fiery, but how clouded in that; — there will be ample promise for the future, not only in the value of the material, but in its exquisite and rich variety. And, even on the surface, how these varieties speak out for themselves, so that it shall not be difficult for a shrewd observer of men to distinguish at a glance, and to declare from what quarter of America the stranger comes, — whether from the banks of the Charles or the Hudson, the Savannah or the Mississippi.

Our orator justly reminds us, while treating of this part of his subject, that, by our compact, the interests of education and literature are left entirely in the control of the States. This vital matter is in our own hands, and nothing but our lachesse or our wilfulness, can possibly lose us the power of moulding the temper of our people in due compliance with our peculiar circumstances, whether moral or physical. We may make our literature what we please if we do not neglect the interests of education. We should confer upon it all the becoming characteristics of our section — our social sympathies, our political temper, and those moral hues and forms which the intellectual nature so happily imbibes from the aspects which surround us in the natural world. The airy structures of our imagination, born of a like sky and atmosphere with that of Greece, should not shrink from comparison with those of Dodona and Hymettus. Our Olympus rises at our will, and the divine spirits which we summon to make sacred its high abodes, clothed in a political freedom superior to that of Athens, with less danger of having their supremacy disputed and their rites disturbed, should surely bring to their altars a priesthood no less great and glorious.

ARTICLE II

THE EPOCHS AND EVENTS OF AMERICAN HISTORY, AS SUITED TO THE PURPOSES OF ART IN FICTION [1]

INTRODUCTORY. TRUE USES OF HISTORY. OBJECTS OF ART. ITS DUCTILITY AND UNIVERSALITY

It was the reply of Sir Robert Walpole, — a shrewd observer of men, a profound politician, and no shallow proficient in those agencies which ordinarily affect human opinion — when, in his last illness, his son proposed to read to him from some work of history, — "No, sir, I have long since done with fiction." Such a reply might well startle and bewilder that blind and credulous multitude, who seem, ordinarily, to confound this species of writing with holy writ, and accord to it a degree of reverence which they are quite unwilling to acknowledge in any consideration of Belles Lettres and the Arts. But the opinions of such men as Walpole, Raleigh, Bolingbroke and many others, of equally brilliant intellect and profound knowledge of human affairs, all of whom speak in very much

[1] [*Simms's note*] This paper forms the substance of certain lectures which were delivered before the Historical Society of the State of Georgia. The purpose for which they were prepared will excuse the somewhat too ornate character of the composition, which could only have been subdued to the usual style of essay or review, by such a thorough revision, as would probably have robbed the performance of all its freshness and freedom. [Simms delivered these lectures in Savannah, Ga., on March 8 and March 10, 1842. A small portion of the lectures was published in the *Magnolia*, n.s., I (July, 1842). A revised version, between the lecture form and that in the third version here reprinted, appeared in six installments between March and September, 1845, in the *Southern and Western Magazine*. This introductory essay to the series appeared in the *Southern and Western Magazine*, I (March, 1845), 182–191.]

the same language in relation to the same subject, might well persuade us to renounce our blind confidence in teachers, whose chief claim to our deference would seem to lie in their overweening gravity; or should, otherwise, conduct us to a more perfect faith in what is due to that art which draws, by a happy judgment, the matured fact from the embryo, and, by a series of successful speculations, leads us to those perfect narratives of life in society which the world has agreed to honour with the name of histories. A little modesty on the part of the mere historian in urging undue claims to consideration, based on grounds which are far less substantial than those which he might assert, — and a more expanded survey of the characteristics and objects of human genius, on the part of those who are much more likely to be impressed with names than with things, — might do much towards a solution of the difficulty under which, in a splenetic mood and moment, Sir Robert Walpole declared himself. The remark of this statesman, — considered the Machiavel of his day and nation, and who is supposed to have suffered great injustice in the final awards of public opinion in respect to his career, — embodied his own experience in the veracity of politics, rather than in that of history. It was the history of a small and selfish partisanship of his own time, and which possibly exists in all times, which provoked his censure; — and it will not need that we should here stop to inquire in what degree he himself contributed to render it deserving of his own sarcasm.[2] His commentary calls for our notice only as it affords us an approach to another discovery which is also due to modern times. From certain venerable Cantabs of our own age we are astounded, for the first time, to learn that there is very little ancient history of any

2 [*Simms's note*] It is to this statesman, the reader will remember, that we are indebted for the political axiom, — true or false, which is so popularly believed — that "every man has his price." This result Sir Robert is said to have arrived at by his own experiments. [See William Coxe, *Memoirs of Walpole* (1798), IV, 369.]

kind that is worthy to be relied on; — that, what we have hitherto been reading with such equal delight and confidence — those exquisite and passionate narratives of Greece and Rome — narratives of soul and sweetness, which have touched our hearts with the truest sympathy and enkindled our spirits with the warmest glow of emulative admiration — are, in reality, little more than the works of cunning artists — eloquent narrators and delicious poets, who have thus dishonestly practised upon our affections and our credulity, making us very children through the medium of our unsuspecting sympathies. Stripped of its golden ornaments of rhetoric and passion, the tale which we are now permitted to believe, is one from which the most hearty lover of the truth may well recoil in disrelish or disgust. Where now are those glowing pictures over which our eyes have glistened — those holy traits of unbending patriotism and of undying love — of maternal courage, and of filial sacrifice — of a valour that knew not self, and of an endurance that confessed no pain? — Those touching instances of social excellence and loveliness which make of the patriarchal life — the first life of civilization, — one of the loveliest periods in the whole broad province of romance; — those instances, fertile in all that is dear to fancy and affection, which have moved us to share in all the ebullitions of joy and of suffering of which we read — now striving with the patriot and now yielding with the lover — enduring with the unshaken constancy of the matron, and kneeling with the pious devotion of the son! Alas! for all these we have no authorities. We are without those grave and reverend witnesses which a court of *Nisi Prius* would suffer in evidence under the general issue — and, thus, we are called upon to deny those histories to be true, which have awakened our souls to the first consciousness of the holiest kinds of truth — the truths of the greatest purpose, — the purest integrity, the noblest ambition, the most god-like magnanimity. We go back with the rigid historian to the axemarks in this antique wilderness, and we look for these generous instances and proofs in vain. We are shown the withered branches and the prostrate trunks, the blasted forms and the defaced aspects, the dry-bones of the perished humanity; but the breath of life is gone from its nostrils, — the heart that beat, the head that planned, the eye, the voice, that willed and commanded. The God-stamped visage and the animating action, are no longer heard and visible!

> Its bones are marrowless, its blood is cold;
> It has no speculation in those eyes,
> Which it doth glare with.[3]

And we may well add, with the terrified usurper — "let the earth hide thee!" — For there can be no friendly or genial influence to man in the resurrection of this miserable mock, and complete wreck, of all that was a people or a life! But not so, say these sage historians of modern times. We are to believe in the drybones, since our eyes have present proof of their existence. We are to recognize the articulated skeleton, — nay, having strung it together on certain wires, and subjected it to a sort of moral galvanism, by which an occasional spasmodic action is betrayed, we shall even be suffered to conjecture that these dry-bones were once covered with flesh, and were informed by sense and feeling. But we may go no farther. When we would demand more, and assert more, we are met by a question as keenly decapitative in historical criticism, as any which debars disquieting debate in the halls of our legislation: — "where are your authorities?" Alas! for the student who lives only by authorities! Alas! for the genius who fears them! The one may become dry-bones himself before he conquers his accidence; and, for the other, if he leaves aught behind him, coupled with his name, it will be in such marrowless

---

[3] A paraphrase of Macbeth's words to Banquo's ghost in *Macbeth*, Act III, scene 4, lines 94–96.

fragments, such empty relics of past emptiness, that even that class of pur-blind chroniclers, of which we have spoken, will scarcely be at the necessary pains to disinter them.[4]

The truth is — an important truth which seems equally to have escaped the sarcastic minister and the learned German, and which the taste that prefers the ruin to its restoration will be the very last to appreciate, — the chief value of history consists in its proper employment for the purposes of art! — consists in its proper employment, as so much raw material, in the erection of noble fabrics and lovely forms, to which the fire of genius imparts soul, and which the smile of taste informs with beauty; — and which, thus endowed and constituted, are so many temples of mind — so many shrines of purity, — where the big, blind, struggling heart of the multitude may rush, in its vacancy, and be made to feel; in its blindness, and be made to see; in its fear and find countenance; in its weakness and be rendered strong; in the humility of its conscious baseness, and be lifted into gradual excellence and hope! These are the offices of art for which she employs history, and it is these which make her not only the most lovely but the most legitimate daughter of heaven. It is through her that the past lives to the counselling and direction of the future, and

---

[4] [*Simms's note*] The allusion here is to that class of modern historians, the professed sceptics of all detail in ancient history, of whom M. Niebuhr is the great example. It is not our purpose to disparage the learned ingenuity, the keen and vigilant judgment, the great industry, the vast erudition and sleepless research of this coldly inquisitive man; — yet, what a wreck has he made of the imposing structure of ancient history, as it comes to us from the hands of ancient art. Whether the simple fact, that what he gives us is more certainly true than what we had such perfect faith in before, is, or should be, sufficient to compensate us for that of which he despoils us, cannot well be a question with those who have a better faith in art, as the greatest of all historians, and as better deserving of our confidence than that worker who limits his faith entirely to his own discoveries. We prefer one Livy to a cloud of such witnesses as M. Niebuhr. [Simms is here referring to Barthold Georg Niebuhr (1776–1831), German historian, statesman, and philologist, the author of *History of Rome* (3 vols., 1811–1832) and *Griechische Heroengeschichten* (1842).]

if she breathe not the breath of life into its nostrils, the wires of the resurrectionist would vainly link together the ricketty skeleton which he disinters for posterity.

Considered with reference to its intrinsic uses, the bald history of a nation, by itself, would be of very little importance to mankind. Of what use to know the simple fragmentary fact, that Troy — a city we no longer find upon the maps — fell, after a siege of years — the proud and polished city before the barbarian and piratical foe? Of what use, or whence the satisfaction, placed upon the summits of Taygetus, to hear the long catalogue of names — names of men and nations — which the historian may, with tolerable certainty, enumerate and perhaps assign to each narrow spot within the range of his vision; — or, astride some block which hopeless conjecture may assume to be the site of the once mighty capital, to turn to our Lemprière [5] and learn that here once dwelt a great people who were overthrown by a greater. We know this fact without Lemprière. Ruins speak for themselves, and, to this extent, are their own historians. They equally denote the existence and the overthrow; — the was and the is not — and the dry, sapless history, tells us nothing, which can tell us nothing more! But, musing alone along the plain of the Troad, — or traversing the mountain barriers of Parnes, Ægaleus, and Hymettus; looking down upon the sterile plains of Attica, — sterile in soil, but O! how fruitful in soul, — or sitting among the dismembered fragments which made the citadel in Carthage, — each man becomes his own historian. Thought, taking the form of conjecture, ascends by natural stages into the obscure and the infinite. Reasoning of what should have been from what is before us, we gather the true from the probable. Dates and names, which, with the mere chronologist are every

[5] John Lemprière (c. 1765–1824), English classical scholar, author of *Bibliotheca Classica* (1788), a standard reference work on mythology and ancient history.

thing, with us are nothing. For, what matters it to us, while tracing hopes and fears, feelings and performances, the greatness which was, and the glories which exist no longer, to be arrested in our progress by some cold and impertinent querist, who, because we cannot tell him whether these things took place, one, two or three thousand years before Christ, — and because we cannot positively assign the precise name to the hero, — accurately showing this or that combination of seven or more letters — forbids our inquiry as idle. The inquiry is not idle, and history itself is only valuable when it provokes this inquiry — when it excites a just curiosity — awakens noble affections, — elicits generous sentiments, — and stimulates into becoming activity the intelligence which it informs!

Hence, it is the artist only who is the true historian. It is he who gives shape to the unhewn fact, who yields relation to the scattered fragments, — who unites the parts in coherent dependency, and endows, with life and action, the otherwise motionless automata of history. It is by such artists, indeed, that nations live. It is the soul of art, alone, which binds periods and places together; — that creative faculty, which, as it is the only quality distinguishing man from other animals, is the only one by which he holds a life-tenure through all time — the power to make himself known to man, to be sure of the possessions of the past, and to transmit, with the most happy confidence in fame, his own possessions to the future.

For what is the philosophy of history but a happy conjecturing, of what might have been from the imperfect skeleton of what we know. The long analysis of probabilities keenly pursued through buried fragments and dissolving dust, is the toil of an active imagination, informed by experience, obeying certain known laws of study, and recognizing, as guiding rules, certain general standards of examination. The dull seeker after bald and isolated facts is no philosopher, nor can he claim even the doubtful merit of being a pioneer. He

is a digger merely; — no more a discoverer than the hireling
whom superior taste and wealth have employed to disen-
cumber the buried city, Pompeii or Herculaneum, from its
ashes; — careless where he explores, indifferent to what he
sees, and only solicitous of the amount of labour done, which
secures him, at the end of the day or week, his miserable com-
pensation. That keen thought and pressing study, which,
heaping conjecture upon conjecture, identifying facts with
their classes, tracing concealed character through a long series
of details, educing causes from associated results, and tracing
upward, step by step, by plausible suggestions, the several poli-
cies by which nations are built up and made famous, or overthrown and dismembered, would disdain the preparation of
history if privileges such as these were denied to the historian.
And, in the exercise of these privileges, he asserts and acquires
more. He learns to speak with a familiar confidence of his subject. His imagination takes part with his judgment, officers and
counsels his thought, wings it to the desired fact, and vividly
portrays to the mind's eye the hero and the event. Thence he
becomes a limner, a painter, a creator; and the picture glows
beneath his hand, and the drama dilates in action under his
glance, and he becomes a living and authentic witness of the
past, and of all the circumstances which he has undertaken to
unfold. Such is the true historian, and such is the sort of genius
which it requires ere we shall dare to say that any history
can live.

To such an intellect, it must be permitted to argue his case
as an advocate, to choose his favourite personages from the
chronicle, and to make perfect his ideals, by a nice adaptation
to their known characteristics, of such as are essential to the
completion of the model. In proportion as his work conforms
to known proprieties and generally recognized probabilities,
and in proportion as it makes favourably for the cause of humanity and virtue, upon the understandings of those to whom

his labours are addressed, are his performances well or badly done, — and in just such degree will he be found to live in the regards of future ages. These, and these only, are his standards, speaking now only with a moral reference; — his taste, his skill, his eloquence, his powers of compression or dilation, of grouping and relief, being of course artistical requisitions, which are all essential to his success in every other respect. It is really of very little importance to mankind whether he is absolutely correct in all his conjectures or assertions, whether his theory be true or false, or whether he rightly determines upon the actor or the scene. Assuming that the means of his refutation are not to be had, that he offends against no facts which are known and decisive, no reasonable probabilities or obvious inferences, — it is enough if his narrative awakens our attention, compels our thought, warms our affections, inspirits our hopes, elevates our aims, and builds up in our minds a fabric of character, compounded of just principles, generous tendencies and clear, correct standards of taste and duty. This, in fact, is the chief object with which all history is studied — the curiosity which impels the desire being equally moral and human, and having reference to the effect, upon character, of lessons drawn from the experience and the deeds of some superior branch or persons of the great human family. We care not so much for the intrinsic truth of history, as for the great moral truths, which, drawn from such sources, induce excellence in the student. The study of mere facts which do not concern our own progress, unless such results are designed to follow, would be as utterly unimportant to ourselves and children, as the solution of the much vexed question — "who built the pyramids, Cheops or Cephrenes?" There they stand, and the philosophical historian, who really knows nothing beyond, has already declared the only really important fact in their history — namely, that they were the work of a merciless despotism — an equal trophy of miserable vanity and of absolute power; — a vanity not less absolute than the power which it exercised, but certainly far less productive of results, since the pyramids are no longer monuments! The philosopher reaches this conviction by a survey of the vast structures themselves. Their useless bulk provides a sufficient commentary on the labour which produced it; — and, even though the veracious chroniclers of the past were here — if we could trace, step by step, the progress of events by which they were raised to what they are — the great moral truth respecting them, of which we were already in possession, would receive no additional weight of suggestion. That moral truth, educed by thought from conjecture, is one wholly independent of details. Nay, even should the details become known, and conflict with the fragmentary facts which we have been accustomed to believe, they could not disturb a faith which they could never have established. To lay bare the tombs of their buried kings, to find their names, to retrace their experience, to declare their histories, would really add no desirable measure to the amount of human knowledge. It would only be multiplying a number of like facts and histories, of which we have more than enough in possession for all the purposes of moral and human analysis. The profligacy of nature, even in her tombs, and wrecks, and disasters, leaves us nothing to desire, in the way of material, whether for conjecture, or philosophy, or sympathy. A natural curiosity may prompt us to inquire, as we loiter beside the unknown tumulus, "who sleeps below?" — but a conviction quite as natural, that there are thousands of inquiries to be made besides, of far more importance even to our tastes, for which life leaves us but little leisure, soon reconciles us to the necessity of yielding the solution of our doubts to that genius which seems especially appointed for such a purpose; — a genius which acknowledges no obstruction in the otherwise dark and frowning barriers set up by the huge and shapeless sphinx of oblivion, which presides over so vast a portion of the globe, — the genius of romance and poetry! — the genius of creative art! And well does he satisfy our doubts. Let us instance one among a thousand histories to which we may refer as pregnant with examples. A statue, one of the most exquisite remains and trophies of ancient art, is rescued from the undeserving but protecting earth. The sages gather round it, the high priests of civilization and philosophy, and each has his doubts, and each has his conjectures. The study is an elaborate one, of some complexity and finish, with certain insignia. One claims it as a Grecian Herald, another will have it a Laquearian Gladiator, while a third makes it a barbarian shield-bearer from Sparta. A host of other graybeards discover a host of other similitudes. Now, the mere conclusion of this doubt, is about the least important of the facts in this exquisite *chef-d'œuvre*. Solve the doubt, ascertain the fact, and we know nothing after all. Yet, what a tale is it found to embody. The poet interposes while the strife is loudest, and furnishes the perfect history.

I see before me the Gladiator lie:
He leans upon his hand — his manly brow
Consents to death, but conquers agony, —
And his droop'd head sinks, gradually low —
And through his side, the last drops, ebbing slow,
From the red gash, fall heavy, one by one,
Like the first of a thunder-shower; and now,
The arena swims around him — he is gone
Ere ceased the inhuman shout which hailed the wretch who won.
He heard it, but he heeded not — his eyes,
Were with his heart, and that was far away;
He reck'd not of the life he lost, nor prize,
But where his rude hut by the Danube lay; —
There were his young Barbarians, all at play, —
There was their Dacian mother — he, their sire,
Butcher'd to make a Roman holiday! — [6]

[6] Lord Byron, *Childe Harold's Pilgrimage,* Canto IV, stanzas cxl and cxli. Simms makes slight modifications in the punctuation.

What a history is here! — how complete — how true! What a long narration of events is brought before us by a word — what a variety of character and fortune, — associations how gorgeous and how terrible, in the few, brief, moving lines which embody the revelation of a great artist. The circus opens upon us as we listen! We see the awful preparations for the strife — we note, with suppressed respiration, the bloody progress of the combat! We wear the buzz of the eager multitude; —

> The murmured pity or loud-roared applause,
> As man is slaughtered by his fellow man.[7]

Rome is in our eyes, — that city of equal crime and empire. We see, at a glance, all her exulting pride and the hellish magnificence of her daily exercises. There are hosts of valiant men, there are troops of lovely women; — there is the pomp of purple, the blinding glare of jewels, and, in the midst, is one, —

> Butcher'd to make a Roman holiday.

But the divine skill of the artist does not suffer us to linger too long upon the guilty glory, and the too seductive aspects of this awful spectacle. The moral requires that we should behold the inevitable concomitants. He hurries us from the scene of terror and of triumph. We fly, with the last thoughts of the dying victim, to the banks of his paternal Danube. His unconscious children are at play. There too is their Dacian mother. She knows not of their father's fate, but her thoughts are still heavy and with him. Even at that moment, a fear of the truth, a dreadful presentiment of evil, is rising within her heart, and she turns away, with a soul that sickens at all she sees, from the sports of her orphan barbarians. Such a history, thus told us, is complete in all its parts. It embodies many histories. Shall we consider it less true because it is attested in

[7] *Ibid.*, stanza cxxxix.

the undying measures of verse! Nay, should it hereafter be discovered that the exquisite performance of art by which the poet was provoked to history, was no victim to the infernal sports of the amphitheatre; — should it be shown that he was a Spartan shield-bearer, or herald, slain by sudden shaft upon the road-side, and not a barbarian dragged from the Danube; — will such a discovery, in any respect, impair the touching truths of such a history? Not a whit! The truth is still a truth apart from its application. The moral objects of the poet and the historian concern not the individual so much as the race, — are not simply truths of time, but truths of eternity, and can only cease to be truths in the decay of all human sensibilities.

The historian then must be an artist. All of the great writers of history deserve the title. Livy in past, and Gibbon in modern times, were artists of singular ability in the adjustment of details and groups, and in the delineation of action. Of the extent of their powers of conjecture, — their capacity for supplying appropriately the unsuggested probability, of filling the blanks in history with those details without which the known were valueless — it needs but to say that the facts in ancient history, compared with what is conjectured of the facts in their connection, were really very few, if not very unimportant. Original, or transmitted authorities, must always have been very vague and uncertain prior to the discovery of printing. Tradition then was the chronicler, and the poet was the historian. What fell in broken, mumbled sentences from the toothless gums of the one, was moulded into undying periods by the peculiar genius of the other, and Homer became a great master of history from no better sources of authority. We should be grateful to such historians and chroniclers. Would that they had left us a thousand more such histories. The language of Wordsworth, is not too fervent for the expression of our gratitude.

Blessings be with them, and eternal praise,
Who gave us nobler loves, and nobler cares, —
The poets; — who on earth have made us heirs,
Of truth and pure delight, by heavenly lays! [8]

But, if the composition of history be the work of an artist rather than of a mere chronicler — if it be permitted to him to speculate upon the unknown, and to assume the fact from the probable — there is yet, in this respect, a limit to his progress. There is a God Terminus for the dominions of art, as there is for each subdivision of earthly empire. The appetite which calls into existence the artist of history, is not satisfied with what he achieves. He provokes a passion which he cannot gratify, and another genius is summoned to continue the progress into those dominions of the obscure and the impalpable, which he fears to penetrate. The one is no less legitimate than the other, — and the province of the romancer, if its boundaries be not yet generally recognized, at least leaves him large liberties of conquest. It is difficult to say what seas shall limit his empire — what mountains arrest his progress, — what elements retard his flight — or

——————— Who shall place,

A limit to the giant's unchain'd strength,
Or curb his swiftness in the forward race! [9]

The liberties of conjecture which are accorded to the historian, become, in his case, liberties of creation. So far as the moral is concerned, the difference of privilege is no ways important. Their privileges differ only in degree. We permit the historian to look from his Pisgah into the land of equal doubt and promise; but the other is allowed to enter upon its exploration and to take formal possession of its fruits. Both, however, are required to recognize a law in common — that, namely, which rules that the survey and the conquest shall be

[8] William Wordsworth, "Personal Talk," lines 51–54. Simms makes slight modifications in the punctuation.
[9] William Cullen Bryant, "The Ages," lines 290–292.

made for the benefit and the blessing of the races which they
severally represent. The fruits of their toil and talents, — by
that decree of providence, which has fitted each of us for a
special and peculiar labour — are meant for the human stock;
— and when they have warmed our curiosity in what concerns
the great family to which we belong — strengthened our faith
in what are its true virtues, and what, under proper cultivation, it may become — excited our sympathies in the cause of
its leading minds — filled our hearts with gentle hopes, and
stimulated our souls to ardency in the grand and unceasing
struggle after perfection which is the great business of the
ages — then have they severally executed the holy trusts of
art which have been committed to their hands. The one employment, in these several toils, is quite as legitimate as the
other. They both demand the most varied talents and the
highest attributes of mind, which have been, or possibly can be,
conferred upon the creature. If the historian is required to
conceive readily, and to supply the motive for human action
where the interests of a State, or a nation, are concerned, — a
like capacity must inform the novelist, whose inquiries conduct him into the recesses of the individual heart. Both should
be possessed of clear minds, calm, deliberate judgments, a
lively fancy, a vigorous imagination, and a just sense of propriety and duty. In degree, both should be endowed with large
human sympathies, without which neither of them could
justly enter into the feelings and affections, the fears and the
hopes, of the persons whose characters they propose to analyze. If the subject of the historian is one of more dignity and
grandeur, that of the romancer is one of more delicacy and
variety. If the task of the one is imposing because of its gravity, and the vast interests which are involved in the discussion,
— the other is more attractive as it admits of so much more of
that detail, in the affairs of a favourite, which brings us to a
familiar acquaintance with the graces of the family circle, the

nice sensibilities of the heart, the growth of the purest affections, and those more ennobling virtues of the citizen, which,
as they are seldom suffered to show themselves beyond the
sphere of domestic privacy, are not often permitted to glide
into, and relieve the uniform majesty of, history. To show
what are the privileges and performances of the romancer, imbued with a just sense of his rights and resources, is to provide
the most ample justification of his claim to rank with the
noblest workers in all the fields of art. On this subject we are
daily growing more and more enlightened. The puritanism
which, (because of certain vague religious scruples of the
class which destroyed the ancient abbey and altar because of
its forms and peculiar service,) felt itself shocked at the story,
is no longer heard to complain; and the stale outcry of a class,
no less bigoted, by which it was supposed that romance was a
disparagement to history, or led only to a perversion of the
truth in history, is pretty much at an end, — silenced by the
certain tendencies of romantic narrative to heighten the taste
for history itself. Philosophy, to say nothing of common sense,
begins to discover that Shakspeare's Chronicles of England,
are not only quite as true, substantively, as those of Hume, but
that they are decidedly more true to the great leading characteristics of society and human nature; and, in more recent
days, it is found that Scott's uses of skeleton history have been
to furnish it with life and character, to reclothe its dry-bones,
and to impart a symmetry and proportion to its disjointed
members, which, otherwise, were as unnatural and formless
as that creation of the shambles, the modern Prometheus of
Mrs. Shelley.[10] It was, for example, only with the publication

---

[10] [*Simms's note*] Let us not be understood as meaning to disparage any
thing in this remarkable production, beyond the clumsy manner in which a
daring conception has been worked out. It is evidently a crude and shapeless
contrivance, which a little more preparation might have licked into better
shape and more reasonable symmetry. In spite of the abortiveness of the details, and the total want of a scheme in the creation of the man, the story

of Ivanhoe, one of the most perfect specimens of the romance that we possess,[11] that the general reader had any fair idea of the long protracted struggle for superiority between the Norman and the Saxon people. Nay, it was not till that stately creation of art, with all its towers and banners, blazed upon the eyes of the delighted nations, that the worthy burghers of London and Edinburgh were made aware that there had been any long continued conflict between these warring races. The general opinion was that the Saxons had yielded the struggle with the fatal field of Hastings, and that the hope of their empire had gone down forever with the star of the intrepid Harold. It was reserved for the romancer to show how very different was the truth — how reluctant was the Saxon to forego his hope of the final expulsion of the intruder, and the restoration of his sceptre in the hands of a native. It is, in all probability, to this very story that we owe the re-opening of the recent inquiry, and the discussion of the events of this period, and in particular the very charming history of the Norman conquest and sway, from the pen of Monsieur Thierry.[12] In this work, the writer, borrowing something of the attributes of the poet, has contrived to clothe his narrative with an atmosphere which confers upon it a rich mellowness not to be found in the works of the ordinary historian; and, with the advance of the popular thought, and the attainment of a just judgment in respect to the legitimacy of art in the delineation of history, shall we recover from the past many more perfect

---

betrays, on every page, proofs of a real genius in the writer. [Simms is here referring to *Frankenstein*, a Gothic romance by Mary Wollstonecraft Shelley (1797–1851), published in 1818, which recounts the catastrophes attendant on the creation of a living monster by a young scientist, Frankenstein.]

[11] [*Simms's note*] Impaired, however, by the single piece of mummery toward the close, which embodies the burial rites of Athelstane and his resurrection. But for this every way unbecoming episode, the romance would be nearly perfect.

[12] Augustin Thierry (1795–1856), French historian, author of *Conquête de l'Angleterre par les Normands* (1825).

narratives concerning periods in our chronicles, of which, at this moment, we scarce acknowledge any want. As it was to Shakspeare's Richard that we owe that of Horace Walpole, so, to similar provocation, shall we be indebted for the restoration of all the British Kings from the old Saxon heptarchy. What glorious histories are in reserve for us, of the Edwards' and the Henrys, — the Tudors and the Plantagenets —

> ———— those rival roses, red and pale,
> That wrought our island's wo, in bloodiest fray.[13]

It will not need, in determining generally the legitimacy of romantic art, to analyze its several classes and distinguish between their rights and privileges. Definitions poorly supply the place of general reading, and, even could ours answer the end proposed, it would make no part of our present design to undertake them. That much of most histories is built upon conjecture — that this conjecture, assuming bolder privileges, becomes romance — that all ages and nations have possessed this romance — that many ages and nations are now known only by its vitative agency — are matters which we have sought rather to suggest than to establish; —and, these being understood, we come now to the question — where, in *our* history, are the epochs, and what the materials, which, in the hands of the future poet and romancer, shall become the monuments of our nation — shall prove the virtues of our people, — declare their deeds, and assert, to the unborn ages, the fame of our achievements? We take for granted that all hearts, not absolutely base and slavish, will yearn for such future chronicles; — will throb, with a natural pulse of enthusiastic hope, in the persuasion that we are to have a song, and a statue, and a story, — which, when our political name shall be an echo, will make it one that the generations will delight to prolong along with those of Greece and Ilium. It would be no less painful

[13] The source of this quotation has not been located.

than unpatriotic to doubt that all who yield to the subject a thought or an affection, will feel with us, that, next to the prayer of a glorious immortality for our own soul, will be that which we prefer to heaven for the soul of our mother country.[14]

In entering upon this enquiry, we discard entirely the supposition that any thing has yet been done with these epochs and materials. We shall say nothing, as well from motives of delicacy as to avoid unnecessary discussion of any of our achievements, whether of pen or pencil, whether of prose or verse. We prefer looking at the country, naked as it is, unadorned, a rough, unhewn mass — shapeless to the eye, — unsightly, perhaps, in other eyes, not blinded by our feelings of sympathy and home! We look at the waste map from Passamaquoddy to the Sabine, and ask, — where are *our* treasures, — our jewels of song and story, — which, when our country shall have become venerable with years, — in ruin perhaps from frequent overthrow, — shall inform the groping nations what she has been, and yield to them, even in her decay and desolation, models of excellence not inferior to those which we owe to the genius of the East; — song and story which shall enchain the ear of future admiration, — telling of our endurance and our deeds — how we toiled and how we triumphed — what bards have sung in our glory, what statesmen have struggled in our behalf, — what valour was in the hearts of our warriers, — what purity and constancy in the souls of our women!

Let your grave lovers of skeleton history ask if these questions have ever been answered by the dry-bones for which they dig. Look for yourselves and behold, — in the long

---

[14] [*Simms's note*] This epithet is employed here in a direct sense, as used by the citizen in reference to our own soil. Our note is intended to prevent the recognition of the old conventional phrase of the provincial, into which, as a people, we are but too ready still to fall.

tract of ages which have vanished — at the mighty nations which have lived and live no longer, — behold the glorious record of the past, preserved to the future, only by the interposition of creative art. The statesman and the chronicler are dust, but the pictured story of the painter still speaks from the canvas, — and what an undying strain of song, peals, echo upon echo falling, — prolonged without faintness, and felt without fatigue, — in the ears of the succeeding ages, from the heaven-touched lips of the inspired minstrel! What a voice for the ages have these! How they clothe their several empires with an unfading halo! How they govern the infant nations with a deathless moral! How they sway our hearts with their sweetness; — how they counsel our spirits with their strength! How we turn to them in our ignorance for our models — how we invoke them in our timidity for our inspiration! They preserve the treasures, — they provide the jewels of a nation, when they embalm, in the "cedar oil" of immortality, the great deeds which have done honour to mankind!

In asking for the materials of art which are afforded us by our own history, we must not be thought friendly to the notion that it is a sort of patriotism, amounting almost to a duty, that the American author should confine himself exclusively to the boundaries of his own country. Every man of genius has a certain character of independence, any attempt to confine which, would be as detrimental to his genius as it would be derogatory to his independence. This independence imparts to his mind an impulse, whose operations are very much like those of instinct. He cannot, if he would, withstand their influence; and if he seeks to obey the old law in such cases, and looks into his heart at all, he cannot help but write after its suggestions.[15] We should regard the doctrine of resolutely

15 [*Simms's note*] "Fool," said my Muse to me, "look in thy heart and write." — *Sir Philip Sidney — Astrophel and Stella.* [The concluding line of the first sonnet.]

restraining ourselves to the national materials as being rather slavish than national, unless the native tendencies of the writer's mind carried him forward in their peculiar contemplation. But, at the same time, it must be remembered that the national themes seem to be among the most enduring. The most popular writers of all periods have been always most successful, whenever they have addressed themselves to either of three great leading subjects, — their religion, their country and themselves! We need not particularize, but such, in great degree, are the themes of Homer, of Dante, of Milton, Shakspeare, Byron, Burns and Scott, and, indeed, of almost every writer who has possessed any marked individuality of character. We state this proposition broadly, without deeming it necessary to suggest the several exceptions and qualifications which a very close scrutiny might detect. That sort of poetry or romance which is of a didactic or merely moral character, never can possess individuality — will be as characteristic of one country as another, and will fail, therefore, to excite a very strong enthusiasm in any. The writings of Cowper — a master in his way — are of this kind. Wordsworth, in our own day, though probably the greatest contemplative poet that has ever lived, labours to a considerable degree under the same deficiency. The thoughtful minds of all nations will yield him a sacred place in their regards. They will go with him to the haunted well in secret — they will linger with him, till after nightfall, for the Egeria of the grove, — and adopt his musings with a ready faith which shall prove how true to the moral nature were the sources of his inspiration. But he will arouse no impulses, waken no heart to enthusiasm, enkindle no generous impatience, lead to no mighty action. His faith is not of a kind to provoke his own fervour, or to move, by his impulse and example, the zeal of those whom he teaches. His faith lacks equally in depth and elevation.

The contemplative writer is usually a phlegmatic in temperament, who kindles no eyes, stirs no souls, touches none of the more vital strings of the passions and the heart. This is reserved for writers who appeal to the blood and the brain in common — writers of great personal courage and character — who seem ever eager for action, and whose themes will be found, as instanced already, either in themselves, their country, or their religion. It is such songs as theirs that become songs of a whole people — it is their names that are never suffered to die from remembrance; and when they yield to the common lot, the voice of their departure thrills through the great world's heart as if an exquisite nerve, necessary to its sweetest functions, were suddenly smote asunder. How touchingly was this illustrated in the feeling among the humbler classes in London, as they gathered silently in groups beneath the windows of the house in which Scott lay dying and pointed out the sacred mansion to one another. They had a personal interest in the genius that had wound himself into the recesses of their own souls, and planted there the choicest seeds of new and grateful emotions. And so of one, of whom the moral world deems far less tenderly. We can all remember what a pang went through this wide western land when the news was brought us that Lord Byron was no more. He had made himself, in spite of his many weaknesses and vices, a part of our personal nature. His genius was a spell, which, speaking through warm and passionate blood, had appealed to similar passions, so effectually, as to command their sympathies even in spite of the truth. To all those to whom poetry constituted one of the necessary ingredients of life, his loss was personal. It was, as if all eyes had, on a sudden, beheld some great and customary light go out in darkness from the sky.

A superficial criticism might object that Lord Byron yielded but a small part of his genius to the illustration of his country's history, and that, of the plays of Shakspeare, the Chronicle Tragedies constitute but a small, and, perhaps, inferior portion of his mighty labours. We trust that we shall not surprise too many of our readers, when we assert that there is very little substantial difference, in reference to what is individual in the revelations of the artist, between the several topics of one's self, one's country, and one's religion! They produce like effects upon the mind of the writer — bring into activity the same intense individuality of feeling, — and, consequently, find that energetic and passionate utterance which will always commend the story to other minds. It is only a more noble egotism which prompts us to speak of our country, — to make its deeds our subject, and its high places our scene. It is because it *is our* country — because its high places have been present to the eye of our childhood, and all its triumphs and interests have been incorporated, by the silent processes of memory and thought, into the very soul of our personal existence. And, what can be more wholly personal to us than our religion? Identified with our country, — for the religion of a nation is the most subtle and widely diffused element in its whole character and history — it is yet the distinct possession and duty of each individual man! It appeals hourly to his hopes and fears, and all his deeds, whether of shame or greatness, necessarily refer to its holy and dread tribunal for that verdict upon which the vast interests of the future life depend. Whether, therefore, the poet speaks directly of himself, his country, or his religion, he speaks in the fulness of his own soul, and from the overflowings of a burdened heart. His song is that of an aroused and earnest mind, deeply excited, and earnest in its least impassioned language. And he who speaks *from* the soul, we need hardly say, speaks *to* the soul. He who shows himself to be in earnest in what he says, cannot fail to produce earnestness in those who hear him. This, indeed, is the great secret of the orator — it is the great secret of success in all labours of the intellect which are addressed to the feelings or the understandings of men. The hearty expression of the Muse of Shakspeare, still declares the thorough English sentiment and feeling, even where his writings fail to contemplate English history; — and so, also, does every breathing of Lord Byron's egotism and passion — his vain pride — his intense kindlings — his stubborn resolution not to do right because his enemies censure his wrong doing — declare the genuine English character. Addressing himself to this character in the usual language of English earnestness, he enters, every where, most readily, into the English sense. The commonest man in England, though he knows and cares little for the Muse, can yet understand such a song as that of Byron. It speaks the language of his own passion — his impulse — his confidence in his own strength — his bulldog powers of endurance — his stubborn consistency in error, from the false pride which makes him reluct at confession, and his resolution to persevere in wrong, for no better reason than because his neighbours have presumed to set him right.[16] All his great characteristics, his strength and his intensity, his scorn of the merely frivolous, his sense of the superior — his appreciation of virtue, even where it is unpractised, — his susceptibility to tenderness even in his pride and selfishness — the boldness of his aim, and the inflexible eagerness with which he pursues it — are embodied in the verse of this great but erring master.

The true and most valuable inspiration of the poet will be found either in the illustration of the national history, or in

16 [*Simms's note*] We have an amusing instance of this characteristic national trait in the notes of a late English traveller in our country. It is Col. Hamilton, we believe, who somewhere tells us that he refused to seek or to hear Daniel Webster, though very anxious to do so, simply because every body in America assured him that this was absolutely necessary. What could be more thoroughly English than this mode of convincing every body that they knew nothing of the matter, and were guilty of impertinence. True, we are too much given to this sort of impertinence, but really Mr. Hamilton need not have punished us so severely. And so, Mr. Daniel Webster — to his own great mortification, doubtless — remains to this day unknown to Col. Hamilton! [Simms is referring to Thomas Hamilton (1789-1842), the author of *Men and Manners in America* (1833).]

the development of the national characteristics. His themes, if unallied to these, will be very likely to lack permanence and general interest. The advantages afforded by national themes, have, therefore, seldom been disregarded by that class of writers whose genius is distinguished by much enthusiasm. They all feel, as if by instinct, the desire of Burns, who tells us, in his own artless manner, that his longing from childhood, had always been to make some song which should live "for poor old Scotland's sake." Putting aside the patriotism of this suggestion, it has its policy also. Poetry or romance, illustrative of those national events of which the great body of the people delight to boast, or of which they have only a partial knowledge, — possesses a sort of symbolical influence upon their minds, and seems, indeed, to become a visible form and existence to their eyes. As in the gorgeous rites of the Catholic Church, the God first enters the mind through the medium of the eye. The passion and the agony of Christ, having a lively representation to the sight, imparts, in turn, a vivid conviction to the heart; and the events of a national history, which we can associate with a place and with a name, endowed with vitality by the song of the poet, — will make that place sacred, as a shrine for far seeking pilgrims, and will render that name famous as a sound, for deep-feeling and warm-loving spirits. A national history, preserved by a national poet, becomes, in fact, a national religion. Taught by him, we every where behold the visible monuments of the agonies of our martyrs. In England, we rush to the Abbey and the Tower, to Kenilworth and the Old Bower at Woodstock. In Scotland, with the help of Burns and Scott, we traverse the fields of Bannockburn and Flodden — we look over the lonely Loch to the ruins of Castle Douglas; and stoop, with shuddering, and half averted gaze, over the blood-stains of Holyrood, which we are told, by the genius of the place, streamed from the heart of David Rizzo. The spell of genius, in thus making sacred the ruins of time, preserves itself from oblivion. What would be the homage of our children, down to the fourth and fifth generation of those, born after, who will love us, — to that inspired bard, who shall conduct them to the high places of our glory — who shall lead them to, and designate, by a song and by a sign, the old fields of Eutaw and Saratoga — who shall say, in a glorious burst of lyrical lament, mixed with exultation — "there, even beside yon hillock, fell the veteran De Kalb,[17] and here — possibly on the very spot over which we stand — the death wound was given to the intrepid Jasper and Pulaski." [18]

ii

BENEDICT ARNOLD AS A SUBJECT
FOR FICTITIOUS STORY [1]

WE assume that the man of genius inclines, by reason of natural affection, to do honour to his birth-place. Such an inclination belongs to the enthusiastic nature, and this is a sufficient reason why it should be indulged, since enthusiasm very rarely expends itself on objects of an unworthy character. Looking forward then to the future labours of the artist who shall preserve and adorn our histories, we turn to the histories

17 [*Simms's note*] The Baron de Kalb was slain near Camden, South Carolina, in 1780.

18 [*Simms's note*] Count Pulaski, the famous Pole, whose attempt upon the person of Stanislaus Poniatowski had so nearly proved successful. Pulaski distinguished himself as a partisan in the war of our revolution, and led a very efficient force of cavalry. He fell, with Sergeant Jasper — a hero in the ranks, whose extraordinary courage and conduct have lifted him into a fixed place in the national memory — before Savannah, in Georgia (where these lectures were delivered) then in possession of the British forces, while gallantly sharing in the assault made upon that city by the combined armies of America and France.

1 A version of this essay was published in the *Southern and Western Magazine*, I (April, 1845), 257–261.

themselves, — even as the sculptor, in whose mind reposes the perfect ideal of the statue, turns to the rude masses of the quarry from which it must yet be hewn. Have we these masses, — does our material answer for such purposes, — and in what quarter does it lie? The artist, it must be remembered, is a *seer!* He must be able to discover that which is hidden from all other eyes — which other minds have not conjectured — which other persons have not sought. If he fail in this, he is not the man to preserve a nation's history. You may be sure he is no genius. He may be clever, and not wanting in a certain sort of talent; but, with all his cleverness, he is not the person for a work like this. He is only an ordinary workman, in common clay, and his achievements will turn out commonplaces. It is in the exercise of the "vision and the faculty divine," that the seer is made conscious of one of the leading difficulties in the way of American romance. What portion of our history remains unwritten? What portion of it is so obscure that all may not equally see? — for, it need scarcely be said to the reader, that, if the ordinary citizen is at liberty to contravene your facts and dispute your premises, there is necessarily an end to your story. There must be a faith accorded to the poet equally with the historian, or his scheme fails of effect. The privileges of the romancer only begin where those of the historian cease. It is on neutral ground alone, that, differing from the usual terms of warfare, as carried on by other conquerors, his greatest successes are to be achieved.

A certain degree of obscurity, then, must hang over the realm of the romancer. The events of history and of time, which he employs, must be such as will admit of the full exercise of the great characteristic of genius — imagination. He must be free to conceive and to invent — to create and to endow; — without any dread of crossing the confines of ordinary truth, and of such history as may be found in undisputed records. He must not expose himself to suspicion by his facts — he must not fear dispute upon his grounds and premises. His materials must be of such a kind as to leave him without danger of rebuke for impropriety; and the only laws and criteria against which he must provide, must be those of good taste and probability, with such other standards as he himself sets up in his progress, as gauges by which to work himself and by which others are to judge of his performances. When we are told that a history is too fresh for fiction, it is because of this danger that it is so. When it is objected that America is too young for the production of a national literature, it is chiefly because of this difficulty, which fetters and defies domestic invention. Genius dare not take liberties with a history so well known, and approaches her task with a cautious apprehensiveness which is inconsistent with her noblest executions. It is asserted of our men of letters, particularly our poets, that their performances are simply English — that they have none of those distinguishing traits which might separate them from their great originals, and identify them immediately with the soil which they claim more particularly to represent. It would, perhaps, be matter of greater surprise were the fact otherwise. The reasons why such should be the case, are obvious when we remember what language it is we speak, and how recent is the period which first severed our ancestors from the great maternal nation. There are yet other reasons, the examination of which would carry us too largely aside, into the consideration of society in general; a task which would be equally inconsistent with our duty and present limits. It is enough to say that our history *is* English down to a very recent period — our infancy and childhood were wholly so, and such also are the most obvious traits in the character of our individuals, — particularly in the southern parts of the republic, where sparse settlements and the employments of agriculture, tenaciously retain for us the tradi-

tional peculiarities of the race. We have a perfect right to
European materials in all moral respects — its histories, its
achievements, its great names; and it is just as legitimate, on
the part of our poets, to model themselves upon the great
masters of the stock to which they originally belonged, and
to employ their fashions and develop their conditions, as it
is with those whose immediate sires preferred the more quiet
and less courageous duty of clinging still to the ancient fire-
sides. We have all our rights, as Europeans, to the stock of
national character as acquired before our ancestors departed
from the soil, as thoroughly as any Briton that remains. The
past is ours, of English history, so long as a common ancestry
toiled together in its acquisition. We shared a common birth,
a common infancy and joint heritage, — and their Chaucers
and Spensers, — their Shakspeares and Miltons, — are ours,
down to the moment when the besotted ministry of George
the Third determined to spoil us of this heritage. As Americans, we sprang into birth, full grown, if not in panoply. Our
political existence, as a nation, is not to be confounded with
our existence as a people. The difficulties of the critics, foreign
and domestic, and most of the blunders which the former
make in regard to our country, are almost wholly in consequence of their confounding two moral propositions which
are wholly irreconcilable. They insist upon an originality in
our characteristics which is incompatible with our condition.
They assume that our peculiarities must be as decidedly foreign to their own as if we were a people of Owyhee, and reproach us with a likeness to themselves, when, in fact, we
claim those attributes and features to be as decidedly our right
as theirs. That we should think and write, according to the
examples and lessons of our ancestors, is not a whit calculated
to impair our originality. As Americans, merely, the case is
different, and there are peculiarities which we may engraft
upon our ancient models, whether in literature or the arts,

which would not impair their symmetry, and would not be amiss as regards our independence. We might also shake off some customs and practices, some laws and fashions, which, brought by our European ancestors to America, are yet unnatural and unfriendly to the soil. Our parents were English, but our garments need not be made by an English tailor. Our language is English, but such need not be the case with our literature. Our sense of liberty is English, but it does not follow that we might not rid ourselves of some of the brutalities of English law. Our education is in some respects too little, in others too much English; and many of our social and political strifes and troubles arise from the strange anomaly of a republican people borrowing their educational forms, their laws and models, from an aristocracy — from those of a nation whose objects do not seem the same as ours, and whose aims and performances have been so repeatedly hostile.

Such being our history as Americans — at once brief in term and deficient in independence — it is very obvious that, as a whole, it will lack, for the purposes of literature, much of that important obscurity —

That little glooming light, most like a shade,[2]

which is so necessary to the invention, and so delightful to the desires and the instincts of the artist. That twilight of time, that uncertainty of aspect and air in history, which so provokes curiosity, and so encourages doubt — that moving, morning hour, grey and misty, which precedes and follows the dawn, but melts away, with all its vague outlines and wondrous shadows, in the broad bright blaze of the perfect day; — or that other kindred period, at its close, when the imperfect shadows reappear, and, in the obscurity of the twilight, once more leave fancy free to her sports, and imagina-

[2] A paraphrase of Edmund Spenser, *The Faerie Queene*, Book I, canto i, stanza 14: "a little glooming light, much like a shade."

tion to his audacious dreams and discoveries; — these are the periods of time, in history, which, illustrated by corresponding periods of light and darkness, afford to the poet or the artist of a nation, the proper scope for his most glorious achievements.

The discovery of America, and its conquest, as a history, seem to have been a day perfect from the beginning. Compared with ancient histories, with those of Greece and Rome and Troy, there is very little of that twilight uncertainty in the events preceding and attending it, which corresponds with our similitude drawn from the history of our solar dawn, and which leaves the romancer at liberty to conceive his schemes, and embody with courage his own inventions. Our country, as a system, sprang up at once before the nations, a wild and wondrous form, rich in all the attributes of European lore, her arts, her philosophies, her religion. We had to pass through no periods of probation in compassing these attainments. There were none of those humanizing superstitions by which the infant heart of the nation was to be oppressed, before it could seek for, or receive the clearer light of a perfect religious inspiration. And the wild struggles of rival chiefs, the reckless passions of opposing despots, conferred upon us no such numerous histories of civil conflict, such as, during the middle ages, furnished unnumbered themes to the eager bard and novelist of every land in Europe. All this period of probation and childhood, of feebleness and ignorance, of power unknown to law, and laws unknown to reason or propriety, through which other nations have had to pass, and by which they have been endowed with marvellous treasures for the employment of superior ages, — was denied to ours. And what was not denied of the bold, the wild, the strange or the terrible, — is, unhappily for present uses, a written record. We may take no liberties with it, — 'nothing extenuate, nor set down aught' — for which there is not proper authority in the state papers. We had our beginning not only in an age when the intellect of Europe was every where active and curious, but after the discovery of printing and when the diffusion of the art had been so general, that, to see, and hear, and publish, beyond recall and suppression, were operations in their nature identical. These influences, while they render our facts less questionable than those of other nations, for this very reason, deprive the artist of his resources and his courage. Tradition is denuded of his stores, and the audacity of invention is paralyzed on the threshold. The poet who sings of Anglo-American achievements, must sing in fear and trembling, — and such a feeling, we need scarcely say, is a sad weight to be carried by the Muse. Her genius is nothing without her impulse, and the caution which ties her wings, keeps her back from that heaven of invention, the exploration of which is the only assurance for her fame. Her facts must be those which inspire doubt, not those which lead to conviction; and the narrowing records which furnish full details of a history, so far from helping her progress, in the construction of her divine fabrics, are, in reality, so many stumbling blocks in her path. The single leading fact in her possession, or the glimpse of such a fact, is worth to her ten thousand of the accompanying particulars. "It is not possible," as Lord Jeffrey somewhere sarcastically remarks, "to invest with epic or tragic dignity, the brigadiers of Bunker Hill or Saratoga, or to shed a poetical halo round a successful cruise of Commodore Rodgers or Decatur." [3] Perhaps not, and for the very reasons which we have given; but the sneer of Lord Jeffrey will equally apply to Generals Burgoyne and Cornwallis; to Captain Dacres and Sir James Yeo. The very fact that we can couple these English names with those of our own countrymen, as sharing a com-

[3] The reference is to Francis, Lord Jeffrey (1773–1850), editor of the *Edinburgh Review;* the idea he often expressed, particularly in his review of Barlow's *Columbiad* and of Campbell's *Gertrude of Wyoming.*

mon unfitness for the purposes of poetic composition, renders it very clear that it is because of the proximity of the events and persons to our own times, by which we are made too familiar with all the details in their histories, and not because of any intrinsic defect in the material itself, — that such is the case. Removed by time from any searching analysis of curious people, — with but a name, and little more of a history, upon record, — a vague tradition alone declaring the patriot hero, or the tyrannical invader — and Decatur and Dacres might occupy a place in epic fiction quite as noble as that of Troilus and Ajax. And, even now, something in the way of song and story may be done with materials even so unpromising as these. If they cannot furnish themes for the epic and dramatic poet, they are yet not wholly ineligible to other artists; and the lyrist, and the novelist, may achieve a triumph in exercises, in which the more rigid laws of the Epopee would provoke failure and contempt. When Campbell sings

Of Nelson and the North,[4]

we do not find our poetic sensibilities set at defiance. Our tastes are not offended. The theme is in unison with the strain, and we acknowledge a pliancy in the rules of art, in this respect, which we should fail to perceive in other branches. It might be more difficult to make Nelson the hero of a drama, or of a poem, the laws of which were even so indulgent as those of Scott's ballad romances. We know too much of Nelson for this, and the author could take no such liberties with his biography as to render his deeds and character symmetrical. The song of Campbell shows us his hero but at a single moment, — speaks of him rather than presents him; and, in terms of vague eulogium, clothed in poetic beauty, renders him a graceful abstraction, the ideal of a hero, rather than *the* hero whom we know — and to this we can oppose no objec-

[4] Thomas Campbell, "The Battle of the Baltic," line 1.

tions whether drawn from propriety or history. The same personage would be susceptible of still better use in the modern novel. Such material would be more corrigible in the hands of the artist of prose fiction. This species of composition, as it combines some of the qualities of almost every species of imaginative art, whether prose or verse, painting or statuary, so is it susceptible of far more various employment than any. More pliant in the hands of the master, it is more universal in its appreciation of the desires of the multitude. It enters more readily into the general sense, and, to a certain extent, has superseded, and must continue to supersede, in some degree, the uses of all others. To its influence may be ascribed, in part, the decline of the drama in popular estimation; and, it is scarcely possible that, while its sway continues, there will be any return to the elaborate works in poetry, which distinguished periods of less diversified forms of literature. That such has been the effect of this species of composition, may be to be regretted by those who confide entirely in the arbitrary manifestations of form in the classic genius; but that such is its effect and influence, must be regarded as no small proof of its legitimacy as a genuine offspring of art. Insisting upon this particular, we shall consider the prose romance of modern periods, along with the attributes of poetic art as known to former ages, in discussion of the pliancy, for their common purposes, of the materials which may be furnished by American history.

We have said, differing from high British authority, that something, even now, might be done with our Brigadiers of the Revolution. A single instance, by way of illustration, may passingly be examined. We will select one of the events whose history we consider particularly susceptible of use, even at this early day, by the novelist; — but by the novelist only, for the mellowing hand of time is necessary to effect its entire preparation for the hands of other artists, whose laws are much more arbitrary, and whose province is necessarily more confined. Our instance shall be drawn from the most exciting period of the Revolution. Our subject shall have been one of its proudest spirits — a gigantic aspect in our ranks — a man who,

> —— in valour proudly eminent,
> Stood like a tower! [5]

His deeds shall have been of the last importance to the country. They shall relate to a series of the most vivid and interesting transactions — distinguished by an action, lively, painful, and pathetic, — uniting the extremes of glory and of shame, the highest and the lowest purposes of human ambition. We speak now of the deeds and history of Benedict Arnold — of Arnold the Traitor!

Perhaps, were the question put suddenly, without concert, to any group of literary men, promiscuously assembled throughout the United States — were they required at once to designate the one man of the revolution, whose history beyond that of all others, furnishes the most obvious materials for the romancer — the probability is that the great majority would agree upon this man! No other series of events, in all that history, seem more naturally to group themselves in the form of story. None were of a more important character — none endowed with a more tragic interest. The fate and fortunes of Benedict Arnold, are, indeed, such as, beyond all others, seem meant "to point the moral and adorn the tale." Brave to desperation, heroism was with him a natural and noble instinct. Among the first to take up arms in the cause of his country, he was the first to lead into the thickest ranks of danger. Privations only seemed to heighten his capacity for endurance, while opposition warmed his valour into a flame

[5] A misquotation from John Milton, *Paradise Lost*, Book I, lines 590–591: "In shape and gesture proudly eminent/ Stood like a Tow'r."

which his own streaming blood could never extinguish. Gallantly leading on the charge, vigorously heading the assault, the epic hero of antiquity never presented a more exquisite instance of fortitude, conduct and audacity of valour, such as bestows animation upon song and imparts impulse to the creative glow of the inspired genius. We behold him at Quebec and at Saratoga, and still he appears the same generous and fearless hero, — as bold as Hector, as unyielding as the greater Ajax. What a character for the first grand opening scenes of the drama — what swelling acts for the great theatres of patriotism and song! — Sure, to secure the admiration of the spectator, as Arnold himself, most certainly, did, at this period, secure that of the American people. Doubtful of their great hope — suffering from privation — harassed by frequent defeat — it is not wonderful that the brilliant career of Arnold — particularly the great share which he had in winning the field of Saratoga — should have dazzled their eyes and baffled their judgments. His star continued to rise in the ascendant, like the sun, —

> —— when his beams at noon
> Culminate from the equator, — [6]

till, almost alone, it fixed the admiration of the people, who began to regard the calmer and the colder Washington as the stalking horse of the pageant — wanting in heroism as conduct, — the mere presentment of the king — the Agamemnon, perhaps, but not the Achilles — the Æneas, but not the Hector, of our Troy! And the cry runs on Arnold.[7] Even those who

[6] *Paradise Lost*, Book III, lines 616-617.

[7] [*Simms's note*] Speaking with strict propriety the cry ran on Gates, with whose name the Convention of Saratoga was more particularly coupled. But, in point of fact, the mere individual makes but little difference, since it was with the caution and prudence of Washington, that the impatience of the public found fault. His Fabian policy did not suit the impetuous temperament of the people, though it saved them. Besides, Arnold was the true hero in the overthrow of Burgoyne, and this is now the popular conviction,

possess an abiding faith in the true virtues and the real greatness of Washington, begin to address him in the language of expostulation, such as the Prince of Ithaca employs when he would provoke Achilles to exertion.

> Then marvel not, thou great and complete man,
> That all the Greeks begin to worship Ajax;
> Since things in motion sooner catch the eye,
> Than what not stirs. The cry went once on thee,
> And still it might; and yet it may again,
> If thou wouldst not entomb thyself alive,
> And case thy reputation in thy tent.[8]

It was the good fortune of America, as it was the true greatness of Washington, that he was not impatient of himself — that he could resist equally the entreaties and the arguments of friends, and the goadings of his own ambition — that, heedless of the cry which ran on Arnold, he could content himself, cased in his tent, waiting his hour, until the time for proper action had arrived; — while his less circumspect rival, encouraged to presumption by success and the adulation of blind worshippers, maddens with an equal blindness; and, first intoxicated by hope, then furious by disappointment, grasps the torch of the incendiary for the destruction of the high temple in which he had been sworn the officiating priest. His hand is lifted, but his deed still cloaked, and the hour is fast speeding whose entire revolution is to bring about the catastrophe, equally fatal to his honest fame, and to the liberties of his country. The interest grows naturally with the struggle which is in progress, equally in his mind, and between the advocates of the rival heroes. The people, like the ancient chorus, clamour their wishes, and bemoan their disappointments. Unlike the ancient chorus, however, they soon begin

---

though it was not so at the time of the occurrences. Gates was never any thing better than a name. His talents were small, and his behavior to Washington extremely little and unworthy.

[8] *Troilus and Cressida*, Act III, scene 3, lines 181–187.

to take an active part in the events of the drama. The result is doubtful. Ambition begins to rear his crest in triumph, while patriotism trembles with numerous and growing apprehensions. Faction exults in confidence, while affection falters in the trust which it once had in the genius of Washington. For a moment — for a moment only — the fate of this great nation swings doubtfully in the balance! The catastrophe follows! — none more sudden, — none more complete in the whole wide world of scenic exhibition. The fall of a great man! — not by death, for death is no foe to the fame that is already sure in past performance! — not by the jealous rival, or the dark assassin; — but by the rapid spreading of the single plague-spot — the inherent baseness in his own soul. And such a fall! — To what utter perdition, not only of all future fame, but of all past achievement — the annihilation of that hope which lived in coming days and deeds, and the overthrow of those high monuments which men had raised up as trophies to denote the deeds already done! A mighty, an irrevocable fall — total to the hero — terrible to the spectator — like that of Lucifer — "never to rise again," — yet not such a fall as would satisfy the catastrophe, or furnish an appropriate dénouement for the dramatic scene. A fall to be stigmatized by the curses of the chorus — to be moralized by the didactic poet into a thousand homilies for the ears of reverent youth; — but utterly insusceptible of use upon the stage — having no outward action, no results corresponding with the crime — no punishment which human eye might follow, proportioned to the extent of his deserving; — a fall of the soul rather than of the frail body which it informs — a conflict of the wild, benighted heart, ending in moral discomfiture and shame, — not of the muscular and mighty frame overborne by superior skill and power, and yielding but fighting bravely to the last.

And with what adjuncts of poetry and feeling — of tears and tenderness — of pride and passion — may that dark conflict be allied! His was not the single ruin. It is coupled with the fate of André — a mournful story of the blight of early promise. Young and full of genius — loving and full of hope — brave and burning with ambition — he too falls with the traitor — is dragged down to the same dreadful moral death! He perishes — a sad catastrophe, — but one from which the human spectator recoils with horror. The chorus must close the narrative. The scene which degrades the hero must not offend the audience. André upon the dishonouring tree, like Hector roped to the car of Achilles, is a spectacle which may be spared the eyes which have previously been delighted with his youth, his beauty, his generous virtue, and his noble valour and devotion!

There is surely much that is dramatic in this history. The leading events, thus grouped in general terms to the entire exclusion of details, are particularly imposing in their aspects, — many of them are startling and full of consequences. The deeds of the hero are as brilliant as his treason is utter and unqualified. Arnold was no imbecile in action. He was only so in morals. His courage was unquestionable, and he exposed himself personally in battle, as was the case with the valiant man in ancient warfare. His audacity was immense, and he entertained along with it a love of approbation, an appetite for praise, which, had his culture been of a better sort, would have been the most impassioned love of glory. But, with all these circumstances in its favour, his story, as at present known, is essentially undramatic. It will not always remain so. The objections to its present employment for the drama arise from our familiarity with the details, many of which, to make the subject available for the stage, must be made to yield place to others more tractable and appropriate. When these details shall be no longer present to the memories of men, — when but little more shall be remembered than the bold, but impressive fact, that one among our bright and shining lights, — one of the noblest in seeming and in promise, — went down from our sky, in shame and darkness, at the very moment when all eyes were fastened upon it in hope and admiration, — then, doubtlessly, the future Shakspeare of our land, — if we are ever to be blessed with such an advent, — will seize upon the event and shape it into some long and enduring chronicle. And this he will do, however his details may vary from the history, by no such violations of general truth as should outrage propriety. He will be conscious of no such barriers as restrain us now. He will exercise such privileges of art, legitimate for his purpose, as the living generations will not tolerate, and the living author, conscious of the true facts, will not venture to assert. He will depict the hero in his day of completest triumph, — no stain upon his shield, — watched, almost worshipped, by the admiring multitude, and with none of those misgivings of success which embitter the hopes and disturb the moral equilibrium of the ambitious nature. The philosophic observer alone may be permitted to see, lurking close, — possibly, in the shape of a virtue, — the single plague-spot in his soul, which is destined to spread, with a rank rapidity, over the growth and freshness of the better nature, — latent, however, — not spreading, — perhaps not to spread, — but depending for its growth or its suppression, upon the chances of a wild and never to be satiated appetite for sway. Grant him what his ambition seeks, and seeks worthily, and we shall see no more of his inherent canker. It will be wholly conquered by the triumphant virtues, which have no need to succumb in the easy gratification of his heart's prevailing passion. Such is the moral portrait of Arnold, as he appears, and may be made to appear, in the opening scenes of the drama. It may be that the future poet who thus undertakes his delineation, — uninfluenced by that feeling of reverence which fills *our* hearts, when we approach the great hero of civilization, — will venture to delineate, as in honourable conflict for the ascendancy, the rival stars of Washington and Arnold. The one, calm, and cold, and haughty, in his serene pride of place; — the other, fiery and impetuous, hot with haste, spurring forward, sleepless always, to that glorious eminence which the jealous fate denies that he shall ever reach. It will not perhaps be difficult, a hundred years hence, to make it appear that Arnold was the victim of some great injustice, — to show that his rightful claims were denied, — at all events, to make it appear that such at least was his own conviction, — a conviction not uncommon to the nature covetous of fame and jealous of any division, however small, of those rewards of glory, on the attainment of which the whole affections of his being have been set. He shall be baffled in these desires. He shall be defrauded of these hopes. Fate shall war against him, — his best merits shall fail of their fruits, — he shall aim in vain, — he shall toil honourably and without purpose; while the better fortunes of his rival carry him onward, with swelling sails, in his own despite, to the haven of their mutual ambition. The star of Washington rises, and gathers hourly increasing lustre, in due degree as his declines from the summit, —waning away, under a cruel destiny, in mockery of all his merits and all his achievements. Such are the frequent vicissitudes of fortune, and no probabilities would be violated by the artist who shall thus depict, to remote ages, the career of this unhappy hero. What follows from such a history? The bitterness of a proud heart, denied! The misanthropy, the jaundiced green of envy and mortification, discolouring to his mind all the objects of his thought, and working, subtly and strongly, upon that little, latent, plague-spot in his soul, till his passions break all bonds, — unleased tigers, — a gnawing fury and a howling hate urging them on, scorning the reason that would guide and mocking the power that would restrain. The temptation follows, — and the fall! That temptation may be made to work upon nobler feelings than any which we are accustomed to associate with the *auri sacra fames!* In this respect, alone, the true history of Arnold should be ennobled for the sympathy and commiseration of less knowing periods. The tempter, clothed in the British uniform and armed with the signet of his king, shall be made to approach the denied and wronged ambition with the deference of an admiration only so far subdued as to forbear offence, — shall dilate only upon the inappreciating injustice of a country which refuses to recognize and properly to honour such superior merits; — shall adroitly exaggerate to the proud, vain man, the paramount importance of his services, the wonder of his achievements and the glory which they have rightly gathered in the world's esteem. Then, by adroit insinuation, the better justice shall be shown which rewards such heroism in the opposing service. It will be part of the tempter's scheme to insist that the war is merely a civil contest between rival parties in the same nation, — a dispute involving only the success of contending factions, not a principle, — not the liberties or safety of a people bravely contending for their rights. It will not be difficult for the spectator to imagine how such a man as the poet has already described, stung by a sense of injustice and neglect, — which, in the case of merit, is the worst injustice, — will give greedy ear to the solicitations and suggestions of the tempter. Supposing the serpent to approach his task with even ordinary ingenuity, it will not be difficult to see that such a man, thus endowed, and with a latent defect of the moral nature already shown, must fall! Thus far, the story, even as we read it now, is dramatic in its character. The difficulty lies in what remains. The treason of Arnold was that of the cabinet, — of the politician — and not the hero. There is no grand action, addressing itself to the eye of the spectator, corresponding with the extreme self-sacrifice of the subject, and the general alleged importance of the events. The mere surrender of an impregnable post, though the key of the country, — and the delivery of a brave army into unmerited capitivity, — are not events which can be made imposing before an audience, however great may be their real interest to the fortunes of a nation. They equally lack the two greatest essentials of dramatic art, individuality of development, and an action, continually rising in interest, to the close of the catastrophe. The flight of Arnold from the scene, and the degrading death of André upon it, are other difficulties which can only be overcome by the dramatist who shall address himself to an audience totally ignorant of or indifferent to these details — which, he may then so vary as to accommodate to the requisitions of the stage. When the grandson of the last revolutionary soldier shall be no more, — when the huge folios which now contain our histories and chronicles, shall have given way to works of closer summary and more modern interest, — the artist will find a new form for these events, shape all their features anew, and place the persons of the drama in grouping more appropriate for scenic action. There will be a more individual character given to the history, — the general events will be thrown out of sight, — the personal will be brought into conspicuous relief in the foreground, — the rival heroes of the piece will be forced into closer juxtaposition, and the treason, detected in the moment of its contemplated execution, will be crushed by the timely interposition of Washington himself. He will be made to have seen the true nature, and to have suspected the purpose of the traitor, even from the moment of his very first lapse from honour, — to have had his eyes upon the tempter, — a stern, cold, silent watch, — keen and vigilant, and the more terrible from its very silence and unimposing calm. His watch will have been maintained with an interest no less personal than patriotic. It will not impair the character of Washington, to show that he too had his ambition; — and, serving glory as well as his country, was filled with a two-fold jealousy of him who, in striving with him for the one, was doing so, fatally and criminally, at the expense of the other. It may be that, in the hands of the future dramatist, the sword of Washington himself shall be made to do justice upon the head of the traitor, — as, by a similar license, Richmond slays Richard, and Macduff the usurper of Scotland, in the presence of the audience. It will only be doing justice to the real merits of Arnold, to show him at least fighting bravely to the last, and proving the possession of a stout spirit, even though he falls the victim of a corrupt and dishonest heart. Or, with a slight variation from this dénouement, and with some nearer approximation to the historical facts, while his sword achieves the death of the foreign emissary, (André) his stern voice, rising pre-eminent over all the sounds of battle, shall send the baffled traitor (Arnold) — hell in his heart and curses on his lips, — to the inglorious scaffold which the audience does not see. The fate of André may be woven in with such a history, in the form of an under-plot, by a process well known to the dramatic artist. You have but to endow Arnold, or his wife, with a sister, who, won by the love of André, shall be made the instrument for bringing about the treachery of the hero. The exercise of her affections and their defeat, may be employed to impart tenderness and animation to the subordinate scenes; while the wife of Arnold, whether described as a patriotic matron, like Portia, or a woman devoted to her lord, like Medora, whether "guilt's in his heart" or not, — will, like the Belvidera of Jaffier, or the unsexed companion of Macbeth, furnish all that is needful for the interest in the domestic relations of the hero. Such departures from the absolute history, as are here suggested, will not offend the spectator some hundred years from now. They would not even now offend a British or a Continental audience who know nothing more than the simple fact, — if they know even that, — that the American Revolution was distinguished by one great traitor whose name was Benedict

Arnold. But such freedoms with details with which we are all so familiar, would scarcely do with us. So fresh in our memories are all the facts in this connection, that any such violations of the written record would convert into a hostile critic every sturdy militiaman from Maine to Mississippi.

But, even with our present familiarity with the particulars in the life of Arnold, it would not be difficult for the art of the novelist to endow them with the highest tragic interest, and to give that dramatic value to his materials, which is the great distinguishing charm, in this form of composition, as it is known to recent times. This could be done without coming into conflict, in the smallest degree, with the written history. In this fact we are led to see how very superior are the privileges of the prose romancer. His realm is wider and more various in its possessions. His wing is more excursive. He possesses a right of way into regions in which other artists possess not — by reason of their own self-made impediments — even a right of entrance. The laws by which he is bound are less rigid and restraining. He may be tragic or comic as he pleases. He may depict in action, or describe in narrative as best suits his purpose. He may employ dialogue in such portions of his work as suggests the use of dramatic materials, and, when the action subsides, be simply narrative and descriptive; while, serving as Coryphæus, he may provoke among his auditors a personal interest in himself, by the running commentary with which he delineates the characters, and discourses upon the moral of the events which he relates. He is neither limited by localities nor by time; — nor bound, as in the case of the dramatist, to concentrate his interest upon the fortunes of some one conspicuous personage. He may carry his story through a period of many years, — may conduct his actors into many countries, — may indulge in numerous digressions, — may require the sympathies of his audience for many persons at the same time, and does not need to hazard his strength upon those events only which conduce to the catastrophe. In brief, the art of the novelist enables him to conform his writings more nearly to the form and aspect of events as they really happen, than can ever be the case with the dramatist and poet, — and this very conformity to nature is a source of vast freedom and flexibility. His laws are not only less arbitrary than those of other artists, but his privileges combine, in turn, those of all the rest. He may contend with the painter in the delineation of moral and natural life, — may draw the portrait, and colour the landscape, as tributary to the general *vraisemblance* which is his aim. He may view with the poet in the utterance of superior sentiment and glowing illustration and description; with the dramatist in his dialogue and exciting action; with the historian and philosopher, in his detail and analysis of events and character. Shall we doubt the legitimacy, or marvel at the progress, of an art, which, while asserting these high powers, not only of its own, but in common with other arts, — conforms, in its delineations, more decidedly than any other, to the various aspects of man, and nature, and society? It is not improbable, indeed, as has elsewhere been suggested, that the decay of the drama, as a popular amusement, is, in some degree, to be attributed to the general prevalence in modern and recent periods of this species of composition. An inquiry into the facts necessary to this suggestion, would be one of immense interest, but would lead us greatly aside from our present argument.

iii

THE FOUR PERIODS OF AMERICAN HISTORY [1]

We have passed over many topics, illustrative of our subject, suggestively, and without seeking to discuss them. Our limits would not suffer more. Having intimated to you that

[1] A version of this essay was published in the *Southern and Western Magazine*, I (June, 1845), 385–392.

the poet and romancer are only strong where the historian is weak, and can alone walk boldly and with entire confidence in those dim and insecure avenues of time which all others tremble when they penetrate; having arrived at the conclusion that, in the employment of historical events, for the purposes of art in fiction, a condition of partial obscurity and doubt in history being that which leaves genius most free to its proper inventions, is the one which is most suitable for its exercise; — it becomes necessary, if possible, to ascertain and to define those periods in our history which are most distinguished by this palpable obscurity — which are the most coupled with this condition of picturesque doubt and uncertainty — and which, hereafter, or even now, may be found most eligible for the uses of the muse. This susceptibility of the *matériel* of fiction, is, of course, a matter of degree. The real genius wants but little of the absolute in fact upon which to work. It is his rare endowment to subject the most stubborn events to his purposes — to mould the most incorrigible forms, and, out of truths the most ungracious and little promising, to evolve the most imposing and delightful fabrics. A happy thought, an inspired fancy, brings out to his mind the form and the colour in the mass, and teaches him to throw off the incumbrance, and in what way to relieve from its impediments, the exquisite ideal that his imagination has pictured in the rock. But, even for him the way may be made smooth, as the French and Italian novelists opened paths for Shakspeare. The grosser difficulties of the work may be overcome, and some of the barriers thrown down, though by the rudest workman, for the uses of the mightiest master.

To facilitate our examination of this subject, we propose to divide the history of our country into four unequal periods. This division, however arbitrary it may seem, is one that belongs naturally to our modes of progress, and would suggest itself to the most casual inquirer into the moral steps by which

we attain the several successive epochs in our national career.
The first period should comprise the frequent and unsuccessful attempts at colonization in our country by the various
people of Europe — the English, French, and Spaniard — from
the first voyage of the Cabots, under Henry the Seventh, —
and should include all subsequent discovery and exploration,
by whatever people, down to the permanent settlement of the
English in Virginia. This period involves a term of seventy-
five years, and abounds in romantic detail and interesting adventure. This was a time when the fountains of the marvellous
seemed every where to be opened upon mankind — when, on
the eve of wonderful discoveries in the natural, the people of
Christendom lent a greedy ear to every sort of legend which
held out similar assurances in the spiritual world — when popular faith reposed without a doubt upon the very bosom of
fancy, and sucked in the wildest superstitions from the
breast of the most prolific invention; — when the search after
the improbable and the impossible prompted a singular disregard to the wonders that were real and every where growing, broad cast, around the very footsteps of adventure. All
the pulses of mortal imagination seemed to have quickened at
this period under a like maternal influence. Man was alive
and eager in the thirst after great truths, and his progress was
in due correspondence with the ambitious and restless nature
of his desires. If he found not exactly what he sought, he yet
laid his hand upon treasures which time has shown him were
inappreciable in value. The real advantages of printing were
then for the first time beginning to display themselves. The
great but degraded masses were slowly realizing its fruits, and
the popular imagination seemed to expand with new wings
and eyes, dilating in the far survey of its newly opened possessions, in all the provinces of art and office. It will be sufficient
to illustrate from one department for the rest — to show, by
the achievements of the muse — as we well may — how active,

on a sudden, had grown that impatient genius of uprising Europe (in England at least) to which the present owes so many trophies and delights. The period we have indicated was the great period in the literary history of Great Britain — vulgarly and improperly called the Elizabethan period. We have but to name the masters of that day — to point to Marlowe, Ben Jonson and Shakspeare; — to Spenser and to Sidney; to Bacon, and to him — a genius no less noble than hapless — whom Spenser has so felicitously called the "Ocean Shepherd." [2] Never was era, in any country, more rich than this, in the one designated — in the abundant variety, the matchless beauty, the masculine pathos, the grace, the strength and the originality of its productions. Nay, never was period half so rich. What was true of its poetry, was scarcely less true in other respects. In fact, it is usually a period most rich in poetry, that is most prolific in progress and discovery. The offices of the imagination are much more various than men ordinarily suppose. It is her eye and her wing that guide and impel genius in all of her departments. It is her sensibilities that quicken the impatient pulses of all adventure — her yearnings that prompt the hopes, and warm the courage of the builder and the battler, whether his province be the conquest of empires, or the more humble desire which contents itself with the planting of towns and the rearing of shrubs and gardens. The spirit therefore which constitutes the soul of poetry, and urges the unwearied labours of the poet, is shared in some degree by all who work, in all the branches of human industry. The labour which is undertaken *con amore*, is a labour which originates in the imagination solely; and we shall take but an imperfect view of the European mind, as exhibited in what may be termed the more national progress of the age indicated, if we fail to see in it the strong proofs of sympathy with that more ethereal working of spirit, in the same nation, to which we

[2] Elizabethan poet, politician, and explorer, Sir Walter Raleigh.

are indebted for its poetry and art. Kindred with the poetry
of a race is its religion; and this also was a period when, in
England, under the impulse of a fresher spiritual yearning, the
religion of the age, taking its direction from the unregulated
passions of the popular mind, grew more than usually active
in the great struggle with the inner world — when, the same
imagination, unschooled and untutored in the popular mood,
grew wild with misdirected enthusiasm — when, accordingly,
the dark spirits seemed to receive a call to new exertions in
consequence of the dangers from this very passionate activity
of the common mind — when there were witches in the land
— sorcerers needing to be baffled — devils to be cast forth —
all angrily striving for continued possession of their ancient
strong-holds in the troubled heart of man. A transition state,
in a people, is thus always one of excited imagination. All the
waters become turbid. But their commotion, though in storm,
is the proof of a new and more hopeful life. It is the sign of a
new spirit abroad. There are clouds — there is blackness —
gloom in the sky — error on the face of the land — but the
winds and the waters sweeten themselves by progress, and the
thunderbolt which rends the spire, purifies the atmosphere
which envelopes the stagnant city. In the history of the being
whose law of life is eternal progress — from province to province, and from empire to empire — it is the calm alone that we
have any need to fear.

The vigorous wing put on by the mind of Europe in the sixteenth century, might well lead the nation into cloud and
frequent obscurity. And thus it is that we find King James —
a sovereign who shared the excursive imagination of his age,
without its judgment — writing with equal enthusiasm against
witches and tobacco. His superstitions were those of wiser
men who did not share in his antipathies. Thus, and then it
was, that Bacon had his superstitions also — that Columbus
meditated the restoration of the Holy City, and dreamed of

the Golden Chersonesus — when Marco Polo was the popular authority — when Sir John Mandeville was the very ideal of the traveller — when Raleigh asserted the existence of the Anthropophagi, and told of a people who wore their eyes in their shoulders, and carried their heads under their arms.

Every working age and people must have their superstitions. Their superstitions are at the bottom of the work and impel it. But for the exaggerations of the imagination, we should lose the chief incentives to endeavour. It is by these that we are deluded to achievement. The objects which reward our toil, are not those which provoke it. The chemist was first a seeker after the philosopher's stone. It was pursuing Raphael that he met with Hermes. We must be careful then, in all our studies of the actual, in the history of the past, not to forget the apparent, by which it was enveloped as in a luminous garment, dazzling the eye from afar, and inviting the enterprise. The superstition is not the less a part of the religion, because, when we have attained to the real, we can separate it from the luminous atmosphere by which it was made to loom out upon the imagination. The faith of a time, by which a people works, is a truth, though it teaches many falsehoods. The artist who would employ the materials of American history for his purposes, must be an earnest student of the lore — must warmly sympathize with the spirit — by which all Europe was governed at the same corresponding period. There are no absurdities in a time, when a people is alive and in action, which the true philosopher can despise. The absurdity which moves the national heart, has always a real foundation, and, to the writer of fiction, it affords the best material by which to work upon the hearts, and lessen the superstitions of other periods and people. He must seek deeply to imbue himself with all the workings of our spiritual nature — what they hoped and what they dreaded — how deep were their terrors, how high their anticipations. It is in the god and the devil of a race that you can behold the truest picture of themselves. Here you may see the extent of their ambition, the degree of purity in their hearts, the things that they are, and the things which are dearest to their pursuit. These subjects, in English history, from the time of the Eighth Henry to the First Stuart, will be best read in the records of the courts, and in the dramatic literature of the same period. They should be studied by him who seeks to turn to account our first American period in history. The analysis of the properties, of the constituents and causes of national character, belongs to the first duties of the philosophical poet, and is absolutely essential to the successful labours of any architect who would build his fabric out of the materials of history. This analysis of the time of which we speak, will lead, as we have already said, to those wonders, crude and shapeless, which embodied in the faith of the past, may become, made symmetrical by the hands of imaginative art, a wondrous study for the future. The popular credulity is so much fairy-land itself — a land of twilight and uncertain shadows — to every shooting star of which a name and office may be given, and whose phosphorescent *ignés fatui*, may each, in turn, be translated to a star.

Our second period should comprise the history and progress of British settlement down to the accession of George the Third, and to the beginning of those aggressions upon the popular liberties in America, which ended in the revolutionary conflict. It will be readily seen what a marked difference of characteristic is that of this period in comparison with the preceding. The discovery of the country has been made, and there is an end to speculation on the subject of those wonders which the popular credulity of Europe was prepared to see. America was no longer El Dorado! — or, if it was recognized as substantially possessing a claim to be considered a land of golden treasure, it was only among that sober, second-thoughted few, whose expectations were based upon the effects

of sturdy labour and industrious enterprise. The idle exploration which set forth on adventures in the vain hope to realize
its own dreams, had given way to a cooler and more reasonable pioneer; and the steel which had been employed by the
one for the slaughter of the savage, was employed by the
other in laying their forests bare to cultivation. The truth remained — a great truth — but freed from its superstition. The
romance which gave impulse to the wing of adventure was
happily diminished, and what remained, though of a character
which might still excite in a subdued period, was of far more
phlegmatic character. But it still possessed the features of romance, was still full of aspects highly novel, persuasive and
interesting, to the European. Adventure was no longer a
phrenzy. It had become a duty. The explorer did not so much
seek for gold, but he sought for that which was still more
precious — freedom. It was not the conquest of a mighty empire that was in his aim — it was a home — a secure and happy
homestead that won his hopes and stimulated his enterprises.
If he no longer went forth glittering in armour, and to the
sound of the trumpet, there was yet a stateliness in his simplicity, a nobleness and a majesty in his firm aspect — a glory
in his strength and hardihood — a brightness in his hope and
a beauty in his faith — such as might well beseem the classical
simplicity of subject as chosen by the old Grecian masters —
such as might well be chosen to adorn and give dignity to the
choicest annals of future song. His career will be found not
without its attractions. The adventure of a life in the wilderness — the lonely travel through unbroken forests — the musing upon the tumulus of ancient and unbroken tribes — the
conflict with the wolf, and the midnight whoop of the savage
— these are all incidents, which, however hacknied they may
seem, shall yet be grouped in happiest combination by the
hand of genius. The period of which we now speak was full
of incident — a rare life, teeming in animation and exertion,

derived from sources of this character— from the inevitable progress of the Anglo-Norman — from the inevitable fate of the Indian — a fate as relentless as that of the victim in the Grecian drama, and which, coupled with the history of his own gods, may be wrought into forms as nobly statuesque as any that drew a nation's homage to the splintered summits of Olympus. Following this almost individual struggle of the white man with the red, a larger field opens upon us. The conflict is no longer individual. New interests have arisen, and Christian Europe finds it politic to send her rival armies across the waters, in search of battle grounds, upon the soil of heathen America. How strange the sight to the savage — that of war to the knife, waged for supremacy between opposing nations in a realm so remote from their own several empires, and upon which they have scarce won foothold. Beneath the same sign of mercy and of blessing, he sees them encounter with hate and curses. He sees, but is not suffered to look on unemployed. He is marshalled in the opposing ranks, and, under the banners of the Cross, the singular and sad spectacle is presented to our eyes of the Christian employing the savage for the murder of his brother Christian. Those old French and Spanish wars, involving the fine trials of strength between Wolfe and Montcalm, the feebler warfare in which Braddock fell, and, nearer home, the frequent conflicts of Virginia, Carolina and Georgia, with the Apalachian tribes, influenced to hostility by the machinations of French and Spanish leaders — are all so many vast treasure-stores of art — stores which you may work upon for ages, yet leave still unexhausted to the workmen of succeeding ages. This period, dating from the settlement of Virginia to the beginning of the popular discontents in the reign of George the Third, will be found to comprise a term of nearly two hundred years.

A third division would cover the preliminaries to the revolutionary war — preliminaries which are not always to be found originating in the aggressions of the British parliament, but will be traced to the increasing power of the colonies, and their reluctance at being officered from abroad — the sentiment of independence growing in their feelings long ere it ripened into thought, and making them jealous of, and hostile to, their foreign governors and officers, long before the popular will had conceived any certain desire of separation. The same period would carry us through the war of the revolution, and include our brief passages of arms with the Barbary powers and with France under the Directory. For the merits of this period, in serving the purposes of art, we have but to refer you to the partisan conflict in the South — the wars of riflemen and cavalry, the sharp shooter and the hunter, and the terrible civil conflicts of whig and tory, which, for wild incident and daring ferocity, have been surpassed by no events in history.

A fourth and last period would bring us to the present time, include our transition experience from the colonial to the republican condition, illustrate the progress of interior discovery and settlement, comprise our Indian wars, the settlement of Kentucky and Ohio, the acquisition of Louisiana and Florida, the war of 1812 with Great Britain; the conquest of Texas, and the final and complete conversion to the purposes of civilized man, of that vast wild tract, that

Boundless contiguity of shade,[3]

spreading away from the Altamaha to the Rio Bravo!

These tracts of time, indicated according to these divisions, may not be equally fruitful and diversified. The materials differ in character, but are in all sufficiently abundant. The future romancer will find them so. With the future Homer, the thousand barbarian tribes by which these woods and wilds were traversed before the coming of our ancestors — their

[3] William Cowper, *The Task*, Book II, line 2.

petty wars, their various fortunes, their capricious passions, their dark-eyed women, their favourite warriors — will, like those of Greece, be made immortal on the lips of eternal song. Their dark and gloomy mythologies — not gloomier nor less pleasing than those of the Scandinavian — will receive some softening lights, some subduing touches, from the all-endowing spells of genius, which shall make them quite as imposing, if not so graceful and ethereal, as those of the people who prostrated themselves in worship along the banks of the Peneus. The future descendants of our line, stretching along the great blue heights of the Alleghanies, may be persuaded and fond to believe that they sprang from the loins of two mighty and rival races — the one, the fierce ViKingr of the northern ocean, — and not less fierce but less adventurous, some haughty Mico or Cassique of Apalachy — the Powhatan, the Pontiac, or the Tecumseh of future romance.[4]

We leave these speculations for another time. Having indicated our separate eras, as suggestive, each of separate resources, and suitable, severally, for distinct kinds of illustration, we will devote the rest of our essay to a brief examination of such specimens, from these materials, as occur to us, passingly, as proper subjects for the exercise of art. These are by no means limited during the first of our epochs. We consider the whole history of discovery, as commenced by the Northmen, as pursued by Columbus, and followed by the Portuguese and Spanish nations with a religious sort of en-

[4] [*Simms's note*] To those who read and confide in the claims set up by Professor Rafn, and others, to the first discovery and partial settlement of America by the Northmen, long before the voyages of Columbus, there is nothing extravagant in this conjecture. On the contrary, the traditions of the northern *savans* are exceedingly plausible, and the poet will make no scruple of insisting upon them if his scheme and genius leads him to their use. The material is susceptible of admirable handling. [Simms is here referring to Carl Christian Rafn (1795–1864), Danish philologist and historian, whose *Antiquitates Americanae* (1837) deals with the discovery by Scandinavians in the tenth century.]

thusiasm that partook of the aspects of a sacred fury, to be, in itself, a long and wonderful romance—furnishing resources the most ample, events the most startling — sometimes grand, frequently pathetic and always picturesque and new: — in almost all of their details, suitable for the poet, and requiring for successful elaboration less of genius than of taste. The artist will need to study the events of this period, not as a narrow student of the events themselves, but in all their connections. The collateral histories must be familiar to his mind. He must exercise the philosophic vision which looks deeply down, for the sources of mere facts, into the hearts of the people whom they concern. A profound inquiry into the moral and social characteristics of the several nations engaged in these discoveries — the English, French, Spanish and Portuguese — is an absolutely indispensable preliminary. Above all, he must *feel* their religious characteristics, in his own spirit, before he can boldly enter upon the delineation of the spirit of their time! This, alone, can lead to a just comprehension of their various motives — their strange phrenzies— their implicit faith — their sleepless jealousies—their fanatic enthusiasm — their curious inconsistency of performance — and the singular union, so frequently found in the same personage, of so much that is base and bloody, with so much that is magnanimous and great! With this preparatory knowledge, the artist possesses that "*open sesame*" of character, without which, as he could not comprehend himself, he could never make his readers feel, the truth or the propriety of those anomalies which would otherwise be crowded in his story. For there is yet a latent probability at the bottom of all that is extravagant among the absolute performances of man; and it becomes a first duty of the philosophical artist to search out, and to find, this latent probability, as a key positively essential to the analysis of his subject.

iv

THE EARLY SPANISH VOYAGERS – HERNANDO DE SOTO AS A SUBJECT FOR ROMANCE [1]

From the first dawning of that era of discovery which led the European to our shores, the aspects were strange and strangely beautiful. We may compare them to those of a day, dim, indistinct, perhaps dark with many clouds at first; — illumined only by occasional flashes of summer lightning; — growing gradually clearer with the day's advance, — the clouds passing off slowly to the distant west, and the gay, bright, oriental sun finally looking down, with the smile of a satisfied conqueror, over the new empires which have submitted to his sway. What happy flights of song, — what bursts of admiration, — may be supposed to have flowed from the spontaneous Frenchman as he watched the progress of this day of revelation in the new world; — and how did the solemn and swelling soul of the Spaniard dilate with immeasurable emotions as he sang Te Deum from the wild and narrow heights of Darien. The very conception of such a scene — the presence of the conqueror, not only in a world which he has conquered, but a world which, so far as he knows, has just come from the forming hands of God — looking down upon new oceans, — beholding a new and subject race, approaching him with a reverence which, in turn, almost makes him feel himself a God! — such a scene is a wondrous story in itself, — a story to burn upon the canvas, and breathe in life and beauty from the chiselled lips of stone! And how many scenes like these — what vast materials are here, — not only for brief description and happy apostrophe, but for elaborate and numerous verse! There are the voyages of Verazzani, of Cartier, of

[1] A version of this essay was published in the *Southern and Western Magazine*, II (July, 1845), 10–16.

Roberval, of De la Roche, and Champlain; — and the history and fate of the French settlements in Acadie, form a lovely story to themselves which may be made the parent of a race of lovely stories.[2] But a still richer and riper interest attends the history of Spanish discovery in our own immediate neighbourhood.[3] Conspicuous as the first, Ponce de Leon was not less conspicuous among the discoverers, when we reflect upon the motive of his adventure. In his mind's eye rose ever the image of a mysterious fountain; its springs in earth, its wondrous properties directly caught from Heaven. The fountain of perpetual youth! Waters of life, and youth, and unfading beauty! What a dream of poetry was this! — none more delicious, none more chaste, or noble, in the whole compass of ancient fable. But the dream was a faith in those days, which, if it led not to the thing it fancied, led to objects and discoveries scarcely less wondrous; and the fountain of youth and eternal beauty which inspired the adventure of Ponce de Leon, may not seem wholly an irrational vision if we regard it as an allegory, promising to the nations a new empire for the liberty of the intellectual man. It may be held as the image of other moral objects scarcely less grateful and attractive when we remember that the infant was already in the cradle whose future fearless voice was destined to shake the mitred city upon her seven-hilled foundations.[4] In those days of gloom, gorgeous and romantic, the image of a glorious fountain rising suddenly upon the landscape, throwing up amidst the dark ancestral shade trees of a thousand years, the gracious and bright waters of a new principle and promise, — drops of pearl and diamond, — drops of fire and of light — sparkling

---

[2] *Evangeline*, Longfellow's poem on the fate of the French settlements in Acadia, was first published in 1847.

[3] [*Simms's note*] Speaking for the State of Georgia. [Simms had already dealt with the Spanish settlements in the Western Hemisphere in the novel, *The Damsel of Darien* (2 vols., Philadelphia, 1839) and in a narrative poem, *Donna Florida, A Tale* (Charleston, 1843).]

[4] [*Simms's note*] Martin Luther.

with myriad scintillations, — blessing with freshness, and an odour that might well have been caught from rosy clouds hanging close about the heights of Heaven! — such a fancy might well allegorize and declare the approaching enlargement of the moral aim, and the religious action of the age; and such a fountain might appropriately grow in the new hemisphere, since the spiritual hopes of men depend so greatly upon the political freedom and the social comforts which they are permitted to enjoy. It is from its faith, even in such visions, that a people advances to achievement. It is from such fancies that the poet plucks his richest chaplets of romance and song. His mines of legendary lore are there — his brightest pendants and pearls of fancy! — and there they still lie awaiting his spells to unveil, awaiting his hand to gather, — the waters untasted, the fruits unplucked, — unsought and unregarded — along the melancholy shores of Florida. Shall the witch hazel conduct any of our brothers, in our time, to these precious but unvalued treasures? Shall we see these jewels of Tampa glittering around the brows of our triumphant minstrel? Shall none of us behold, — shall none of us partake them? Will there come after us the Bards who shall grow great and glorious in spoils which might have been ours, and mock that blindness which leaves to them, what had given to us the perfect realization of the very faith which moved the enterprise of Ponce de Leon — youth, life and perpetual beauty? We must not wait for the answer!

The fate of Ponce de Leon — the fading of his dream of youth — the baffling of his fervent and phrenzied hope — the pang of his defeat — the loss of his life, — these are things of which the artist may weave the most beautiful forms and substances which shall delight the souls of coming generations.[5] We pass over the adventures of Diego Miruelo, of Grijalva,

[5] Simms had dealt with Ponce de Leon in an historical sketch in *The Book of My Lady, a Melange* (Philadelphia, 1833). This volume contains six sketches of Spanish adventures in America, all indebted to Washington Irving's style for their whimsy and to his *Companions of Columbus* (1831) for their subject matter.

and Garay. We must pass without regard other names, which, hereafter, shall be guide-stones to many a buried treasure. We can only sample from the vast masses which lie around us. We linger for an instant upon the two voyages of Lucas Vasquez de Ayllon, since his adventures have for us a local interest, and would of themselves furnish materials for a story equally picturesque and tragic.[6] The scene of his story is in our immediate neighbourhood. His business was that of a piracy which cupidity had legalized. He enters the waters of the Combahee in Carolina, beguiles the unsuspecting natives on board his vessel, and suddenly sets sail carrying two hundred of them into captivity. One of his vessels founders with the loss of crew and captives. Such of the latter as survive are doomed to perpetual bondage in the slave markets of Hayti. But his profits far exceed his losses, and he determines upon a repetition of the game. His honourable achievement is rewarded by his monarch with a commission which confers upon him exclusive powers of robbery along the shores which he has already ravaged. He prepares himself for the conquest of the country, and appropriating his whole fortune to the enterprise, descends with a powerful fleet to his cruel work. But he came not to conquer. He was destined, under the decree of a mightier monarch, to a far different reward. As if by the overruling will of Providence, his largest vessel was stranded in the very river where his first crime had been committed. In the moment of storm and peril, while his people are struggling in the waters of the sea, they are set upon by the natives of the country. Mercy is none for the unmerciful, and the people of Combahee amply avenged themselves in the blood of the pirates. But few escaped the slaughterous hands of the savage, and we may fancy the wild whoop of the red man,

[6] Simms dealt with this subject in "Lucas de Ayllon, A Historical Nouvellette," *Ladies Companion*, XVII (May, July, and August, 1842), 36–40, 147–152, and 184–190. The story was reprinted in *The Wigwam and the Cabin, Second Series* (New York, 1845), pp. 196–238.

as, with hand wreathed in the hair of his victim, and knife at his
throat, he recognized the pale features of the mercenary
spoiler who had dragged from him, into hopeless foreign
captivity, the sister or the brother of his love. The peculiar
fate of De Ayllon is left in doubt, but is supposed to have been
suited to his deserts. That he perished here is understood. The
tradition is that, less fortunate than his comrades, he was made
captive by the Indians, and reserved for the terrific horrors of
the fiery torture. At all events, whatever may have been the
manner of his death, it is involved in that happy obscurity
which leaves the poet at perfect liberty so to shape his catastrophe as to adapt it to the general exigencies of his story.

The fortunes of Pamphilo de Narvaez, interesting as they
may be made in the hands of a skilful artist, will not detain us;
but passing rapidly over our records, we pause and linger
upon the history of an expedition, of which, it appears to us,
the material for romance is at once conspicuous and complete. Hernando de Soto was an accomplished cavalier and
an ambitious warrier. He had won the laurels of battle, — he
had won the favours of the court. He was generally regarded as a fine ideal of the noble Spanish gentleman! A
courtier in high esteem, the smiles of beauty had not enfeebled
his military enterprise. As a companion of the famous Pizarro,
he had acquired high reputation in Peru; — had surpassed his
comrades in valour, and returned to Spain equally fortunate
in the spoils and the honours of adventure. But these do not
suffice. He is unsatisfied. The glorious deeds of Cortés and
Pizarro keep him feverish and sleepless; and he is seized with
the fancy of finding, in Florida, a second Tenochtitlan or
Peru. Florida, in that day, it must be remembered, was considered, *par excellence*, the peculiar world of romance. A
melancholy cloud-land it was, not the less suited because it
was cloud-land, for the purposes of fiction. Its sun-bright hues
and sullen shadows, mingled in singular unison, seemed to

promise the possession of vast and mysterious treasures. Washed by the blue waters of the Gulph, itself a wonder — its shores dotted with innumerable little, sudden uprising islands, that lay like so many bright gems along the surface of the deep — its margins covered with rich wild flowers that perfumed the summer breezes an hundred miles from land — its forests, and green tracts of equal sea and forest [7] — filled with birds of strangest voice and most glorious plumage, that rose in flight, at the approach of the stranger, almost unscared in chattering clouds whose wings seemed borrowed of the rainbow and the sun: — these, and other wondrous peculiarities, were only so many proofs of an indefinite and attractive promise. Surely, said the European, — surely, there are great cities, empires like those of Peru and Mexico, hidden deep among these mighty retreats of shadow. These dark grey mountains along the Apalachian chain, are surely fruitful in the precious minerals and metals! Such were the convictions of De Soto, — and, with a mighty train, — men in armour — shining with the rich plumage and gay panoply of a court, — wearing the spurs of knighthood, and decorated with the favours of beauty — a thousand noble cavaliers! — he set forth, as if upon some pleasant masquerade, — some gay carnival procession — to explore those dark, mysterious forests, — to find out those hidden cities of the Floridian — to conquer their wild, plume-browed warriors, and to dive, with greedy haste, into the bowels of their treasure-keeping mountains. From first to last, his progress is a long and touching story. Seeking empire, his first step is made upon the neck of affection! He heeds neither the prayers, nor the tears of love, and dreaming only of the sordid objects of his search, he tears himself away from the wife of his bosom. Such are the usual sacrifices which diseased ambition is called upon to make. It is not wealth, nor life merely, that he risks. He sets at hazard the

[7] [*Simms's note*] The Everglades.

dearer treasures of love in his insane search after more precious jewels, — as if any jewels of the sight deserved to be named as precious with the priceless jewels of the heart! What must have been his parting with that wife! How touching, — if he held in her heart the same high place which he seems to have held in the hearts of all others. She, — sinking forward, sinking downward, in her agony — with outstretched arms, and streaming eyes which vainly strain and follow, long after the white sails have set which bear him forever from her sight. He, — looking only along his path — hurrying his departure, — proud in hope, and flinging from him the sweet restraints of love with as much haste as if they had been so many fetters keeping him back from his true performance. Thus he passes from Cuba to the sea, and our next scene beholds him descending upon the lonely shores of Tampa, — that wild but lovely region, whose subdued but picturesque beauties have been married to a sweet song by one of our own Southern minstrels.[8] But the plaintive musings of our Bard are not those of the fierce, ambitious Spaniard. The thoughts of De Soto do not dwell on the decay of mortal life, or the disappointments of human hearts. These are musings from which he rather shrinks, whether in scorn or self-rebuke, as by no means suited to the purpose in his soul or the adventure which lies before him. If his mind meditates at all upon the blue waters of the gulf as they break, mournfully sounding, upon

Tampa's desert strand,[9]

it is with no moral contemplation. He thinks only of the golden treasures which they wash, and of the proud, opulent

[8] [*Simms's note*] Richard Henry Wilde [(1789–1847), Georgia poet and biographer of Torquato Tasso.]

[9] From line 18 of Wilde's best-known poem, "Stanzas (My life is like the summer rose)," also called "The Lament of the Captive." It was first published in 1818.

cities which are supposed to lie, hidden deep, among the far hills and forests from which their tributary streams descend. A fearless and high-spirited warrior, there is a touch of lofty character, visible even in the most mercenary movements of his mind. Uninfluenced by any such necessity as governed Cortes — for the soldiers of De Soto shared in all his hopes and expectations, and eagerly adopted the adventure, — he yet emulates that admirable conqueror in one of the grandest acts of his life. De Soto does not destroy his shipping, but he as effectually deprives himself of its help. He dismisses it, — peremptorily commands its return to Cuba, leaving himself no means of flight. It was not that he distrusted his people or himself. It was in the dilatings of a proud soul that he thus resolved, emulous of a career and deeds like those of Cortes and Pizarro. He will not suffer any feeble longings for home to baffle his ungovernable ambition and, depriving himself of all motive to fear, cutting himself off from all succor, he turns his back upon the vacant sea, and gives the signal for his march to conquest. To this moment, all is bright and encouraging before his eyes. Who, looking on such an array, — a thousand gallant warriors — the very pride and flower of the court of Spain, — could otherwise than feel exultation! With less than one hundred men had Pizarro commenced his march through the empire of the Incas. What was that force to his? — those men, the outcasts, and offscourings of earth, to the high-spirited chivalry which he commanded. He had but to compare them, their character and numbers, to rejoice in all the assurances of hope. He did not ask, — though this inquiry was of the very last importance — whether the people of Apalachia [10] were like the descendants of Manco Capac. He

[10] A word derived from Choctaw, referring to Indian tribes in Florida. By 1839 it was sometimes used as a substitution for United States. See entries, "Appalachee" and "Appalachia" in Mitford M. Mathews, *A Dictionary of Americanisms* (Chicago, 1951). Simms's spelling, with one *p*, was fairly common in his time.

was yet to learn the vast difference between the most timid and the most fearless races in the world; — between the gentle people, whose nature seems to have been drawn in the likeness of their own innocent animal, the Llama, — and that fierce nation, whose kindred tribes, stretching from the mountains of Virginia to those of Guatemala, were as tenacious of their soil, as impatient of intrusion, and as deadly in their blow, as their own emblematic rattle-snake. The Floridian warrior met De Soto on the very threshold of his country, and never failed to meet him at every step which he took into the interior. The days of the Spaniard, from the first of his landing at Tampa, were numbered by battles — his path-way, every where, was mapped out in blood! Still he marched, still he battled, and still he bled! It was the saddest sort of consolation, to himself and followers, that he always conquered. A conquest which secures nothing but a temporary respite from blows and exertion, is scarcely cause for human exultation.

We follow him through this march of conquest as through the second act of a great drama. He reaches the mountains of Apalachy. He looks down on the waters of the Mississippi. He finds a great city! — but not such as were great in Peru! — great in wealth and splendour, the magnitude and durability of their fabrics and the gorgeousness of their materials; but great in great hearts, brave warriors and sagacious men! — a sort of greatness which most effectually baffles the ambition of the adventurer, and subdues the audacity of Spanish knighthood to the unwonted modesty of fear. The stern savages of the Mississippi, while the Spaniards occupy their city from which the proprietors have been expelled, — anticipate that wondrous achievement of the Russian, which, in recent times, baffled the genius of Napoleon and drove him homeward, palsied, panic-stricken, pursued by arrows of ice and fire. In the still hour of midnight, while sleep hangs heavy over the camp of the wearied conquerors, while the sentinels drowse, satisfied that the victory is complete and all is secure, — the brave and still undiscomfited warriors of the Chickasah, gather in silence to their prey. In a moment, at a given signal, — the wild howl of the wolf which calls for the corresponding clamours of the herd, — they surround their enemies and apply the torch to the crowded tenements of thatch and reed. The conquerors awaken in a sea of flame. A sky of fire is above their heads, a bed of fire is beneath their feet, and the terrible war-whoop of the desperate savage, rings, peal upon peal, resounding in their ears. What a scene for the poet and the painter! The fright of the conquerors as they start in terror from their sleep — seeking for flight with outstretched arms — stunned and blinded — running to and fro, amid the flames, pursued by their thousand tongues, — shrieking with feeble cry, — stammering with bewildered question — while, all in vain, the voice of discipline strives to recall and rally the scattered senses of valour. Over all, that terrible cry prevails — a howl fit only for the midnight — by which the savage increases the terrors of his foe, while announcing his own desperate revenge. Amidst the clamour and confusion, he alone preserves his senses! With busy hand, and greedy hate, and prompt direction, he penetrates the narrow streets. With stone hatchet and shortened lance, he rushes from victim to victim, with a fury as wild as that which his own brands have kindled. He has no mercy in his mood. All is death and vengeance, and the Spaniard can save himself only by the veteran resolution — the better armour — the more efficient weapons of his time and country. That was a night for the painter of the wilder passions! — a night not less terrible and cruel than the famous *triste noche*, so proverbial for the retreat of Cortes over the causeways of Mexico. It will glow upon the canvas a fit parallel with that, — so like it in its cause and consequences — the struggle of the freeman against the tyrant — the citizen against the invader — in both cases, the victim being the Spaniard, and the conqueror, in all probability, the descendant of a common stock. The streets of the Apalachian, traversed by fire and watched by the savage warrior, formed passages as grim with death as the narrow causeways of Mexico, the sluggish lake on either hand, and the fierce Mexican crowding close in his canoe for the first glimpses of the hated fugitive. In both cases, the Spaniard could boast of a victory in his escape. But the victory was like that of Pyrrhus, which leaves the conqueror undone. The scene closes in the momentary triumph of the European — discipline, which succeeds always, enabling De Soto to shake himself free from the flames and from his enemy, and to rally his surviving warriors for newer marches, and perils equally severe.

The last act in the melancholy drama of De Soto's fortunes is at hand. But, even while dying, he is not permitted the mournful consolation of feeling that he remains the conqueror. A messenger from the warriors of Apalachy seeks his bed of death. He comes, as the Spaniard fondly believes, to make submission — to tender the earth and the water of his realm in tribute to the superior genius of European civilization. But he has mistaken the spirit of his foe. Instead of submission, — instead of bent knee and suppliant aspect — the fearless representative of this fearless race, breathes nothing but defiance! Standing over the miserable couch which sustains the feeble form of the dying Hidalgo, he sounds within his shuddering ear the fearful war whoop of his tribe — that cry so well known, so suddenly heard, so terribly remembered, in the awful conflict of the melancholy night; — then, dashing through the assembled but astounded captains, regains his native wilderness in safety.

What a death bed was that of Hernando de Soto! There, on the banks of the Mississippi — his most memorable discovery — in whose waters he is to find a grave — his hopes baffled —

his people thinned by slaughter to a timid, trembling few —
conscious himself of approaching death — dreaming no longer
of empire and conquest — gold or golden cities — but only
how the remnant of his band shall be rescued from the savage! That savage, too, even in that moment, plumed and
powerful, bending down above his couch, and shrieking in
his ear that proverbial whoop of death which has so often
chilled the heart of valour, and palsied the arm of strength.
How easy to associate and to contrast this scene with the first;
— this scene of hopelessness, defeat and death, with that first
setting forth, all music and exultation, of his gorgeous expedition.[11]

But the moral rests not in this single contrast. The eye of
the poet will not confine itself to these. He will look above
and beyond them. He will go back to the desolate wife, —
meek and mournful, — standing on the shores of Cuba, and
looking forth, late at evening, for the return of the dusky
white sail which her eyes shall never see. Oh! how dearer to
him, where he lies, than all his dreams of ambition, were she
but nigh in that parting moment — bending over his bed of
death, wiping the cold dews from his clammy forehead, and
catching the last broken accents of his late returning love!

[11] In late 1824 or early 1825, on a visit to his father in the Southwest,
Simms once fell asleep and awoke to find that he had slept on a grave
marked with a crudely carved cross. He imagined it to be that of one of the
followers of De Soto. This event from his youth he described in an address
at the University of Alabama, December 13, 1842; the address was published
as *The Social Principle: The True Source of National Permanence* (Tusca-
loosa, Ala., 1843). He also gave a highly colored rendering of the event in
"The Grave in the Forest," *Odd Fellow's Offering for 1853* (New York,
1852), pp. 188–194. His most successful Spanish romance, *Vasconselos* (New
York, 1853), deals with the De Soto expedition. Simms had written a good
portion of *Vasconselos* in the late 1830's.

V

THE SETTLEMENTS OF COLIGNY [1]

COMPREHENDED within the same period of time which we have ventured to describe as the most valuable in all our history for the general purposes of art in fiction, are to be found a series of events, which, as they took place in our own neighbourhood, and seem to be singularly susceptible of poetic arrangement and illustration, will demand our passing consideration. Our allusion now is to the famous settlements — famous because of their objects and melancholy termination — which were made in Florida, under the auspices of Gaspard de Coligny, Admiral of France. These colonies were composed wholly of that class of religionists who were known as Huguenots — a name, the origin of which, though universally employed then, and since, in designation of this people, is buried in impenetrable obscurity. We take for granted that it will not need that we should dwell upon the history of this people, or upon the particular policy which governed their great leader in determining to plant them in Florida. We have no reason to suppose that a period of such great importance in French history, to say nothing of our own, has been left unexamined by any intelligent American. Enough for us to remind him of the single event that most concerns us, — the fact that such a policy was carried out to experiment, — to a series of experiments, — which, under the most cruel auspices, failed entirely of their expected fruits.

The Huguenots, led by Ribault and Laudonniere, appear to have traversed no inconsiderable portions of Carolina, Georgia and Florida — countries, all of which were, at that time, dis-

---

[1] A version of this essay was published in the *Southern and Western Magazine*, II (August, 1845), 87–94.

guished by the common name of the latter. Finally, settling on the frontiers of the former State, they proceeded to entrench themselves and to explore the country. These leading facts are sufficiently well known. It is not so well known, however, what a fine series of romances belongs to this history, needing only the most ordinary developments of art, to render them as highly distinguished and delightful as those of any history, the foundations of which were laid in the most adventurous and primitive periods of society. Let us trace, with hurried pencil, the events in this connexion. The spot is chosen for the fortress of our Huguenots — an island in the friendly waters of an Indian territory, to which, from the magnificence of the bay, the French give the name of Port Royal. The fortress of La Caroline springs up amid the shade. Its cannon are mounted, its magazines prepared, its cabins raised, its provisions stored, and then, the duties which he had undertaken being all completed, Ribault departs for France, leaving a small colony of twenty-four men under the command of one Captain Albert. His purpose is to report progress at home, and to return with new supplies. Our interest lies not in his path, along the dark waters of the deep, but lingers over the spot which has so strangely, of a sudden, been transferred from the care of its savage to that of its Christian masters. A colony so small, and so thoroughly isolated from its accustomed world — thousands of miles from home and help, surrounded by herds of savages, — few in number, feeble in resource, — poorly supplied in provisions, and depending, in so many words, purely on themselves for all the comfort and safety they could know — would, — so one might reasonably suppose, — harmonize in their objects, and yield a hearty and affectionate support to the common interests. This would seem to be due equally to the social tendencies, as to the obvious necessity, for security, of a perfect and habitual unanimity among them. Such, however, was not the case. It is not so sure, at this late period, and in the imperfect condition of our authorities, where and with whom the error lay by which this hopeful scheme was defeated. By the colonists themselves, such as survived the expedition, the guilt of its failure is ascribed to their superior. Albert, their Captain, seems to have been one of those ordinary men whom it is easy to spoil by elevation. He soon converts his authority into a despotism. With a feeble and wanton passion for the display of his power, — under some slight provocation, — he singles out one of his men, who happens to be a favourite among the people, as a proper object for its exercise; and subjects him to a penalty, — something short of death, indeed, but which, in the condition of the colony, seems to have been worse than death itself. At least, it appears to have been thought so. He sends the offender into banishment. He is exiled from his Christian comrades, consigned to the dangers from wild beasts of the forest, or to dangers scarcely less terrible, at the hands of the capricious savage. It is the cruel resolve of Albert that he shall perish. No food is allowed him beyond the supply for a few days, with which he is furnished when first expelled from the walls of La Caroline; and his comrades are forbidden, under like penalties, to extend him any relief. It is the hope and the conviction of the cruel despot, that his victim must die of starvation. He is deceived; — he lives. He is provided against hunger, — he is consoled by society. We know this from the chronicles, but nothing farther. The poet alone, or the romancer, can declare boldly by whom he is succored — who brings him nourishment and food, — who cheers him in the lonely haunts of the forest, who encourages him to live and to hope, in despite and defiance of that tyrant who had decreed that he should despair and die. Was not his exile shared by some gentle damsel of the woods — some Pocahontas of St. Helena — nay, was it not because of the smiles of some such bright humanity that he first suffers the doom of banishment. There is some faint tradition that will justify this conjecture. Now, — should the poet ever avail himself of this suggestion — should he venture, in song, to insist upon this, as, in truth, the history, where is the Niebuhr to start up and gainsay it with a solemn chronicle? Where is the critic who, if the artist shall have performed his work with reasonable skill, shall dare to insinuate a doubt of his veracity? It is by the excellence of the art that the fiction is converted into truth; and all malleable conjecture, not conflicting with the unquestionable and the known, is truth sufficient for all the purposes of poetry.

But the exile is consoled and succored — we will suppose, in the absence of any certain particulars, by the sympathies of the Indian damsel. But this is not all — he is avenged. Hated by his commander, he had qualities to endear him to his comrades as well as to the dusky beauty of the savage. They rise in arms against the tyranny which oppresses them, and Albert perishes in the conflict which ensues.

Such a story might end here. Properly grouped, and with the addition of such other persons of the drama as the action must have possessed, — though history does not deem it necessary to record their names — and the parts have quite a dramatic finish, and maintain the epic fitness and dependency. The action being single, that of the recall of the banished man from exile, and the overthrow of the oppressor, affords the happiest opportunity to the artist to introduce and ally with the events, whatever adjuncts of terror or of tenderness he pleases. Captivity by the Indians, his rescue by the dusky maiden, — their mutual loves, — the jealousy of Albert, etc., — these are all topics which suggest themselves naturally for employment, in the development of this little history, in a form either narrative or dramatic.

But this story of Albert forms but a single scene in this domestic history. The residue, if less dramatic, will prove it-

self scarcely less full of susceptibilities for other forms of art.
Let us continue the narrative. Albert being slain, the insur-
gents choose a successor; but this event, though it quiets the
strifes among themselves, is very far from bringing peace to
the little colony. Their exile has been protracted — their supplies from France have failed them — they have made enemies
among the Indians, and, yearning with the *maladie du pays*,
they resolve upon returning to their European home. But
how? They are without ships and without architects. But
where the inclinations of the heart are fervent, the mind readily furnishes, in most cases within human power, the agents by
which its desires may be realized. The simple narrative which
tells us of the modes and substitutes which they employed in
building and rigging up their little brigantine, with which to
traverse the long ways of the Atlantic, is pleasingly pathetic.
How, without artificers of any kind, they yet ventured upon
one of the most noble of the mechanic arts. How they gathered from the oaks the moss, and from the pines the resin,
with which to make tight the seams of their vessel — how the
Indians brought them cordage for tackle, made doubtlessly
out of moss also; — and how their own garments furnished the
frail canvas. These are all minutiæ which, however, work upon
our sympathies with an influence such as belongs to the pages
of that dear little book of details, the Robinson Crusoe of our
childhood. Drunken with joy, according to the old chronicler
— a joy that grew out of the simple fact that they had once
more turned their eyes in the direction of *La belle France*, —
they put to sea, rashly, like greedy and thoughtless children,
without any adequate supply of food, without giving any
heed to the aspects of wind and weather. The usual narrative
of ocean caprice ensues. Tossed about and baffled by storm,
— out of provisions and out of water — despair seizes upon
their hearts; and here follows one of those terrible events
which we shudder to imagine can ever occur to add to the

thousand humiliations which sometimes track the footsteps of unfortunate humanity —

> Savagely
> They glared upon each other — all was done —
> Water and wine and food – and you might see
> The longings of the cannibal arise,
> (Although they spoke not,) in their wolfish eyes.

One of their number is demanded, as a victim, to pacify the now frenzied appetites of the famished wretches who remain. —

> At length one whisper'd his companion, who
> Whispered another, and thus it went around,
> And then into a hoarser murmur grew
> An ominous, and wild and desperate sound;
> And when his comrade's thought each suff'rer knew,
> 'Twas but his own, suppress'd till now, he found;
> And out they spoke of lots for flesh and blood,
> And who should die to be his fellow's food.[2]

Lots were not necessary in the present instance. The brave fellow whom they had rescued from the tyranny of Albert, proves his gratitude, and justifies the interest which they had shown in his behalf, by voluntarily subjecting his own bosom to the knife. Here is the exhibition of a magnanimous soul, surrounded by terror and agony, yet rising up without fear, and utterly superior to both. What a model of manly defiance, and strength of heart, for the genius of painting or sculpture, — what a scene for Michael Angelo or Fuseli. How the poet of the terrific and intenser passions, Milton or Danté, would have given this terrible scene, in a few bold touches, as Byron has given it in details. What a picture of the wild phrenzies of the heart — its deep desolation — its fierce despair — its degrading willingness to prolong life on any terms, — and its individual example, worthy of record in all ages, of that

[2] Lord Byron, *Don Juan*, Canto II, stanzas lxxii and lxxiii. Simms makes his customary slight changes in punctuation.

sublime resignation of soul, which scorns to struggle against fate with the impotent blindness of fear, and disdains the life which can only be preserved by a loathsome sacrifice of all its humanity. The offer of the victim is accepted. The sacrifice of their brave companion is made; and, strange to say, these miserable outcast Huguenots — denied, as it would seem, by the shores of two continents — finally reach Europe in safety.

But this issue does not conclude the enterprise, the history of which is much more full of the tragic than has been shown already. Ignorant of the fate of the former, and too late to afford them succor, a second colony repairs to La Caroline. Laudonniere, their new Captain, finding the place abandoned, is discouraged from any attempt to renew the settlement in the same spot. He views it as of evil omen and, proceeding farther south, builds a second fortress, and the Indians, as in the case of his predecessor, gather to his assistance. An error in his policy and humanity, is yet a source of poetic and romantic material, which the imaginative writer will readily conceive. Laudonniere foments wars among the natives, selects one tribe for his alliance, lends the force of his arms to the support of one faction against another, and converts crowds of willing friends into troops of watchful enemies. It is not easy to secure the affections even of the tribe which he sustains. The Indians withhold their supplies, and his people suffer accordingly. Insurrection, among them, is the natural fruit of privation. They conspire against him — penetrate his tent in armour, at midnight — drag him on shipboard, and, with weapon at his throat, extort from him a regular commission of piracy. How they coursed, whom they captured, and by what means they were finally destroyed, are all facts of curious interest and value which may be found in the record. It is not for us to dwell more particularly on them, or to do more than suggest their susceptibilities. It needs not even that we should say, that — in the materials indicated, — in the nov-

elty of the events — their exciting character, — the daring temper of the persons concerned, — the various passions brought
into play, and the final and highly tragic issue which closed
the deeds of the adventures — to say nothing of the privileges
afforded by that condition of palpable obscure which is due to
the absence of all details — will be found all the resources and
facilities, which, in the case of preceding histories, have been
as the canvas and the colour in the hands of the successful
artist.

But the truly sublime and terrible catastrophe to this sad
tale of colonial enterprise, is yet to follow. The closing portion of this history is one of peculiar grandeur — bright with a
lurid sort of brightness, — a strange, wild mixture of glare and
gloom, such as startles us at first, then half offends and repels,
and half delights, in the audacious pictures of John Martin.[3]
We have said that the colonists of the French were Huguenots
— another name for a sect of religionists professing the prot-
estant faith. We need not remind the reader of history, of
the melancholy truth, that religious conflicts are, of all others,
distinguished by the most shocking disregard of all the principles and precepts of humanity. That these poor adventurers
were protestants and French, were twofold reasons why they
should be put under the ban of the Spanish Catholics, by
whom, in the name of Spain, a vague title was asserted to the
whole of the vast country, into a few acres of which they
had driven their stakes. This claim was now to be asserted,
and this hate satisfied, by deeds which seem to have been almost peculiar to the Spanish practice in America. There was
a famous, or rather an infamous, Captain of that time — a man,
cold, dark and designing, who was chosen to assert the rights
and the religion of Spain, in reference to the Huguenot set-

---

[3] John Martin (1789–1854), British historical and landscape painter, noted
for his wild imagination in such famed pictures as *Belshazzar's Feast* (1821)
and *The Fall of Nineveh* (1828).

tlers in Florida. Brave, indeed, as was unquestionably the Spanish distinction in those days, this man was totally wanting in those gentler graces of character which subdue the asperities of valour, and soothe, where they cannot soften, the severities of war. Pedro Melendez was not less a bigot in religion, because he had been heavily amerced for crime. He prepared to atone, to his king and his religion, by the commission of a darker crime than any in the already long black catalogue of his past offences. He descended upon the Huguenot settlement with a superior power. Unhappily, the forces of the latter were divided. One portion maintained their fortress, while another, and the larger, kept the sea. The fierce valour of Melendez, aided by a cruel fortune, and stimulated by the fierce fanaticism of religious hate, enables him to storm the fortress. That he conquers, offers no reason to his bigot nature, why he should spare his foes. Such of them as escape the sword in the assault, and yield to his mercy, are hurried to the neighbouring tree. None were permitted to live who confided to his faith. In this bloody manner nearly two hundred persons perished. This *auto da fé* accomplished, High Mass was celebrated upon the scene of massacre; and while the earth was yet smoking with the blood of the innocent, the place was dedicated to God by this miserable butcher!

The fate of those who had sought safety on the seas, was not more fortunate. Pursued by the Spanish armament, and scattered by storm, they abandoned their stranded vessels and sought safety along the shore. They had weapons in their hands, they could fight, they were still free, and resolved with desperate valour that they would die like men. It was in an evil hour that they altered this resolve. But the constant pressure of ill fortune had chilled their hearts and subdued the courage in their souls. They hearkened to, they treated with, the murderer. They knew and feared his faithlessness, yet they listened to his words. The false-hearted Spaniard invited them to seek his mercy. A few of them suspected, as well they might, the value of his assurances. These held themselves aloof, and found their safety only as they did so. The greater number, worn with toil, sinking from famine, and hopeless of better things, resigned themselves to their fate, rather than prolong the exhausting conflict with necessity. They complied with the invitation of the Spaniard to treat for their surrender. A curious scene now followed. A small river ran between the opposing armies, while the conference between their chiefs proceeded on its banks. On one side stood Melendez, sternly phlegmatic, coldly resolute in all his requisitions. He provides a boat, and offers to the French officers every facility for passing to and fro, while the treaty is in progress. Nay, he even goes farther — he sets food and refreshments before them, and, with a rare exhibition of the demoniac spirit, he conducts them to the plain where lie the carcasses of their comrades, yet ungathered, in their gore; and, after all, coldly requires that they shall confide in his mercy — that mercy, of which, he himself, in the same moment, affords them the most terrible spectacle. In vain do they expostulate. He demands that they shall surrender at discretion. Certainly, with this bloody evidence before their eyes, it was the strangest fatuity, that which prompted them to give ear, for a single instant, to the cruel monster. But that despair which enfeebles the heart, asserts a still more tyrannical force upon the judgment. Perhaps they even gathered hope from that frank exhibition which he presented them of his former cruelties. It would seem by this that he meant to say, "my anger is pacified." At all events, by whatever process of thought they were persuaded to a compliance with his will, it is very certain that they yielded for themselves and people. In small detachments, just so many as the boat can carry, they are ferried across the river. Each division, as it arrives, is conducted out of sight, to the plain where their comrades were butchered, and there, man by man, subjected to the same bloody doom. Melendez superintends the execution. He is described as deliberately drawing, with his cane, a line along the sands, and thus designating the precise spot where the butchery must be done. He has no relentings. No generous impulses soften his stony heart, at any moment, in this dreadful execution. He spares none — placidly superintends the crime till it is finally complete in the silence of the last expiring victim, and turns away with the spirit of one well satisfied that he has done a work as acceptable to Heaven, as it was to the kindred soul of his sovereign.

It is grateful to know that all were not thus confiding — that all did not perish in this wretched manner, the tame victims to their own imbecility and the tiger fury of their foe. One small body of men, endowed with a nobler spirit than their comrades, confiding to their own weapons rather than to the words of the Spaniard, compelled him to terms of safety and comparative indulgence. Another band of twenty men, following the suggestions of their brave captain, disdaining the terms which their comrades had secured — perhaps, and properly, despising their securities — preferred rather to trust themselves to the deep thickets of the wilderness, with all their savage possessors, than the faith of their Christian enemies. Separating themselves from those who submitted, they disappeared from sight. The Spaniards sought for them in vain. Their farther history is a blank. They were never heard of more! What was the fate of this little band of Huguenots? There may be an answer, hereafter, to this question. It may be that their probable fortunes, rich in variety of adventure, and glorious by the golden tints of romance, shall yet delight the fancies of our children. *They* may be made to see, in all the colours of the Epic muse, that terrific picture of sacrifice which we have feebly shown — that strange, dark strife — so cruel yet so picturesque. In the fore-ground, that fierce fanatic warrior, standing, cane in hand, upon the shores of the San Matheo, and marking along the sand that slight but dreadfully intelligible line, to be afterwards made more legible in blood. In the distance, the little boat bringing the captive Frenchmen, ten by ten, little dreaming of the fate that awaits them, unconscious, like sheep to the slaughter, moving on to perish by sudden stroke where that unseen line is drawn.

It is something to know that this massacre was avenged. The soul feels a fierce delight, which even Christian tuition does not always subdue, when it is told of the vindictive retribution which follows the deeds of the cruel upon the unoffending. Man's blood, shed by his brother, does not often cry in vain to Heaven! A hero as religiously resolute in vengeance as Melendez had been in crime, took upon him the work of retribution, and carried out the ends of justice, in punishment, upon the murderers. The single spirit of retributive justice by which the valiant Gascon, Dominique de Gorgues, was led to peril himself in battle with the Spaniards of Florida, to forfeit the protection of his own country, and win the admiration of all the states of Christendom but Spain, has given him a rank in chivalry not inferior to that of Bayard and Duguesclin.[4] It might be no difficult matter, even now, to make his deeds the subject of story, and himself the hero of an epic song!

We must not linger upon this period, nor dilate upon its incidents, passionate and touching though they be. If we insist that there are thousands such during this epoch in our history, we deal in no unfounded exaggerations. It would be easy for the romancer even now — the poet — such poets as we already possess — pursuing the proper methods, devoting himself, soul

4 Seigneur de Bayard (c. 1473–1524), French knight, known as "*Chevalier sans peur et sans reproche*," was the subject of a book-length biography by Simms, *The Life of the Chevalier Bayard* (New York, 1847). Bertrand Du Guesclin (c. 1320–1380), a constable of France, was known as "the Eagle of Brittany."

and body, to his art, and properly sustained by the sympathies, and encouraged by the obvious wants of the people, to work such details into a thousand exquisite and truthful fictions. He need not turn his eyes for the crude material to the obscure chronicles of foreign lands. That which we possess, is not less susceptible of artistic elaboration; nay, in many instances, it is not only quite as good as the exotic, but rudely developed in the block, and ready to our hands. The outline of the statue is already in the stone — the image is half starting from the shade, and the divine conception looks out from its cloud, with eyes of sweetest soliciting, only waiting for the endowing hands of art to become a living and a loving soul. The studies yielded to the master of fiction by our moral progress, are not less numerous than those which the painter may gather, on every hand, from the matchless forest land through which he wanders. He has but to follow a like direction — to cut away the under growth — to cast down the offensive and obtrusive object — to bring out into bolder relief such forms as merit to be made particular — to be raised into superiority, and elevated by appropriate tributaries — and the work is done as he could wish it. The creation is here — already in our possession! — it is the *clearing* — the *clearing* only — which has need to follow.[5]

[5] Simms utilized this material later in *The Lily and the Totem, or, The Huguenots in Florida, A Series of Sketches, Picturesque and Historical, of the Colonies of Coligny, in North America, 1562–1570* (New York, 1850). This work was originally planned for the Wiley and Putnam Library of American Books and was announced for the series as *The Huguenots in Florida.*

vi

POCAHONTAS: A SUBJECT FOR THE HISTORICAL PAINTER [1]

W<small>E</small> have already dwelt so long upon the events of the previous periods, that we shall be compelled to hurry somewhat rapidly over those which remain. It will be conjectured, from what has been already said of the characteristics of this epoch, that we regard its materials, not only as decidedly superior, at present, to those which follow, but as being quite as much adapted, even now, to the purposes of fiction as those of any other history. The events are equally curious and copious, full of vivacity, and glowing with the most various and striking traits of human passion and performance. Leading personages may be found in their development, endowed with all those attributes of character which constitute the moral of the heroic. Their deeds provide as noble and imposing action as romance has ever esteemed the most proper upon which to build her inventions of "lofty rhyme" and "stately tragedy," — and there is quite enough, in the detail, of that ductile obscurity, which we have insisted upon as so necessary to the full exercise of all the privileges which are asked by the original artist. We commend the study of this period, down to the date of English settlement in Virginia, to the peculiar care of the American student — satisfied, as we are, that he cannot fail to find among its chronicles a body of crude material, virgin and fertile, fresh and blooming with the beauty of its dawning youth, and susceptible to all the maternal uses which grow naturally from the embrace of the prolific genius.

The epoch which follows is one of more narrow privileges,

[1] A version of this essay was published in the *Southern and Western Magazine*, II (September, 1845), 145–154.

circumscribing our progress by the absolute and well known in those facts, which are of value in proportion to their obscurity, quite as much as because of their intrinsic capabilities. Its aspects are sharper and more repulsive — its outlines more decisive and angular — its incidents too clearly stated upon the record, and abridged by those definitive boundaries of the real, which impair the courage of him who seeks after the ideal. The softening effects of distance, and the mellowing influence of time, are equally needed to reconcile us perfectly to the beautiful in its aspects, and the pliant and the graceful in its forms. There are intrinsic deficiencies also. We feel, as we examine the moral of its history, that a harsher and a severer judgment has made its way among men, lessening their faith in the fancies of the past, disparaging authority and tradition, and disturbing that repose among ancient things in which the meditative and endowing genius takes most of its delight. Chivalry had given way to more mortal politics, and, standing in the presence and beneath the freezing countenance of the bigoted Philip of Spain, or wearied with the caprices of one quite as selfish, if less bigoted — Elizabeth of England — we feel those frigid influences which were destined to pass like a blight over the social character of Europe. Not that we mean, now, to indicate any preference, except in a simple reference to the objects of art in fiction, for the condition of the social world in the days of chivalry over those of the reformers of the Christian Church. On the contrary, the study of the middle ages, obliges us to conclude with Sismondi,[2] in disregard of Burke — "*Cet heroism universel, nous avons nomme la chevalerie n' exista jamais commes fictions brillantes.*" But it is precisely because of the paralyzing influence of these and other powers, upon the habits and condition of the world,

[2] Jean Charles Léonard Simonde de Sismonde (1773–1842), Swiss historian, author of *Histoire de Républiques Italiennes du Moyen Âge* (16 vols., 1803–1818) and *Histoire des Français* (31 vols., 1821–1844).

then and afterwards, that we are made conscious of the want
of the proper materials for a fiction as brilliant as was found,
the spontaneous production of society, in the previous epochs
of its history. We have now reached a period when commerce
begins to assert a claim to be an estate among those long before
acknowledged among the powers of Christendom — helped
wonderfully in the assertion of this claim by the sudden and
surprising progress of maritime discovery. We are on the eve
of those great social and moral changes which led to the catastrophe in the career of Walter Raleigh — to the heartless
and senseless profligacy of the Stuarts — to the substitution, in
England, of French for English poetry — the clinquant of a
false, for the hearty ring of the genuine metal — and — not to
class things so utterly dissimilar in every point of view — the
anomalous growth of the demure and sly, the daring but cal-
culating ambition of the Puritans. Virginia has been discovered, named and colonized — inadequately colonized, as were
all of the settlements in America; — a fact which led to that
deplorable waste of blood and treasure, that prolonged struggle in arms, which naturally ensued from the painful contest
for ascendancy, between the red men of the country and their
pale invaders. But this, which provokes the censure of the
philosophical statesman, as the very last of social misfortunes,
is hailed as a source of invention and exercise by the professor
of art in fiction. A vast store-house of material is laid open to
us by the struggles between these warring races; and over its
heaps the future genius of our romance shall hang with the
fond avidity of him who gloats above the discovery of an unknown treasure. Our limits will not suffice to enable us to
indicate more than a single topic in the history of our sister
State; but this shall be one admirably adapted to the purposes
of poetry and art. This story is that of Pocahontas, with
which every native is familiar. It is one which has been frequently attempted, and unhappily, in most cases, by very fee-

ble hands. It has never been put to proper use by the pen or pencil of any; yet there is scarcely one, in all our history, at this second period of which we speak, which seems to us better adapted to the equal purposes of the painter and the poet. Let us endeavour to sketch from it a single scene for each. The painter, it must be remembered, has but a moment of time for his delineations — but a single moment — and if he fails so to select this moment as to compel the picture to tell its own story, the subordinate merits of exquisite elaboration will not avail to maintain his claims as a *builder* and a master. The dramatic requisitions of his art — which are the most stringent, for the just reason that the department which delineates human passion is necessarily the most noble — require that he shall seize upon that moment in the event he seeks to celebrate, which, because of the intenseness of the interest felt by the several parties to his group, shall present the spectator with the most impressive and intelligible action. It is when the struggle is at its height, when face and form, and eye and muscle, in each of the dramatis personæ, are wrought upon by the extremity of the action — when the crisis is reached of human hope, or fear, or endurance, and nothing that follows, can, by any possibility, add to the acuteness of that anxiety with which the beholder watches the scene — that the artist must snatch the occasion to stamp the story in life-like colours upon the canvas. It is the judgment which he exhibits in this particular — in thus choosing his moment — in the sensibility and the imagination which prompt him to catch the vivid emotion and the hungry passion, ere they subside into the repose which follows from natural exhaustion — that he establishes his pretensions as the poet of his art. To show his story at the extreme and doubtful instant, when hope can no longer admit of increase, when fear can bear nothing more without pain, and both, in the spectator, begin to merge in that anxiety to behold an issue, the approaches to which he can no longer endure without suffering too deeply for any sentiment of pleasure — this is the great merit which places the dramatic painter far above all other professors in his art. That moment, in the history of Pocahontas, is when Smith is rescued by her interposition from the stroke of the executioner. Our artists, generally, have shrunk from this subject. We know not one, endowed with any of the necessary attributes of genius, taste and imagination, by whom it has been attempted.

Mr. Chapman, a southern artist, whose large and peculiar merits it gives us pleasure to acknowledge and assert, has given us a lovely picture of the reception of the Indian princess into the bosom of the Mother Church; but it is to the reproach of this gentleman[3] that he has avoided the nobler event which first brought us to the knowledge of her character. Certainly, it is one of singular difficulty, demanding the highest powers of art, and an imagination equally warm and courageous, to say nothing of the inevitable requisites of the exquisite colorist and draughtsman; but it is this very difficulty, and the danger which attends it, which commend the subject to the affections, and stimulates the ambition of the proper genius. He, therefore, whether painter or poet, who shrinks from the task because of its hardships or its dangers, has a better reason for his timidity in the absence of his capacity. He is not the genius to obtain a mastery over the grand — not the soul to conceive

[3] [*Simms's note*] Mr. Chapman is one of our best painters. He has a vivacious and an abundant fancy, an exquisite taste, and more industry than half of our artists put together. We are indebted to him for several Indian pictures, in all of which he has been singularly successful. But his genius inclines him rather to the pleasing than the passionate—rather to the soliciting and the sweet in nature, than the stern and terrible. Pocahontas, entering the English settlements at night to warn the colonists of the intended massacre — or the same lovely creature made captive by the artifice of Argall and the treachery of Japazaws — would be subjects more agreeable to his genius, than the terrible scene in which she rescues Smith. Still, we should like to see the attempt, made by his hands, upon this difficult but noble subject. [Simms is referring to John Gadsby Chapman (1808–1889), American painter, born in Alexandria, Va., whose *Baptism of Pocahontas* is in the rotunda of the Capitol, Washington, D. C.]

what belongs to the sublime and the majestic — not that seer
who alone carries the true divining rod — upon whose eye the
dim creation of the mind irresistibly fixes itself, not only as
the unavoidable presence, but as one which can be treated
only in one manner. It is when the subject forces itself, with
all its particular aspects, unchangeably, before the eye of the
imagination, that we can be altogether sure of its grandeur,
its efficacy, and the propriety of that attempt which seeks to
embody it in physical material in the sight of eyes to whom its
beauties never came before even in their dreams.

Let us now endeavour to suggest this event by a skeleton
draught of its deeper outlines — to sketch this picture, feebly
of course, and very faintly — in crayons rather than in oil —
but sufficiently, we trust, to commend it to those by whom
the elaborate achievement may yet be wrought. We trust, in
what we say, to make good the assurance with which we set
out, that the subject of Pocahontas, rescuing Smith from the
executioner, is worthy of the great historical painter.

Our back-ground is one familiar to you all. It lies in the
unbroken forest, yet undishonoured by the axe. Great oaks,
moss-bearded and grand, like Hebrew prophets and patriarchs,
stretch their shadowy arms above the scene. Gigantic pines
group themselves behind them, and tower up and away in
emulation of the hills. There you may see the green vine
gadding fom bough to bough; — the green thickets are burdened with the weight of blossoms which persuade us that the
atmosphere is faint with a sweetness all its own. The sward is
similarly rich beneath our feet — a carpet of emerald with
tiny flowers, purple and yellow, here and there saddening into
brown under the melancholy smiles of autumn. Such is our
landscape, the still life present, unavoidably perceptible, but
not in its details, and only as subordinate to the human action.
That fixes and fascinates the glance. There we see, crowding
the intervals beneath the trees of the forest, a thousand human

forms — the wild people of the woods — stern and dark, proud and fiercely frowning warriors, armed after their own fashion, looking the more terrible, perhaps, because of the absence of all armour; — with — only half seen among the groups — some less dusky visage which heaven has benignly touched with features of more human sweetness. Woman appears upon the scene, half shrinking back even while she advances, as fearing to be seen while anxious to see; — and boyhood stands forward, eagerly, before all the rest. Curiosity is in all, anger and exultation in many, faces. All eyes turn to one centre, where, conspicuous in the fore-ground — the sunlight streaming down through a broad opening of that natural amphitheatre upon the spot — lies one

Destined to make an *Indian* holiday.[4]

It is the pale, the European face, that lies beneath that oppressive sunlight. The captive is bound and prostrate upon the earth — the strong man, conscious of all his strength, in the same moment in which he feels all its impotency. He constitutes the centre of that eager group that fascinates every glance — to whom every eye addresses itself — some with hate and eager ferocity, some with curiosity simply, and, possibly, some few with pity and regret. Perfectly helpless, quite hopeless, his face turns upward to that sun which is about to set forever on his sight. Such, at least, is his conviction. The pity which has power to save rises not in that dark assemblage; and he has prepared himself with the courage of the soldier, and the patient confidence of the Christian, to await the cruel death which hangs above his head. His manly cheek does not pale with apprehension. His eagle eye makes no appeal for mercy, and, when his lips unclose, it is only to utter themselves in the language of defiance. His muscular form, though

4 A paraphrase of Lord Byron's line, "Butcher'd to make a Roman holiday," *Childe Harold's Pilgrimage*, Canto IV, stanza cxli.

fettered with gyves from the neighbouring vines, subsides nevertheless into an attitude of grace, consistent with the reputation of the courtier. Patiently he awaits the stroke of death. A jagged rock sustains his head. The executioner stands above him with his mace — a stalwart savage, who has no shrinkings of the heart or muscles — who will be only too happy when bade to strike — who will drink in, with a fierce phrenzy, the groans of the victim — nay, bury his hand within his bosom and pluck the heart from its quivering abode, while life yet speaks in the pulses of the dying man! *He* waits, he looks, with impatience to the savage monarch for the signal when to strike. That signal is made — the word is spoken! —

> The arm that holds the mace is bending,
> The heavy stroke of death descending.[5]

What arrests the blow? Why does the eager savage, anxious for blood, panting for vengeance, forbear to execute the bidding of his cruel sovereign? Lo! the miracle, at once, of loveliness and mercy! What has arrested the stroke of the murderer, so frequently, and in all lands and ages? What, but the interposition of an angel! A form of light — that loveliest creation of mortal beauty, a young girl just budding into womanhood — is this interposing angel. With what a sinking, terror-stricken heart, has she sat at her father's feet, watching the whole dark proceedings. What a strife has been in progress the while, between her timid sex and years and the holy strength of maternal nature in her heart. The maternal nature is at last triumphant. She darts from her seat — voiceless — gasping with new and convulsive emotions, which lead her, she knows not whither, while she flings herself between the captive and the blow. One arm is thrown upward to prevent the stroke — one covers the head of the victim — while her dilating but tearless eyes, turn in fear and entreaty to the spot

[5] From section 14 of Simms's own poem, "The Forest Maiden," *The Book of My Lady* (Philadelphia, 1833), p. 57.

where sits the fierce old monarch, Powhatan! This is the moment of time for the painter. It is the crisis in the fortunes of the scene. Will the interposition of that angel prevail — will the sire relent — will they not drag her from the prisoner, heedless of her entreaties — heedless of her shrieks and prayers? These are the enquiries in every face. All eyes turn with hers to the rock where the monarch sits — all eyes, but those of the captive! *He* looks only upon *her*. He has forgotten that he is to die in the advent of that unexpected vision of light and beauty. A pleasing wonder is in his heart — he doubts, indeed, whether the blessed form has not really descended from the skies; and his memory carries him backward to the days when a like vision of beauty in the east, once cheered him with delivery even in a moment of trial as terrible as that which still hangs above him in the west.[6] From this recollection he gathers hope and heart, and the most assuring auguries — and they do not betray him!

And what of Powhatan, that hard-souled, iron-browed old despot! What are his emotions? He has started from his seat. The conflict in his soul speaks fully out in his countenace. To be thwarted in his vengeance, and by a child, is something new in his experience! But the child is *his* child, and *such* a child! Her sweet nature is written in her most innocent deeds. He looks upon her kneeling form, and his face is full of surprise and anger. His right foot is thrown behind him — his arm, grasping the tomahawk, is uplifted to strike — his form swings upon its centre, to give fatal impetus to the blow! Shall he strike or spare? Here is another issue of doubt and curiosity, most favourable to the painter. How shall the question be de-

---

[6] A reference to Smith's having been befriended in Constantinople by Tragabigzanda, the mistress of the satrap Bogalius. Smith, in the dedication of his *General Historie of Virginia, New-England, and the Summer Isles* (1624), links his indebtedness to "the beauteous Lady Tragabigzanda" with his indebedness to "Pokahontas, the great King's daughter of Virginia." Simms gives an account of the episode in chapter ix, Book I, of his *Life of Captain John Smith* (New York, 1846).

termined? What hopes, what fears, depend upon this question. What feelings of vengeance and of mercy, of hate and tenderness, are in conflict. How completely would such a picture, though grasping but a single moment of time, tell its own history! Need we say that the angel of mercy must finally prevail?

With these, our examples must conclude. Our limits do not suffer us to carry out our first design of presenting such an analysis of this delightful story, as would show its admirable susceptibility for poetic illustration. For the border romance — the free and easy narrative of the wild and startling, such as Scott has rendered so familiar to us, in that happy combination of the epic and the ballad which is destined to a long association with his peculiar genius — the life of the Virginia princess furnishes other materials like this, and not much inferior to it in dramatic respects — which are fully equal, in intrinsic capabilities, to any of those which have been employed by Scott. The tone of the story may be pitched with that of the Lady of the Lake — the characteristics of the people and the country are not dissimilar — but the events in our Virginia legend are of a nobler sort; and the wretched failures which have followed every attempt to work them into song, are due entirely to the inadequacy of those writers who have presumptuously addressed themselves to the task. When our people shall really have acquired some intellectual appetites in sufficient number to make and mould the popular taste; and books shall have become an aliment as absolutely necessary to us as brandy and tobacco — we shall then have the poet and the song.[7] The laws of demand and supply govern this subject, in most of its respects, as thoroughly as they govern in

[7] Simms attempted the poetic treatment of this material in "Pocahontas: A Legend of Virginia," in *The Missionary Memorial: A Literary and Religious Souvenir* (New York, 1846), pp. 199–220, re-issued as *The Evergreen*. The poem is reprinted in Simms's *Southward Ho! A Spell of Sunshine* (New York, 1854), pp. 110–123.

the market place. It is a consoling part of the faith which it is the purpose of these papers to teach, that we shall not always slumber — that we are at last to have an awakening — not, certainly, to be put off to the indefinite period of the *Greek Kalends.*

It needs not that we should review the remaining periods of time which have been assigned to the materials of our history, in considering them with regard to their susceptibility for the purposes of art. We have not the leisure for this task, nor, indeed, is it at all essential to our purpose. Having already indicated the disabilities of these epochs, in general terms, such a performance would seem unnecessary — the more particularly, indeed, as the task would be endless of sampling from our staples, and distinguishing the most eligible and excellent for the use of the artist. Besides, the independence of character which every where makes the individual mind, would render this a gratuitous and unwelcome labour. The subject must suggest its own modes of treatment to him who conceives it. What would strike one mind as singularly suitable for the uses of the artist, would scarcely commend itself to the peculiar genius of another. Of these periods, therefore, which we leave unexamined, it will suffice to say, that, however inferior to the two first, they are yet very far from deficient in that boldness of event, and warmth of colouring, which are demanded by the worker in the fields of fiction. Their chief difficulties lie, as we have said before, in their too close proximity to our own time. But these difficulties are neither permanent in their duration, nor total in their exactions. It would be easy to enumerate hundreds of events, in the wars of the Revolution, which would amply answer for the experiments of novelist and poet. Partisan warfare, itself, is that irregular and desultory sort of life, which is unavoidably suggestive of the deeds and feelings of chivalry — such as gave the peculiar character, and much of the charm, to the history of the middle ages. The sudden onslaught — the retreat as sudden — the midnight tramp — the moonlight *bivouack* — the swift surprise, the desperate defence — the cruel slaughter and the headlong flight — and, amid the fierce and bitter warfare, always, like a sweet star shining above the gloom, the faithful love, the constant prayer, the devoted homage and fond allegiance of the maiden heart! These are all to be made available, as the ordinary characteristics — all of them highly susceptible of the uses of romance — which must inevitably distinguish a domestic warfare carried on in a country such as ours — full of forests, sparse of population — where the march must needs be wearisome and long — where the foragers must wander far in search of provisions with dangers necessarily increasing at every mile in their progress, and where no army can be secure from capital misfortunes, even through a single night, unless by an equally stern energy and a sleepless vigilance. The comparison of such a warfare to that of the middle ages, derives no small additional force from the fact that so much of it must needs be performed on horseback. The partisan warrior combines, in his own person, the man at arms and the bowman of ancient chivalry. He is at once the cavalier and rifleman, uniting in himself the eye and the wing of battle, having the unerring and fatal directness of the one, with the untiring velocity of the other.[8]

It will have been seen, in the progress of these pages, that we have confined our examination entirely to such events as have taken place within our own geographical limits.[9] We have, in order to take the subject in its least copious and least

[8] This passage describes very clearly Simms's intention and subject matter in his seven loosely connected romances of the American Revolution: *The Partisan* (1835); *Mellichampe* (1836); *The Kinsmen* (1841), later renamed *The Scout; Katharine Walton* (1851); *The Sword and the Distaff* (1852), later renamed *Woodcraft; The Forayers* (1855); and *Eutaw* (1856). In 1844 Simms had published a book-length biography of General Francis Marion, the most important partisan leader.

[9] The limits that Simms intends here are national rather than sectional.

prepossessing aspects, recognized the political boundaries of
our republic as boundaries also for its muse! We have not
yielded any consideration to the vast resources, for the artist
who works in the realm of fiction, which lie, broadcast,
among the countries between us and the Pacific. Peru with
her wealth of tradition and history [10] — Mexico with her pictured treasures — and the collateral and dependent provinces,
many of which possessed a sway and a story which may be
yet found to be very far superior even to those which we find
so wonderful in the greater states by which they were afterwards overshadowed. These are empires which, in future days,
shall be far more prosperous and productive in the hands of
fiction, than they were in the iron grasp of their Spanish conquerors. Nor has that race, rapidly tending to the chambers
of the setting sun, but still lingering like a mournful shadow
upon our horizon, left the student of the muse no treasures. Their melancholy story, even in our own day, will
yield to the gleaner the living sweetness of some touching
song. As yet we do no justice to this material. We see nothing
but the squalid poverty, the wretched destitution, and the
baser passions of this failing race. We have yet to learn the
truth in regard to their characteristics, in many particulars
equally important to the poet and the philosopher. We are
burdened with many conflicting and false ideas of their moral
and social constitution, which have hitherto furnished barriers, and not helps, to the progress of discovery. With solemn
gravity we have pronounced upon their insensibility to the
ordinary passions of mankind. We shall grow wiser upon reflection, and gather, as we proceed, from the lips of tradition,
some of those better histories which shall long survive the
certified chronicles of the historian. Much of those that we
have already at its hands, may resolve themselves into the
finest notes of fancy. The very fortunes of their people —

[10] Simms had dealt with Peru in *The Damsel of Darien* (1839).

doomed, as they are, and desolate! — their fierce wars and faithless loves, — their unbending justice — their primitive love of truth — their firm endurance of toil and torment — their tenacity of purpose — their sleepless vigilance — wonderful self-esteem, and never-dying thirst of revenge! Nay, the very doubt and obscurity which envelop their history — the who, the whence and the whither of their race — their long legends of strife and invasion, seen only in the most imperfect glimmerings of assertion — these, not only yield scope, but furnish provocation to conjecture. The imagination, left free to spread its most daring wing, darts forward with the Phœnician adventurer on the countless ocean. Taking a bold flight from the pillars of Hercules, it never rests till it places a free foot on the highest peaks of Chimborazo and Darien! With such a wing, and such a flight, what a bird's eye view of wonders shall we attain! What a world of romance and song shall then lie open before us! We shall then trace the fortunes of those very people whose great cities lie buried among the mountain passes of Guatamelá. We shall pursue the story through the chambers at Palenque, and around the strange altar places, raised to false gods, in the desert regions of Copan!

We do not despair of these discoveries; but they will be due, rather to the Homer than the Champollion [11] of future times. We doubt not that, even now, we are on the eve of the most wonderful discoveries — treasures of story and of song which we may not live to enjoy, but which shall gather our children together, in sweet suspense and tearful expectation, around the family altar-place. No nation of our magnitude — sprung from such famous stocks — having such records of the past — having such hopes of the future — with our enthusiasm of character, and with our boldness of design — can long re-

[11] Jean François Champollion (1790–1832), French Egyptologist, discoverer of the clue for deciphering the Rosetta stone, author of *Précis du Système Hiéroglyphique des Anciens Egyptiens.*

main without its *Genius loci!* It is in our hearts, that, even now, he breathes and burns! — for, what are all these strivings and aspirations, which, every where, in our day and country, are bringing together the select few — working in their academies, their societies, their libraries and their lyceums — to emulate the good and the great things of older nations. It is the struggle of that infant genius of place — the only genius which makes place holy, and preserves it from degradation and decay! That genius, thus feebly striving now, and with a faint torch burning in his infant grasp, is yet destined to grow mighty — yea, mightiest among the mighty. Already we behold his chosen altar-place on the blue summits of Apalachy! [12] — already we gaze upon his marble watch-towers and golden heights. The flame, lighted from heaven, sheds its crimson splendours, far off, to the hills of New Hampshire, and glows, with the triumphant beauty of an unclouded sunset, over the purple waters of the gulf. We may see his worshippers, as they march in ceremonial procession from our kindred republics, bringing tribute and music, and incense to his shrine! Nor, last among these — nor least — we may count among the proudest of these shining hosts, our own dear brothers of the south — our offspring — the blessed sons and daughters of the muse; — stately in step, noble in aspect, and with eyes that flash like the lightning from our own summer heavens. They march, as to a conquest! Their banners waving — their music sounding — their high hearts beating — in holy sympathy with that white robed genius of our land, which alone shall confer upon it the richest trophies of renown — the renown which follows from the achievements of creative art. We have a faith in this vision! We cannot — we dare not — for your sakes — for the sake of our common mother — be unbelievers! We

---

[12] A reference to the Appalachian Mountains. For the several nineteenth-century uses of this word see "Appalachee" and "Appalachia" in Mitford M. Mathews, *A Dictionary of Americanisms* (Chicago, 1951).

feel that we are men — sprung from the greatest men — and destined to execute all the trusts, and to secure all the triumphs, that God has ever permitted to the powers of humanity. This is a faith which will most surely realize its own predictions. We must enjoy these triumphs — these treasures must be ours. We should believe, though our eyes may never behold them! It is by a blessed instinct from heaven that we feel and *know* this prediction *must* be true! We know that we shall yet behold the advent of this genius of place; — that, penetrating the antique forests, he shall drag the old tradition from his Druid cavern, and compel him to deliver up his secrets. We shall yet hear the incantation uttered by some mighty voice, not unworthy of the greatest masters who have spelled the departed in their urns. We shall see the cavern unsealed, its ponderous jaws distend, and, in a dim glory like that which hangs about the line of successive kings on the vision of Macbeth, we shall number the great spirits of the past, issuing forth and trooping in review before us! We shall see the Montezumas, the Quaghtimozins, and the Atabalipas of our own land, re-enacting their exploits — exploits not less marvellous than those which have already found their Homer! The hope which is based upon a noble ambition, is always sure to realize itself. The faith which is felt in sincerity, and which leads to work, is a faith which will assuredly bring down the god to its temples! Let this faith be ours and we shall be sure of the deity to whom we proffer the service of our hearts. We have but to build the altar, and he will send us the prophet and the priest. Let us only prepare the sacrifice with clean hands, and the fire which is to consume it, thenceforth to become our peculiar and eternal light, will, as surely as the rising and the setting of the sun, come down to us from heaven.

ARTICLE III

LITERATURE AND ART AMONG THE AMERICAN ABORIGINES.[1]

I. — ONEOTA, OR THE RED RACE OF AMERICA; Their History, Traditions, Customs, Poetry, Picture Writing, &c. By Henry R. Schoolcraft. New York: Burgess, Stringer & Co. 1845.

II. — ALGIC RESEARCHES. By Henry R. Schoolcraft,[2] 2 vols. Harper & Brothers. New York [1839.]

THE vitality of a people, their capactiy to maintain themselves in recollection and to perpetuate a name through all the ordinary vicissitudes of empire, is in just proportion to their sensibilities; and these are shown in due degree with their susceptibility to the impressions of art. The highest manifestations of this susceptibility are those of invention — the faculty to combine and to compare, to adapt, endow, and, from the rude materials furnished by the experience of the nation, to extract its intellectual and moral resources, whether of pride or of pleasure, of triumph, or simple consolation. The humblest manifestation of this sensibility is that of music, since this is one of the most universal known to man, and may be entertained, even in large degree, by nations wholly barbarous in every other respect. There is, perhaps, no primitive people so very rude and wretched, as to be wholly without one or other of these manifestations. In all probability music is one of the first. If not exactly a substitute for thought — as one of the British poets would seem to affirm,[3] — it is yet apt to pre-

---

[1] Originally published in the *Southern and Western Magazine,* I (March, 1845), 153–164.

[2] Henry Rowe Schoolcraft (1793–1864), an American ethnologist, was a leading authority on American Indian culture.

[3] Among the many poets Simms may have had in mind is Milton, in "L'Allegro," lines 131–150, and "Il Penseroso," lines 151–174.

cede the toils of thought, and, possibly, to pave the way for it. Appealing directly to the senses, it serves to chasten and refine them, and, by subduing or mollifying the passions, it leaves the intellectual nature free to assert itself, and to maintain, by other processes the ascendancy which it thus acquires over the brutal. Other developments follow which are more or less modified according to the circumstances and condition of a country. These declare themselves, first, in rude attempts at material art; in outlines upon the wall; in figures wrought in clay; in uncouth attempts to connect narrative with music; — the germs, not to be overestimated in the analysis of a national mind, of its romance and poetry. These are all bald or copious, fluent or constrained, wild or soft, according to the necessities, the habits, and the climate of a people. Where the nation, either directly, or through individuals whom it sends forth, have contact with strangers who are superior to themselves in art and civilization, the exercise of a rude faculty of imitation necessarily precedes all native and original endeavour. Where this is not the case, the art springs, slowly and painfully, from the usages of the tribes, from their sports, their toils, their religion, the egotism of the individual, or the pride of the stock, — to all of which it imparts, or seeks to impart, by little and little, the attributes of form, grace, colour and dignity. At first, no higher object is aimed at than simply to reconcile the struggle and impatient nature, yearning for better things, to a fate which seems unavoidable, and to a toil which needs assuasion. The shepherd is thus taught to find a solace, and perhaps a charm, in his rustic and wretched life among the bleak passes of the Alps; persuaded by his Melibœus of the superior loveliness of a condition, — with crook, and pipe, and dog — from which he feels it impossible to escape; — and the squalid fisherman who draws his nets, and pursues his miserable occupation, along the gloomy edges of the northern seas, may well yield himself to those assurances of song

which can only reconcile him to his own land and labour by
disparaging those of other nations as more wretched still. And
thus it is that the poet becomes the first minister of a people,
either to find a solace for the present, or to provoke prouder
and more attractive hopes in another and more fruitful condition. Thus it is that we have the pastoral and piscatory Muse,
— the Muse of a humble nature and inferior pursuits — to
which it seeks to impart beauty and a grace which nothing but
the growing fancy, under this tutelage, enables the miserable
labourer to behold. In this manner are the rude nomadic tribes
hurried forward under the stimulating entreaties of the lyrist,
— himself a hunter and a warrior, — to the invasion of distant
forests. Thus the young savage grapples with the grizzly bear,
and confronts the she wolf in her den. War thus, is made to
look lovely in spite of all its terrors; its dangers are wooed
with the eager impetuosity of the bridegroom — its achievements form the objects of glory which a tribe most sedulously
preserves for imitation — and the Bard justifies the crimes
which are committed with this sanction — stimulates resentment, and impels the passions of the living to emulate, by similar atrocities, the terrible actions of the dead. The Greeks,
sung by Homer, were neither more nor less than highwaymen
and pirates; — the chiefs and demigods of the northern nations, honoured by Odin with highest places in Valhalla, were
of the same kidney; — and both find their likeness in the hunter
of the American forest — the dark, fierce, barbarian, Choctaw
or Cherokee — whom we are apt to consider nothing more
than the barbarian. But he too had his song, his romances and
his deities — good and evil — even as the Hellenes and the
Northmen; and his deeds were just as deserving as these, of
their Saemund and Melesigenes. That they would have found
their poet and historian to have given them as admirable a
record as any of those which recount the deeds of Greek and
Trojans, was a certainty to have followed hard upon their

progress to that degree of civilization which would have brought with it the higher efforts of invention. The Greeks had no Homer till their wanderings were over; and, with the concentration of their affections and their endowments upon a fixed abode, the American aboriginals would have then looked back upon the past, gathering up, with equal curiosity and industry, its wild fragmentary traditions. These, in process of years, they would have embodied in a complete whole, and we should then have been as rigidly fettered by its details as we are now by those of Livy and Herodotus. First, we should have had the crude ballads, the border minstrelsy, of the several tribes, descriptive of their wild and bloody encounters for favourite hunting grounds, or for the revenge of a wrong done to the honour of a proud ambitious family. These would have been welded together by a better artist in a more refined period, and a still superior genius, seizing upon this labour as so much crude material, would have remodelled the action, improved upon the events, brought out the noble characters with more distinctness, adorned it with new fancies and episodes, and sent it forth to admiring posterity, stamped with his own unchallenged impress. The rough story from which he drew, would, in the course of a century, have been as completely forgotten as were the still ruder ballads from which that was originally wrought; and nothing would have remained to future history but the symmetrical narrative, too beautiful for fact, which we cannot willingly believe, yet know not how to deny — a work too rich for history, yet too true to art, to be approached with anything short of delight and veneration.

That these materials were in the possession of the North American Indians, — that these results might have followed their amalgamation into one great family, — in a fixed abode — addressed to the pursuits of legitimate industry, and stayed from wandering either by their own internal progress, or by the coercion of a superior power — are conclusions not to be denied by those who have considered the character of this people. They had all the susceptibilities which might produce this history. Eager and intense in their feelings, lofty and courageous in spirit, — sensible in high degree to admiration, — ambitious of fame, — capable of great endurance, in the prosecution of an object, or in the eye of an adversary, — they were, at the same time, sensible to the domestic influences — were dutiful to the aged, heedful of the young, — rigid in their training and hopeful of their offspring, — with large faith in friendship, — large devotion to the gods, — not cold in their religion, and with an imagination which found spirits, divine and evil, — as numerous as those of the Greeks or Germans — in their groves, their mountains, their great oceans, their eternal forests, and in all the changes and aspects of their visible world. Their imaginations, which carried them thus far, to the creation of a vast pneumatology of their own, did not overlook the necessity of furnishing their spiritual agents with suitable attributes and endowments; and a closer inquiry than has yet been made into their mysteries, their faiths and fancies, will develop a scheme of singular imaginative contrivance, with wide spread ramifications, and distinguished by a boldness of conception, which will leave nothing wanting to him who shall hereafter contemplate a dream in mid-summer for his Chickasah or Choctaw Oberon. These traits and characteristics of mind and temperament, constitute the literary susceptibilities of a people. These susceptibilities are the stuff out of which Genius weaves her best fabrics, — those which are most truthful, and most enduring, as most certainly native and original — to be wrought into symmetry and shape with the usual effects of time and civilization. Cultivation does not create, nor even endow the mind with its susceptibilities; — it simply draws them forth, into sight, and stimulates their growth and activity. Nor, on the other hand, does repose lose or forfeit the germinating property which lies dormant in the core. Like those flower seeds plucked from the coffin of the mummy of the Egyptian Pyramids, where they have lain sapless and seemingly lifeless for three thousand years, — they take root and flourish the moment that they feel the hand of the cultivator — springing into bud and beauty, as gloriously bright as the winged insect darting from his chrysalis cerements with the first glimpses of that warming sunlight which is kindred in its sympathy to the secret principle suspended in its breast. Time and change are necessary to these results. As the flower seed which had no light in the waxen grasp of Egyptian mortality, transferred to the sunny plains of Italy, or even nursed in the warm flower palaces of England, shoots out into instant vitality — so, the nature of the savage, sterile while traversing the wide prairies of Alabama, or ranging the desert slopes of Texas, subdued and fettered by the hand of civilization among the hills of Apalachy, becomes a Cadmus,[4] and gives a written language to his hitherto unlettered people.[5] The most certain sources of a national literature, are to be found in the denseness of its population, in its readiness to encounter its own necessities — in other words, its willingness to labour in the domestic tendencies of the citizen — in the growth of intellectual wants — in the necessity of furnishing a stimulus to pampered and to palsied appetites, and in the sympathy of the community, thus needing provocatives, with the talent which is required to provide them. These conditions obtained, — with the sensibilities already insisted upon, — and the literature of a people is a growth too natural in its rise, too gradual in its progress, to be traced easily in its transitions.

[4] A mythological prince, reputed to have invented the Phoenician alphabet.

[5] [*Simms's note*] The allusion here is to the invention of the Cherokee Alphabet by Gess, a half breed — an event quite as worthy of commemoration among his people, as the achievement of Cadmus was among the Greeks. [Simms is referring to Sequoyah (*c.* 1770–1843), the inventor of the Cherokee alphabet from 1809–1821. Sequoyah took the name George Guess, after a white trader Gist, who may have been his father.]

All other conditions fulfilled, and its growth follows the requisitions of its people. In their summons, in their sympathy, the poet finds his birth and provocation. He scarcely asks their rewards. The eagerness of the Athenians after news — an eagerness which moves the patriotic indignation of the orator — was yet one of the prime sources of the popular intelligence, — by which the orator himself obtained his audience — which furnished strings to the grand organ of Æschylus, and filled the mouth of the Bee of Colonus with that honey which other bees can find there still. To this very appetite, this thirsting for the novel, they owed the beginnings of their drama, and all their other glorious arts. The exquisite finish of their first conceptions, was the duty of successive periods. As invention began to stale, taste ripened into fastidiousness. The massive outline, wholly beyond human ability to rival or surpass, was left in its acknowledged supremacy; and Genius, exhausted in the struggle for original conquest, settled down to the perfection of details. This is a history. These are all achievements of the city, of the crowded mart, of struggling, toiling, conflicting masses. It is the progress of those masses, writing itself in stone, in tower, in temple, in all sorts of monuments. These are the signs of permanence, of a fixed condition, drawing resolutely from itself and from the narrow empire to which its domain is circumscribed. We can hope for nothing of this sort from a wandering people. They build no monuments, rear no temples, leave no proofs behind them that they ever had a faith, or an affection, a hero or a God! The hunter, and even the agricultural life, is necessarily thus sterile. Their capacities, — such as depend on the studious cultivation of their sensibilities, — are deadened and apathetic by disuse. But that we reason from first principles and just parallels, we have no right to know that they ever had sensibilities, — that they are not obtuse and incapable by nature, — an inferior order of creation having different uses, and a far inferior destiny. But we know

better, and justly ascribe to pursuit and condition that which
the unobserving judgment would refer to native incapacity.
That sort of mental flexibility and aptitude, which, in a state
of crowded society, is the necessary result of attrition with
rival minds, conflicting temperaments, and continually arising
necessities, yields, in their cases, to a cold shyness of character,
a stern and jealous self-esteem, a hard and resolute reserve and
haughty suspiciousness of mood, which leaves the individual
wholly deficient in all the arts of conciliation. Confident in
himself, his own strength and individuality, he lacks that love
of approbation, that concern for the opinions of others, which
is at the bottom of much of the ambition by which poet and
painter are drawn to their tasks. He asks for no sympathy,
does not expect it, perhaps scarcely cares for it in any degree.
Is he not himself? — Equal to his own wants, fearless of foes,
wholly indifferent of friends? It matters not much what you
think of him, so that you do not question him. If he has a
merit, a faculty, it is enough, for his own gratification, that
he is conscious of its possession. He does not feel or find it
necessary that you should quaff at his fountains. His light, if
it burns at all, is carefully hidden beneath his own bushel.
He has virtues, but they are not those which belong to, or
spring from society. He is proud, and this protects him from
meanness; generous, and capable of the most magnanimous actions; hospitable, — you shall share his bread and salt to his
own privation; — loves liberty with a passion that absorbs almost all others — and brave — rushing into battle with the
phrenzy of one who loves it — he prolongs the conflict, unhappily, long after mercy entreats to spare.

Such is the North American Indian. He probably bore an
equivalent relation to the original possessors of this continent,
with the barbarians of the Northern Hive to Italy, in the days
of her luxurious decline. At the time of the discovery of
America, he was very much the sort of savage that the his-

torians represent the Gaul, the Goth, and Cimbrian to have been during the wars of Camillus and of Catullus, of the Scipios and of Caius Marius. The Teutones — the great German family, with all its tribes — were all of this complexion; — neither braver, nor wiser, nor better, nor more skilful in the arts, nor possessed of a jot more of imagination and letters, at the moment when they first became known to civilization. The Saxon Boor when first scourged by the Norman into manhood and stature, moral and physical, had given scarcely more proofs of intellectual endowment than the red men of the great Apalachian chain. He was a Christian, it is true, after a fashion; but Christianity is properly the religion of civilization, and he was not a civilized being [6] — far less so, as we know, in the time of Rollo, than was the Mexican during the reign of Montezuma. Of all these nations, North and South, the North American Indian — keeping in mind the parallels of time already indicated — was probably the superior person. He was quite as valiant, quite as venturous — had probably overthrown the more civilized nations of Central and of South

[6] Simms is here unquestionably overstating the case, and, in fact, making a statement contrary to his customary attitude. His position is ambiguous in the nineteenth-century movement in America praising the Anglo-Saxon language, literature, and political attitudes. Certainly he was in sympathy with Jefferson, an ardent "Saxonist," who would have had the great seal of the United States bear the images of Hengist and Horsa to remind us of our Saxon heritage (see *Familiar Letters of John Adams and his Wife, Abigail Adams, During the Revolution*, ed. C. F. Adams [New York, 1876], p. 211), and who introduced the study of Anglo-Saxon into the American college curriculum by including it in the course of study at the University of Virginia (C. R. Thompson, "The Study of Anglo-Saxon in America," *English Studies*, XVIII [1936], 242–246). On the other hand, Simms as a Southerner had high admiration for Norman chivalry. At this time, too, the *American Whig Review*, a hated rival of the Young America group, was publishing much strongly pro-Saxon material (for example, I [March, 1845], 250–257; III [April, 1846], 425–441; IV [September, 1846], 240–241), and the *North American Review* was also very pro-Saxon (see XXVIII [January, 1829], 18; XLVII [July, 1838], 91; L [January, 1840], 148). The tone Simms takes here toward Saxon and Norman probably reflects, in some part, the bitterness of the literary war.

America, and, as dim glimpses seem to assure us, had been the conqueror of a highly civilized and even white people in North America. He was fleet of foot, strong of frame, capable of great enterprises; of great powers of endurance; equally erect, large, and symmetrical — a model, according to West, for the conception of a god; [7] — and not without some few of the arts of civilization, whether acquired by conquest, or by his own unassisted genius. His bow and arrows, his war club, his canoes, his own garments and decorations, were wrought, not only with considerable dexterity and ingenuity, but with an eye to the beautiful and picturesque. He had a picture-writing like the Mexicans, and was not without very decided beginnings of a literature. This may have been rude enough, — not so rude, however, as we are accustomed to think it — but it is sufficient that he had made a beginning. His genius answered for the rest. This differed considerably in the several families. Among these, the Catawbas and the Natchez, seem to have been most distinguished for an elasticity and grace of manner, which separated them widely from the sullen and ferocious Muscoghee. The Cherokees, however, had taken the most certain steps towards civilization. Their structures were more permanent, their towns more populous, and a large portion of their people had engrafted the farmer upon the hunter life. The laws of nature are so mutually provocative, that one step cannot well be taken without another. The moment that the habitation and limits of the barbarian become circumscribed, he begins to labour. This is of necessity. The extension of the abodes of man, and the increase of his

[7] [*Simms's note*] The reader need not be reminded of the famous anecdote of the American painter West, who, on seeing the statue of the Apollo Belvedere, exclaimed, "My God! how like a young Mohawk warrior!" The coincidence was not in the mere symmetry of frame. It was the eye, the breathing attitude — the mind and music in the air, action and expression. [Simms is referring to Benjamin West (1738–1820), an American artist. Among his notable paintings are *The Death of Wolfe, Death on the Pale Horse,* and *Penn's Treaty with the Indians.*]

numbers, is fatal to the wild beast of the forest, — to the forest itself — and it becomes really easier to find food from labour, in the earth, than to wander remotely, into distant regions, to the probable encounter with superior enemies, furious at any intrusion upon their hunting grounds. This, in fact, was the secret cause of the moral improvement of the Cherokees. The Creeks boasted to have made women of them. They had whipt them into close limits, where they were compelled to labour, — and labour, — a blessing born of a penalty, — is the fruitful mother of all the nobler exercises of humanity. Hence, the progress of the Cherokees — their farms, their cattle, their manufactures, their discovery of the alphabet, their schools, their constitution, and newspaper, — all the fruit of their subjection, by the Muscoghees and other nations, just before the first English settlements in Virginia and the Carolinas. Had these English settlements been such as a mighty nation should have sent forth — had the colonies been such as issued from the fruitful ports of Carthage, — thirty thousand at a time, as were sent out by Hanno, — what would have been the effect upon the destinies of the red men of America. They would have been rescued from themselves and preserved, — a mighty nation, full of fire, of talent, of all the materials which ensure long life to the genius and to the eminence of a race. The good people of England were not the morbid philanthropists that they have become in latter days — latter day saints, putting to the blush such poor pretenders as those who read the golden plates of Mormon, and look out for the fiery advents which disturb the dreams of Parson Miller.[8] They would have subdued the aborigines, as William of Normandy subdued the

---

[8] The followers of the Mormon religious sect are called "Latter-day Saints"; they follow a revelation supposed to have been written on golden plates by the prophet Mormon at the dictation of the angel Moroni. William Miller (1782–1849) believed that he had found the key to biblical revelation and that the second coming of Christ would occur in 1843. His followers were known as Millerites or Adventists.

Saxons. An European colony of ten thousand men would have done this. They would not have paltered with the ignorant savages, flattering their vanity in order to conciliate their prejudices and disarm their anger, as was done by the feeble settlers at James Town, and other places. They would have overrun them, parcelled them off in tens, and twenties, and hundreds, under strict task masters, and, by compelling the performance of their natural duties — that labour which is the condition of all human life, — would have preserved them to themselves and to humanity. Properly diluted, there was no better blood than that of Cherokee and Natchez. It would have been a good infusion into the paler fountain of Quaker and Puritan — the very infusion which would put our national vanity in subjection to our pride, and contribute to keep us as thoroughly independent of the mother country, in intellectual, as we fondly believe ourselves to be in political respects. But we are becoming too discursive.

Our imperfect knowledge of the Indian, — the terror that he inspired, — the constant warfare between his race and our own — have embittered our prejudices, and made us unwilling to see any thing redeeming either in his character or intellect. We are apt to think him no more than a surly savage, capable of showing nothing better than his teeth. The very mention of his name, recalls no more grateful images than scalping knife and tomahawk; and, shuddering at the revolting associations, we shut our eyes, and close our ears, against all the proofs which declare his better characteristics. We are unwilling to read his past as we are unable to control his future; — refuse to recognize his sensibilities, and reject with scorn the evidence of any more genial attributes, in his possession, which might persuade us to hope for him in after days — for his natural genius and his real virtues — when, shut in by the comparatively narrow empire which we have allotted him — barred from expansion by the nations which are destined to crowd upon him on every hand, — the people of Texas, of Oregon and Mississippi, — he will be forced to throw aside the license of the hunter, and place himself, by a happy necessity, within the traces of civilization.

Regarded without prejudice, and through the medium even of what we most positively know of his virtues and his talents, and the North American Indian was as noble a specimen of crude humanity as we can find, from history, any aboriginal people to have been. There is not the slightest reason to suppose that he laboured under any intellectual deficiency. On the contrary, the proofs are conclusive, that, compared with other nations — the early Romans before their amalgamation with the great Tuscan family; the Jews prior to the Egyptian captivity; — the German race to the time of Odoacer, — the Saxon, to the period of the Heptarchy, and the Norman tribes in the reign of Charlemagne; — he presented as high and sufficient proofs of susceptibility for improvement and education, as any, the very noblest stocks in our catalogue. In some respects, indeed, the Indians show more impressively. The republican features in their society — their leagues for common defence and necessity, and the frequency of their counsels for the adjustment of subjects in common — led to the growth of a race of politicians and orators, of whose acuteness, excellent skill in argument, and great powers of elocution, the early discoverers give us some of the most astonishing examples. The samples of their eloquence which have come down to us, are as purely Attic as the most severe critic could desire — bold, earnest, truthful — clear in style, closely thought, keenly argued, conclusive in logic, and, in the highest degree, impressive in utterance. That their action was admirable, and would have delighted Demosthenes, we know from authorities upon which we would as cheerfully rely as upon the assurances of the great Athenian orator himself. Now capacious and flowing, now terse and epigrammatic, adapting the manner to the matter, and both to the occasion, — sometimes smooth and conciliatory, anon searching and sarcastic — now persuasive and adroit, and again suddenly startling because of their vehement force and audacious imagery; — these were the acknowledged characteristics of their eloquence, which awed the most fearless spectator and would have done honour to the noblest senate. An eloquent people is capable of taking any place in letters — in mastering all forms of speech, in perfecting any species of composition — history, or poetry — the one faculty, indeed, somewhat implying all the rest, since to be a great orator, imagination must keep pace with thought, — and reason, and the capacity for historical narration, must contribute to the embodiment of the argument, to which a warm fancy must impart colour and animation, and which great energies of character must endow with force. All of these qualities and constituents were in possession of our aborigines. They had all the requisites, shown by their speeches only, even if there were no other proofs, for intellectual development in every species of literature. Tecumseh was a very great orator, — so was his brother, the prophet. The Cherokee, Attakullakullah, was one of the most persuasive and insinuating of speakers; and the renown of Logan, of the Shawanee, is already a proverb from the single speech preserved by Jefferson.[9] Some of the sayings and orations of the Seminoles and Creeks, are equally remarkable for their significance and poetical beauty. Of the Six Nations we have numerous fragments, and the Catawbas had a reputation of this sort, among the tribes of the South, though but few specimens are preserved to us. Wether-

[9] Thomas Jefferson gives the speech of Logan (or Tahgahjute), a Mingo chief and warrior, in Query VI and Appendix No. 4 of his *Notes on the State of Virginia*, ed. William Peden (Chapel Hill, 1955), pp. 63, 226–258. Note that Jefferson compares the Indian with the Gauls in the days of the Roman Gallic Wars in the paragraph that immediately follows Logan's speech (pp. 63–64). This paragraph possibly suggested Simms's comparison of the Indians to the "Saxon Boors."

ford, who roused the Southern Indians to war, while Tecumseh and his brother were fomenting the western nations, was not inferior to either of these as a statesman and an orator. His speech to Jackson, when he surrendered himself, voluntarily, a willing sacrifice, in order that his country should obtain peace, is at once one of the most touching and manly instances of eloquence on record; and, in recent times, Osceola of the Seminoles, and Mooshalatubbee of the Choctaws — the one a bold, and the other an adroit speaker, — are proofs in point, showing that the faculty was not one to die utterly out in the emasculation of their several people. We should be pleased, did our space suffice, to give examples from each of these remarkable men. Enough to say, that they betrayed the possession of a power of logical thinking, lively fancy, subdued good taste, cool judgment, and lofty imagination, such as, addressed to literature, in a community even partially civilized, would have been worthy of all fame and honour in succeeding times. And that we should doubt or be insensible to this conclusion, is only to be accounted for by reference to our blinding prejudices against the race — prejudices which seem to have been fostered as necessary to justify the reckless and unsparing hand with which we have smitten them in their habitations, and expelled them from their country. We must prove them unreasoning beings, to sustain our pretensions as human ones — show them to have been irreclaimable, to maintain our own claims to the regards and respect of civilization.

We commend to some of our clever compilers, — Mr. Griswold,[10] for example — the plan of an Indian miscellany, in which choice specimens of their oratory, their fable, their poetry, — shall appear together, in judicious opposition. The material for a goodly volume is abundant. Colden, Hecke-

---

[10] Rufus W. Griswold (1815–1857), Poe's literary executor, was the compiler of *The Poets and Poetry of America* (1842) and *The Prose Writers of America* (1847).

welder, Adair, Jefferson, Hewatt, Lawson, Duponceau,[11] and many others, may be examined with this object; and, among recent writers, there is Mr. Schoolcraft, — a host in himself — whose passion for the subject will make him a willing contributor to any plan for doing it justice. Such a miscellany will prove the native North American to have been an artist, a poet, a painter, and a novelist. His abilities were not confined to oratory alone. His faculties were exercised in other kinds of composition. He was no barren churl — no sullen, unproductive savage — such as we are too willing to suppose him. He had the necessary sensibilities for literature, and was not wholly without the performance. His affections were deep and lively, and stimulated his genius to other utterances than those of the Council House. These sensibilities, though perhaps less nice and active than they would have been were he less the hunter — less fierce and intractable in war — were not utterly subdued by his more prevailing passions. His superstitions alone are in proof of his spiritual susceptibility. It has been commonly insisted that these were of a cold and brutal character, at best resembling those of the Northmen — a savage mythology, filled with gods like Odin and Thor, — bloody, dark, malignant, and gratified only by the most horrid rites and festivities. This is only true in part. They had gods of terror it is true, as the Etrurians had — but like these people and the Greeks, they had others of gentle and benignant in-

---

[11] Cadwallader Colden (1688–1776) wrote *The History of the Five Nations* (1727). John G. E. Heckewelder (1743–1823), a Moravian missionary to the Indians, wrote *An Account of the History, Manners, and Customs of the Indian Nations Who Once Inhabited Pennsylvania* (1819) and *A Narrative of the Mission of the United Brethren Among the Delaware and Mohegan Indians* (1820). James Adair (*c.* 1709–1783) wrote *The History of the American Indians* (1775). Alexander Hewat (or Hewatt) (*c.* 1745–1829) wrote *An Historical Account of the Rise and Progress of the Colonies of South Carolina and Georgia* (2 vols., 1779). John Lawson (d. 1711), founder of New Bern, N. C., wrote *A New Voyage to Carolina* (1709). Pierre Étienne Du Ponceau (1760–1844) wrote *Grammatical System of the Languages of the Indian Nations of North America* (1838).

fluence, smiling, graceful, fantastic, who watched over the happier hours of the race, promoted their kindlier fortunes, and gave countenance to the better feelings and habits of the individual. Their pantheon was quite as well supplied as the Greek, though they had not lived long enough to have it arranged, and made immortal, by their dramatists and poets. They had their ruling, their unknown god — their good and evil genii — their demons of the elements — of earth and air, of fire and water, of hill and valley, and lake and wood; and the lively genius of the people, in moments of danger or delight, created new deities for the occasion, consecrating the hour and the place to that worship which had been ordained by their passing necessities or moods. For all of these they had names and veneration. Offices were assigned them, adapted, each, to their several attributes and station, the analysis of which constantly reminds you of those so common among the Germans, by means of which their modern writers have framed so many fanciful and delightful histories. The Kobolds, and Ondines, and Salamanders, might find their parallels among the personifications of the Indian — and their spirits of the mine and the river, of the forest and the mountain, bearing Indian epithets quite as musical as any in the language of the Teuton, attest all the preliminary conditions of an intellect that needed but little help from civilization to grow into a vast and noble literature. His gods were hostile or benignant, cold or affectionate, hateful to the sight and mind, or lovely to the imagination and the eye. He addressed them accordingly. To some he urged solicitations, and implored in song. Others he deprecated, and addressed in prayer and expostulation. He had his burnt offerings also, and no idea could have been more happy, than that of fumigating his deity with the smoke of that precious weed, whose aroma, so pleasant to himself, was to be extorted only by his own lips. The operation was thus never wholly in vain, whether the god accepted the sacrifice or not. The spirit of the cape and headland, of the battle and hunting ground, of peace, and war, and fortune; of love, and of hate; — commanded thus his homage, and received his devotions. Extraordinary events or achievements; a spot rendered peculiar by circumstance, or by its own aspect; the wild beast that baffled his skill, or the bird that appeared to him on frequent occasions, when he was troubled, or very joyful; — these were all fixed in recollection by some spirtual name and emblem. His omens were not a whit less picturesque, or imposing, less reasonable, or less impressive, than those of the Greeks and Romans. The vulture spoke to him in a language of command, as it did to the wolf-suckled children of Rhea Sylvia. His prophets were quite as successful as the augur, Attius Navius, and practised, with equal success, the art of bringing the gods to a participation in the affairs of State. The favourable response cheered, and the unfriendly paralyzed his valour — and, altogether, with faith and veneration, the character of the North American Indian exhibited, not merely in common but in large degree, all of those moral and human sensibilities, out of which art has usually fashioned her noblest fabrics. The capacities and the sensibilities were there, present, in mind and heart, waiting but the hour and the influence which come at length to every nation, thus endowed, which is permitted to survive long enough in independent career. Their growth and just development, must have followed the first steps of civilization. We have noted their oratory, and their spiritual exercises; but their songs might teach us something farther. What was the song of war, of victory, and the death song, but strains, each, like those of the Jews and the Northmen, on similar occasions, under similar exigencies, combining history with invocation. The exploits of their warriors, thus chaunted in the hearing of the tribe, and transmitted through successive generations, would, if caught up, and put in the fashion of a living language, be not unanalogous to those rude ballads, out of which Homer framed his great poem, and the German his Nibelungen Lied. They embodied the history of the race, with its groups of gallant warriors, and one great commanding figure in the foreground. If the chief filled the centre, emulous and admiring subordinates grew around him, and the correspondence of all furnished a complete history. How such a history, chaunted by a famous chief on his bed of death and glory, could be made to ring, trumpet like, in a modern ear, by such a lyre as Walter Scott. We should not need a Milton, or a Homer, for the performance. The material would have suited Scott's poetical genius better, perhaps, than that of better bards. And how rich must be that material! How wild were the conflicts of our Indians — how numerous — with what variety of foes, under what changing circumstances, and how individual always! What is there improbable in the notion that Powhatan, in his youth, was at the sacking and the conquest of some of the superior nations in the Southwest — the Biloxi for example, — of whom the tradition goes that they were a rich and populous people, accomplished in the arts, who were overrun by an influx of strange barbarians and driven into the sea. His ancestors may have brought their legions to the conquest of Palenque — may have led the assault upon the gloomy towers of Chi Chen — may have been the first to cross the threshhold of those gloomy and terrible superstitions, whose altars have so strangely survived their virtues. It is a somewhat curious fact, in connection with this suggestion, that Opechancanough — a famous warrior — a man of very superior parts who usurped the sway of the Virginia Indians after the death of Powhatan, and probably disputed it while he lived — was described by them as having been the "Prince of a foreign nation," — and as having "come to them a great way from the southwest." Beverly [12] adds, — "And by their accounts, we suppose him to have come from the *Spanish Indians, somewhere near Mex-*

[12] Robert Beverley, *The History and Present State of Virginia*, ed. Louis B. Wright (Chapel Hill, 1947), p. 61 (originally published in 1705).

ico, or the mines of St. Barbe: — but be that matter how it will, from that time (his usurpation) till his captivity, there never was the least truce between them and the English." [13] We reserve to another paper our notice of the miscellany, by which the preceding remarks have been occasioned. Mr. Schoolcraft is an authority, in Indian history, upon which we are permitted to rely. He has passed more than thirty years of his life, chiefly in an official capacity, among the red men of the continent. He married an Indian woman of great intelligence and beauty, and was thus placed in a position to see her people, if we may so phrase it, without disguise. He was admitted to their privacy, and informed in their traditions and character. He has accordingly written, at frequent periods upon these subjects, and, we may add, exhibits no larger predilection in their behalf, than the proofs which he produces can fairly justify. A few years ago, he put forth two interesting volumes of Indian traditions, under the title of "Algic Researches." We doubt if the publication attracted much attention, though quite worthy to do so in the eyes of the student. The title probably discouraged the ordinary reader. Of the work before us, we are in possession of the first number only, though a second has recently been published. A detailed notice of these shall be given in future pages, when it will be seen that nothing has been urged in our text, whether for the capacities of the red men, or their actual performance, for which there is not good warranty in the records.

[13] [*Simms's note*] Itopatin, the brother of Powhatan, succeeded to his empire, but was dispossessed by Opechancanough, who was remarkable for his talents, his address, his large stature, noble presence, and the terrors of his name. Here now is material for fiction. Why should not Opechancanough have been a prince in Mexico, flying from the Spaniards? Why should he not have been a captive to the sire of Powhatan, while he and the latter were yet children? How easy to form a romance upon this conjecture! How easy to convert his ceaseless struggle against the English invader into another story. Then, there is the overthrow of Itopatin — but —

ARTICLE IV

DANIEL BOON – THE FIRST HUNTER
OF KENTUCKY [1]

Of all men, saving Sylla the man slayer,
  Who passes for in life and death most lucky,
Of the great names which in our faces stare,
  The General Boon, backwoodsman of Kentucky,
Was happiest among mortals any where;
  For killing nothing but a bear or buck, he
Enjoyed the lonely, vigorous, harmless days
Of his old age in wilds of deepest maze.

DON JUAN [2]

THESE verses are not to be counted among the very happiest of Lord Byron's muse, and he has, in one small particular at least, sacrificed the truth to the rhyme — a matter in
which poets are supposed, though incorrectly, to be somewhat
privileged. It is for us to correct these errors. Our Boon was
never more than a Colonel. We are, as a people, so liberal in
conferring this distinction, that it has ceased almost to be one;
and this is one reason why we are rather slow in getting beyond it. Whether Boon was even a Colonel, except by the
courtesy, is another question which it is scarcely possible at
this late day to answer. It was as a Captain, that he received
Governor Dunmore's commission in ante-revolutionary times,
during the war with the Shawanee Indians; and, in his frequent conflicts with the Indians, he rather led in the sudden
emergency, at the head of his neighbours, aroused by savage incursion, than because of any military commission or special legal authority. In such cases, distinguished by promptness
of character, coolness and ready courage, and frequently sum-

[1] Originally published in the *Southern and Western Magazine*, I (April,
1845), 225–242. See note 5 below for "Boon."

[2] Lord Byron, *Don Juan*, Canto VIII, stanza lxi.

moned to the field, a leader receives his title, as such, by the spontaneous impulse of those whom he conducts. He is their Captain, their Colonel or their General, as the case may be; and such, in all probability, was the origin of Boon's military title — deserved, certainly, much more than that of thousands more formally bestowed; for our backwoodsman did famous good service without beat of drum, and probably was one of the most modest leaders of men that the world has ever seen. That he ever won the style of General, even by the courtesy, is, however, very doubtful.

Lord Byron has committed another error of much more importance. Boon's rifle occasionally made free with much nobler victims than bear and buck. He was a hunter of men too, upon occasion. Not that he was fond of this sport. His nature was a gentle one — really and strangely gentle — and did not incline to war. But he had no shrinkings, no false tendernesses, no scruples of feeling or of conscience in the moment of necessity. He was a man, albeit one in whose bosom the milk of human kindness still flowed copiously and warm. He could be a warrior, ay, and take his rank among warriors, where the stakes of the game were death. He smote the savage man, as well as the scarcely more savage beast of the same region; and, though the fact is not expressly written, yet there is no reason to suppose that he forbore to do battle after the Indian fashion. He could take a scalp with the rest, and might feel justified in the adoption of a practice which, when employed by the whites, had its very great influence in discouraging the Indian appetite for war. With these exceptions our epigraph may stand, and we make two-fold allowance in the case of a poet and an Englishman, in all matters that concern history and America. They both claim privileges in these respects, with which, at this moment, we are in no mood to quarrel. Boon was all the rest that Byron writes him — lucky that he lived to a good old age — that his heart was not ren-

dered callous by strifes or years, but was true to the last hour
to the holiest humanities — that his desires were few, his appetites modest, his ambition humble, and his manhood prolonged to the latest moment of his existence. His fortunes
were thus far good, though he died penniless.

Boon was one of those remarkable men whom Providence
seems to have endowed with a special restlessness of character, in order to the performance of certain tasks necessary
for the human race, but from which the greater proportion of
mankind shrink in dismay. He was born to be a pioneer. It is
useless to talk about training here. A man like Boon is as much
the creature of a special destiny as the poet or the painter. He
has his office appointed him — and the mere influences of the
community in which he is reared, though these may contribute to his passion, cannot at any time subdue it. In an age of
chivalry — during the Crusades — Boon would have been a
knight errant, equally fearless and gentle. That he would have
been much of a Squire of Dames, is very uncertain — but he
loved his wife, and he risked his scalp more than once to
rescue beauty from the clutches of the savage. His native
mood prompted his adventure. He had an eye for the picturesque in nature, as is the marked characteristic in all very
great hunters — a characteristic of which Mr. Cooper has
given us an exquisite ideal in Leather Stocking.[3] His mind was
of a contemplative character, and loved to muse undisturbed
by contact with man, upon its own movements, as influenced
by the surrounding atmosphere. A constant desire for change
of scene and object, is the natural growth of a passion for the
picturesque, and an impatience of the staid and formal mo-
notonies of ordinary life, springs with equal certainty from an
eager temperament, great elasticity of muscle, great powers

[3] That Cooper was modeling Natty Bumppo, at least in part, on Boone is
a truism of Cooper criticism. See Thomas R. Lounsbury, *James Fenimore
Cooper* (Boston, 1882), p. 72, and Allan Nevins' introduction to *The Leath-
erstocking Saga* (New York, 1954), p. 15.

of endurance, and an eye that seems to discern and detect, rather by an instinct of its own, than by the ordinary exercise of vision, objects in forest or prairie much too obscure for the common sighted mortal. These were among the mora. and physical characteristics of our hunter. Add to these, that he was a dead shot, an active man with the tomahawk, tall, erect, of powerful frame and exquisite symmetry, and you have one of the most perfect specimens of the class to which our adventurer belongs.

Daniel Boon was a Virginian, born somewhere about the year 1737.[4] Of his early life nothing is known. He emigrated to North Carolina in his youth, and here we find him, in 1769, a married man, with children, on the banks of the Yadkin. It is at this period that his own narrative begins.[5] This production is a small octavo pamphlet of thirty or forty pages, and embodies his adventures from the period of his arrival in Kentucky to the close of the year 1782. It is probably not the production of his own pen, since it bears marks of ambitious com-

[4] [*Simms's note*] Marshall, in his History of Kentucky, represents him as born in Maryland, somewhere about the year 1746, and emigrating, without his parents, to Virginia while yet in the gristle of his youth. With regard to his birthplace, we have followed the more popular account. The period of his birth, as set down in the text, is estimated from the supposed period to which he had reached at the time of his death. He was then said to be eighty-five, and he died in 1822. His oldest son was killed by the Indians, fighting bravely, on his second visit to Kentucky, in 1773. Supposing this son to have been sixteen, and Boon to have been a father at twenty — both reasonable estimates — and we arrive at a very probable result. If he were born in 1746, he could scarcely have had a son old enough for Indian warfare in 1773. [Simms is referring to *The History of Kentucky*, by Humphrey Marshall, published in 1812. Boone was born in 1734.]

[5] Simms is here referring to a pamphlet of 36 octavo pages, *Life and Adventure of Colonel Daniel Boon*, Written by Himself (Brooklyn, 1823). This narrative first appeared in John Filson's *The Discovery, Settlement, and Present State of Kentucky* (Wilmington, 1784), where it is apparently taken down by Filson from Boone's dictation. It was reprinted in the *American Museum* (Philadelphia, 1787), II, 321–328. The Brooklyn edition, which Simms apparently used, spelled Boone's name without the final *e* and reprinted Byron's stanzas on Boone from *Don Juan*. It is most accessible in *Magazine of History*, XLV (Extra Number 180, 1932), 7–29.

position quite unlike our hunter — sometimes it aims at eloquence and poetry, and at all times it lacks that simplicity of
manner which belonged to the character of Boon. In all like-
lihood he furnished the material to some young lawyer or editor, who dressed it up with rhetoric and made it fine for
company. With all these (supposed) advantages it is an exceedingly unsatisfactory performance. Its details are wholly in its
flourishes, and never in its facts, and this is perhaps a sufficient
reason why we should deny the paternity of it to Boon himself. The events are meagre and few — a skeleton only of a
biography, which, properly filled out, would no doubt have
been as ravishing as any romance. But we must make the most
of it, such as it is.

"It was on the first of May, 1769," that our hunter "resigned his domestic happiness for a time, to wander through
the wilderness of America, in quest of the country of Kentucky." He assigns no motive for the pursuit. He urges no
reason for this "resignation of domestic happiness." He simply
acknowledges an impulse and he must obey it. His companions
were five in number — John Finley, John Stewart, Joseph
Holden, James Monay and William Cool. Finley, of whom
unfortunately nothing more is known, had visited the country
two years before. He was now something of a pilot. The
party was on foot. They burdened themselves neither with
clothes nor provisions, with no unnecessary equipage, whether
for day or night. The curtains of heaven and the trees of the
wood were their canopy, and they slept among the long
grasses of the slopes, or amongst the dried leaves of the forest,
without fear. Their food was taken by the way-side. Their
stealthy feet came upon the deer as he couched in the stunted
thicket, and the wild turkey was easily shot from the branches
of the high tree under which they had slept throughout the
night. In this manner they went forward in a westwardly direction, until they crossed the wilderness bordering on the

Cumberland mountains. At last, standing upon a gentle but commanding eminence, on the seventh day of June, they looked down with delight upon the lovely levels of the Kentucky. Here they paused and proceeded to encamp. The weather was growing unfavourable, and they built themselves a rude but sufficient shelter. Their temporary settlement prepared, they sallied forth to reconnoitre the country and seek their game. The forest had never before echoed to the footsteps of the white man. Wild beasts of all sorts were in abundance, the deer, the bear, and mighty herds of the buffalo, cropping the herbage of the plains or browsing upon the cane tops in the morass. From June to December, did our hunters prosecute their sports with great satisfaction, and in perfect safety. But a change was at hand. On the twenty-second of the latter month, Boon and John Stewart went forth together. The scene had never been more grateful to the eyes of our adventurer. The day was a pleasant one, and their rambles brought them to a close of it, through a region of incomparable beauty, upon the banks of the Kentucky river. Here, at sunset, as they ascended the brow of a hill, they were descried by a party of Indians concealed in a neighbouring cane-brake. These rushed suddenly out upon them. Their surprise was complete, and the next moment found them prisoners. But Boon and his companion betrayed no uneasiness. The manly philosophy which teaches to wait patiently and to endure without complaint, was that which constituted the chief strength of our hunters, as it is that of every heroic nature. They submitted without a murmur to captivity, and were kept for seven days in the usual Indian sort of confinement. The cheerfulness which they manifested, their fortitude and gentleness, disarmed something of the watchfulness of their captors. They relaxed in their vigilance, and Boon was soon enabled to take advantage of the change. In the dead of night, as the party lay in a thick cane-brake by a rousing fire, our hunter touched his companon quietly and thus awoke him. The Indians were in a deep sleep. A whisper sufficed for a proper uuderstanding between the captives. They rose to their feet and departed, leaving the savages to take their rest. And here we see a proof of the gentle nature of our hunter. Many of the fierce spirits of our forest land, soured by captivity, and reared with a constant hate and apprehension of the Indians, would have been as eager for revenge as for escape, and, once in possession of their freedom, with their foes sleeping around them, would never have been satisfied to leave them in possession of their scalps. They would have deepened, with their hatchets, those slumbers which the more human nature of Boon forbore to disturb.

Our hunters returned to their camp, but found it abandoned. Their companions were dispersed and on the way for home. While they hesitated, to the surprise of Boon, his brother, Squire Boon, accompanied by a stranger, made his appearance in the camp. The party now consisted of four, but was soon to be thinned. The stranger who came with Squire Boon, soon left them and returned to North Carolina, and John Stewart was shortly after killed by the Indians. The little party of three suffered surprise. The first intimation which they had of the proximity of the foe, was by the fire from a cane-brake. Stewart fell mortally wounded. The two Boons remained unhurt, but the Indians showing themselves numerously, with a shout, they were forced to precipitate flight, compelled from a distance to behold the savage as he stripped the fresh scalp from the bleeding skull of their comrade. They were only too well satisfied at being able to save their own. Stewart was the first anglo-norman victim of the red man, in the lovely wilds of Kentucky. Hitherto, it had been their practice to make prisoners of their foes, rather than to despatch them. They preferred bondsmen, and the triumph, such as always awaited them, when they brought home captives to the wigwam. But they had grown embittered by intrusion. The party assailing them may have lost in recent combat one of their warriors, whose *manes* it was necessary to appease by a victim; or they may have recognized their former captives in Stewart and his companion. Enough, however, that the tradition asserts the blood of John Stewart to be that of the first white man ever shed upon a soil which was destined, for long years after, to be annually watered from the same generous fountains.

The two Boons succeeded in making their escape. Their disasters did not discourage them. They fled, but did not leave the wilderness. A howling wilderness it was, but, not without its attractions for the peculiar nature with which they were endowed. If we can believe our hunter, they were still quite happy. "You see," said Boon to the Squire — "You see how little human nature requires. It is in our own hearts, rather than in the things around us, that we are to seek felicity. A man may be happy in any state. It only asks a perfect resignation to the will of Providence."

It does not appear that Squire Boon disputed this philosophy, which was no doubt felt by his brother. But they spent no time in the discussion. They built themselves a cottage against the winter, and devoted themselves wholly, day by day, to the one, but various toil, of hunting. They remained without disturbance through the winter. On the first of May, 1770, Boon sent his brother home for supplies and recruits, leaving him, as his narrative mournfully expresses it, "by himself, without bread, salt or sugar, without company of his fellow creatures, or even a horse or a dog." A few days of this lonesomeness were passed uncomfortably enough, exercising all the courage and philosophy of our hero. Thinking of his wife made him melancholy; for, as Childe Harold has it —

Thinking on an absent wife
Will blanch a faithful cheek.[6]

A thousand vague apprehensions filled the brain of our hunter, but he was not the man to indulge them long. Besides, he had really too many pleasures where he was. His life was one of excitements, and a certain sense of insecurity heightened his enjoyment. He lived in sight of loveliness, but on the verge of danger. Beauty came to him, with Terror looking over her shoulder. The wilderness was charming to the senses and the mind, but its thickets of green concealed the painted and ferocious savage; and he who hunted the deer successfully through his haunts, might still, while keenly bent upon the chase, be unconscious of the stealthy footsteps which were set down in his own tracks. With the dawn of day he arose from his couch of leaves or rushes, and started upon the chase. New groves, and woods, and hills, and·plains salute his vision with each returning dawn. He pursues no old paths, but, reconnoitering the country, gathers a new horizon with every sunrise. Boon describes these wanderings as perfectly delicious. The swelling of the breeze, the repose of the leaf, the mysterious quiet of the woods, the chaunt of the birds, or the long melancholy howl of the wolf at evening — these are among the objects, the sights and sounds, which stir his sensibilities and move him to the happiest meditations. He tells of the delight which he feels as he ascends the great ridges, and looks over the fertile vallies, and the ample wastes before him. How he follows the Ohio — *la Belle Riviere* of the French — in all its silent wanderings — how he sits and studies the huge mountains as they cap their venerable brows with clouds. That he should find a pleasure in such contemplations, declares for his superior moral nature. He was not merely a hunter. He was on a mission. The spiritual sense was strong in him. He felt the union between his inner and the nature of the visible

[6] Lord Byron, *Childe Harold's Pilgrimage*, Canto I, lines 164–165.

world, and yearned for their intimate communion. His thoughts and feelings were those of a great discoverer. He could realize the feelings of a Columbus or a Balboa, and thus, gazing over the ocean waste of forest which then spread from the dim western outlines of the Alleghanies, to the distant and untravelled waters of the Mississippi, he was quite as much isolated as was ever any of the great admirals who set forth, on the Atlantic, still dreaming of Cathay. His fire at noon is kindled near some sweet water, and his meal is made from the loin of the buck which his rifle has just stricken in the forest. And his fast broken, he goes on his way rejoicing, ignorant of fatigue while the day lasts, still pressing forward, so long as the scene is lovely, and the wild deer darts across his path. With the approach of night he retires to the cane-break rather than to his camp. He sleeps there infrequently. He has reason to believe that it is visited in his absence, and a new resting place receives him every night. How this very insecurity sweetens his adventures! He sleeps not the less soundly under these circumstances. He does not fear, for, in his own words — "How unhappy such a situation for a man tormented with fear, which is vain if no danger comes, and if it does only augments the pain." It is his boast to be free from this humiliating passion — he speaks of being "*diverted*" by the wolves howling about his den by night; and it was at their own peril they crossed his path by day. "I had plenty," he says, "in the midst of want; was happy, though surrounded by dangers; how should I be melancholy? No populous city, with all its structures and all its commerce, could afford me so much pleasure as I found here."

And thus, lonely but not unhappy, he remained until July, when his brother returned to him at his old camp. Here it was now thought imprudent to linger longer. The Indians were probably awakened to his proximity. They set out accordingly for Cumberland river, bestowing names, like other founders of nations, upon heights, and plains, and waters. No event occurs of interest in the life of our hunter, until, in the latter part of 1771, we find him once more at home, from which he had been absent more than two years. He finds his family in happy circumstances, but is not satisfied to leave them so. The destiny must be obeyed. That restless impulse to change will admit of no excuse, and he sells his farm on the Yadkin, and all his unnecessary baggage, and, with five families more, leaves home in September, 1773, for a final remove to the lovely forest land which has delighted him so much. Before the party had left the settled regions, it was joined by another, consisting of forty men. The solitude of Kentucky was about to be broken. The seal had been taken from the fountain. But the numbers which increased the strength of the Colonists diminished their security, and left them fewer chances of concealment and escape. A melancholy finish was about to befall this journey. On the tenth of October, they were surprised by the Indians. The rear of the party — probably less vigilant than the advance — was attacked, and six of the whites were slain. The Indians were repulsed, yet the cattle was dispersed, and the company so dispirited that they retreated forty miles to a settlement on Clinch river.

But Boon ceased to be alone in this march of discovery into the Kentucky wilderness. There were other spirits like himself, destined to open the way for the thronging multitudes that began to cry aloud for homes of their own. In 1770, an expedition consisting of forty stout hunters, set out from the western settlements of Virginia, for the purpose of trapping and shooting upon the other side of the Cumberland mountain. Of these, thirty may have fallen by the hands of the Indians. We lose sight of them altogether. Nine of them reached Kentucky under the command of Col. James Knox. They were so long gone from home, that they acquired the proverbial name of *"the Long Hunters."* Thus it was that Boon was not the sole white occupant of Kentucky as he imagined. The two parties never met. They might well pass each other a thousand times in those pathless wilds, as ships scattered over the broad waste of ocean, yet never come in sight of their mutual fires. From this period, every successive season sent forth its new explorers and many of them men of remarkable courage and capacity; but our consideration must now be yielded entirely to one. Boon continued with his family at Clinch river until 1774, when he accepted an appointment of Governor Dunmore, of Virginia, to conduct a brigade of surveyors from the falls of the Ohio into the new settlement. His reputation was evidently spreading. Without the slightest ambition for notoriety, flying, as it were, from his kindred and society, he was rapidly and in spite of himself acquiring fame among them. He executed his mission with success and in safety, completing a tour of eight hundred miles, through a wilderness, in sixty-two days. His duties were so well performed, that his Excellency extended his confidence, and conferred upon our pioneer the military command of no less than three garrisons, with the rank and commission of Captain. These garrisons were upon the Virginia frontiers, and meant to protect them from the incursions of the Shawanees, who had broken out in bloody war. This outbreak is one that will be remembered by the reader, when told that it originated in the wanton butchery, by Colonel Cresap, of the family of the friendly chief Logan. The speech of this famous warrior, as preserved by Jefferson,[7] will never be forgotten, so long as natural eloquence, enlivened by the most cruel provocations, and sharpened by justice, holds a place among the recollections of men. This pathetic performance furnishes the justification of a war begun by the Shawanees. They were defeated, but not till after a bloody struggle. Several severe bat-

[7] Thomas Jefferson, *Notes on the State of Virginia* (Chapel Hill, 1955), pp. 63, 226–258.

tles took place between them and the border militia, and one, in particular, at the mouth of the Great Kenhawa, in which the Indians were heavy sufferers. What share Boon had in these conflicts is not told us by himself. His modesty only permits us to know that he had a responsible command in the hour of danger; and we know that he acquired the confidence of the authorities for the execution of his trusts. He gives us no details, and as his position was a subordinate one, the chronicles are silent on the subject of his claims. But his fame had spread and was still spreading. Already the tradition had reached the settlements of a great and fearless pioneer — the first white man who had ever dared to pass alone into that howling wilderness, upon which even the Indians themselves had agreed to confer the terrible name of the "Dark and Bloody Ground." Such is the signification of the Indian word, "Kentucky" — a name conferred rather in regard to the uses of the region, than to its real characteristics or external appearance. It had been the battle ground for a thousand years, of as many different nations. Unoccupied by any, it was a debatable land, to which they wandered constantly, in squads varying from three persons to as many hundred, with a view to the spoils of the chase or of war. War, in short, is an absolute necessity of all the Indian tribes, as it is the simple consequence of the life of the hunter. When, in pursuit of game, two tribes encounter in the same hunting grounds, conflict is inevitable. And in proportion to the increasing scarcity of game, will the feelings of hate become embittered. A people who live by the chase must always be savage.

Our hunter next appears in a somewhat more dignified capacity. He is solicited by a company of North Carolina gentlemen to attend a treaty at Watauga, to negotiate with the Cherokees for the purchase of a tract of land on the south side of the Kentucky river. He did so in March 1775 — made the purchase, and was appointed to explore the country and open the way for the proprietors. Discretionary powers were given to our hunter, and with a number of chosen men, well armed, he sets out upon the expedition. At the treaty thus made at Watauga, when the instrument was signed, a venerable Indian took Boon by the hand, and said to him — "Brother, we have given you a fine land, but I believe you will have much trouble in settling it." The first step which he took for this purpose, proved the justness of this opinion. Within a few miles of the site of Boonsborough, a settlement which he subsequently made, the party was fired upon by the Indians, two men slain and two wounded. Boon stood his ground and beat off the enemy. Three days after, they had another attack, in which two more were slain and two wounded. The Indians were again defeated, and the party succeeded in reaching the Kentucky river without further loss. On the first day of April, they struck the first axe into the timbers from which rose the fortress of Boonsborough. On the fourth day, the Indians slew one of their men, but the work advanced to completion. Boon then proceeded to remove his family to the spot, which he did in safety. "My wife and daughter," he exclaims, with, as we may suppose, a natural exultation, "were the first white women that ever stood on the banks of the Kentucky river."

But the establishment of the fortress was the signal for war. It immediately drew, as to a centre of attraction, the roving tribes by which the country was traversed. They harassed the settlers while building it, and now maintained almost constant watch about the precincts; and every inadvertence of the emigrant — if he forbore for a moment his precautions — if he wandered beyond a certain limit — he paid the penalty with wounds or death. Their hostility was still farther stimulated by British and Tory influence. The revolutionary war had begun, and our benign mother of Great Britain had already filled the forest with her emissaries, fomenting their always eager jealousy, and the common appetite for war and plunder.

While Congress were making the declaration of independence, at Philadelphia, Boon was already waging the conflict. One of his severest trials was now at hand. On the fourteenth of July, 1776 — his daughter, with two other girls, the children of Col. Calaway, were made captives by the Indians, within gun shot of the fort. The alarm was soon given, and Boon, with a small party of eight men, immediately began the pursuit. A keen hunter, well versed in Indian customs, cool and determined, he pressed the chase with an acuteness and earnestness that soon brought him within sight of his object. He overtook the Indians two days after, brought them to battle, slew two of their number, and recovered all the girls. These are the simple facts. The reader must conceive for himself the feelings of the father, the terrors of the children, the skill of the hunter, the courage of the pioneer — all brought into liveliest action, and forming a natural romance not less full of interest because, in the history of our forest settlements, it has become a very common one.

The year of 1777, found Kentucky sprinkled with settlements of the whites — rude block-houses, isolated out posts, that specked the wilderness imperceptibly, like dots that stand for islets on some great map of the nations. Among the new settlers following the example of Boon, may be mentioned as particularly distinguished by the chief characteristics of their predecessor, the names of James Harrod, Benjamin Logan, and Capt. Thos. Bullitt. Harrod, like Boon, was a man framed in the very prodigality of nature. He was six feet high, and straight as an arrow. His muscular power and activity were immense. His eyes and hair were dark, his face animated, but his deportment grave — as is usually the case with persons of great pride of character, who have been reared in seclusion. This is a trait of the aborigines, and of all people living in communities sparsely occupied. Gentle and conciliating in manner, frank in conversation and very fluent, Harrod, who had never known any thing better in the way of education than an "old field school," was yet a highly accomplished gentleman. He was schooled by those influences that best bring into exercise the capacities of the man. He had lived among men, and had been taught by the pressing necessities of life, and what he knew was known thoroughly, as the result of his own experience. His courage was generous to the last degree. He seemed as superior to selfish fears as to selfish gains, and was ever on the alert to serve and to save the suffering. Tidings are brought him that a party of Indians, four miles off, have murdered one of their neighbours. "Boys," he says to those about him — "we will go and punish the red rascals." He is the first in danger, the last in retreat. Does a poor family need food, he volunteers his rifle in their behalf, seeks the forest, kills the game and brings it home to the destitute. Does a horse wander beyond the range, and into forests in which the savage is just as likely to lurk as not, he mounts his own, and dashes boldly into the thicket. Harrod was a true specimen of our forest gentleman — a man above meanness — a frank and earnest nature — with impulses the most generous, and a courage the most spontaneous — independent in thought, fearless in action, frank in council, modest in opinion, and always manly in behavior. His memory, as it should be, is still properly honoured in Kentucky.

Not unlike him, in many respects, were the other pioneers, whose names have been given. Benjamin Logan aimed at high distinctions in military and civil life. He was a man of thought as well as action — a firm, clear-headed man, of large executive mind, a decided will, great fortitude, courage and judicious conduct. He was of Boon's exploring expedition, in 1773, and subsequently had a share in that of Lord Dunmore, in 1774.

Of Captain Bullitt we have a few particulars which sustain fully his claim to rank honourably with the first and master spirits of this forest region. He was one of the first to approach the rapids of the Ohio — a scene of terror to the inexperienced boatmen of those days, in their boats hollowed from logs, or in the frailer vessels of bark employed by the Indians, which effectually paralyzed the courage of those who sought to descend the stream. A torrent that rushes at the rate of ten miles an hour, down a succession of rocky ledges, foaming white through their dark passages, and sending up a roar as of dreadful strife, might well discourage and daunt the inexperienced boatman. But Bullitt explored the channel, and was the first to conduct the bark of the way-farer to security in a port, in the very mouth of the warring waters — a safe and commodious harbour on the side of the Kentucky river — safe from the danger and rendered more lovely by the contrast of its sweet repose with the chafing billows beside which it seemed to nestle. Here, the explorer made his settlement. He died prematurely, after having won, by his judgment, his courage, his address, and great resources, the complete confidence of all with whom he came in contact. Other names might be given, bold, strong hearted and adventurous spirits, framed like these for enterprise and endurance, who had already dotted the face of the great Kentucky wilderness, with the fires of a rude civilization. Their settlements united the fortress with the wigwam. The fort of the white man, in those days and regions, consisted of a central block house and contiguous cabins enclosed with palisades. The woods were cut down within a given distance, and none were permitted to straggle beyond certain limits. These were the places of safety and rendezvous — the stages made by all new comers — the places of refuge upon alarm — points of as much importance as the isolated chalêt among the mountains of the Swiss.

While Boon was rescuing the girls from a small party of the savages, this wily enemy had simultaneously scattered numerous bands over the wilderness. These, at nearly the same moment, proceeded to attack the various settlements. The general movement was politicly conceived, in order to prevent the relief of one post by another. They did not succeed against any of the posts, except in the murder of an occasional settler, and the destruction of cattle; and the year passed off in continual alarms, unattended by any serious injuries. But, on the 15th April, 1776, Boonsborough was beleaguered by a considerable force. Indian weapons and warfare are not particularly adapted to sieges. They have neither battering rams nor cannon, and that caution which is one of their characteristics, forbids any attempt at escalade, even if the use of the scaling ladder were known. In besieging an armed station, therefore, the Indian seldom exposes himself to danger, and as seldom betrays his real numbers. But every shrub and hollow in the neighbourhood, tree or rock, dell or dingle, conceals its man — vigilant in watch, prompt to take advantage, and ready for flight or conflict, according as opportunity or necessity counsels. He crawls from bush to bush in his approach, he crouches behind stump or shrub — his patience is inexhaustible while his prey is before him, and while it is possible that victory will reward his vigilance. His wars were seldom bloody until he encountered with the Anglo-Norman, and then he paid the penalty of an inferior civilization. The loss of a warrior was a serious event — the taking of a single scalp was a triumph. To gain but one shot at a foe, an Indian would crouch all day in a painful posture; and the loss of five warriors, would greatly discourage a daring war party. To contend properly with such foes, needed a patience and vigilance like their own, and the exhibition of these qualities on the part of the whites, very soon depressed their audacity. Boon was too familiar with their character to be led into error, and they soon abandoned the leaguer of his post. He lost but one man slain and four wounded. Their own losses were carefully concealed from the garrison. A second attempt was made by double their former number — two hundred Indians — in the July following. They maintained the siege but forty-eight hours and had seven men killed, when they departed precipitately. The loss of the garrison was but one man slain, and two wounded. Boonsborough had a garrison of but twenty-two men. Logan's fort was besieged on the nineteenth of the same month, by another party of two hundred Indians. The garrison consisted of fifteen men; of these, two were slain and one wounded. The assailants were baffled in every instance, but nevertheless wrought considerable mischief to the infant settlements. But these were now beginning to be strengthened from the frontiers. Emigrants frequently joined their ranks. Boon had scarcely been freed from the immediate presence of his foes, when forty-five men came in from North Carolina, succeeded, a month after, by a party of one hundred under Col. Bowman from Virginia. But, in due proportion to their increase of numbers, were the increased hostility and numbers of the savages; and, for the term of six weeks from this accession of strength, scarcely a day passed without some skirmish, in some quarter, between the parties. But the "Long Knife," as the borderers had been for so long a time called by the Indians, at length proved their superiority in spite of their inferior numbers. The latter no longer ventured on open warfare — no longer attempted sieges, but, placing themselves in ambush along the paths, lay in waiting for chance successes. Boon was destined, in person, to reward the patience and vigilance of one of these parties. He had been fighting day by day against the enemy, and always with success. He tells us none of his achievements. But he who has any conception of the peculiarities, the terrors and the vicissitudes of savage warfare, can readily conjecture the scout by night, the ambuscade by day, the surprise, the sortie, the fierce hurra of the borderers, and the ghastly whoop of the savage. Our forest hero had braved or displayed all these, with the coolness of one whose composure of nerve nothing could disturb, and the enemy had disappeared from before his face. His fortress was no longer threatened, and the infant colony began to flourish in such a manner as to inspire the inhabitants with too much confidence in their fortunes. Whether Boon himself too soon relaxed in his vigilance — whether it was by his own or the neglect of others that the event happened which we are about to relate — cannot now be determined. But on the seventh of February, 1778, he was captured by a party consisting of one hundred and two Indians and two Frenchmen. He had gone out with a force of thirty men to the Blue Licks, on Licking river, to make salt for the several garrisons. Finding himself without power of escape, he capitulated for the safety of his party, and was treated well by his captors. How the Frenchmen came to be assailants against the American settlers, at a time when France and the United States were on friendly terms, and about to form an alliance offensive and defensive against the British, it is not easy at this time of day to guess. In all probability, the Frenchmen in question were mere renegades, indifferent to all European authority, and seeking the gratification of a passion for strife and plunder fully equal to that of the savages; or they may have been captives to the Indians on some previous occasion, and, adopted into the tribe, had readily amalgamated with the red men. It is known that the French, in all their intercourse with the Indians, proved themselves much more flexible than the more stubborn Anglo-Saxon, were more popular with the natives, and frequently led their warriors to battle. In the Cherokee wars of 1757–8, French officers were scattered all over the interior, counselling and fomenting the savages to strife.

Boon and his party were treated with kindness by his captors. They were conducted first to Old Chilicothe, the principal Indian town on Little Miami, and, subsequently, Boon, with ten of his men, were conveyed to the British post of

Detroit, held by Governor Hamilton. On these two journeys, Boon's deportment was such that the Indians became absolutely charmed with him; so much so, that they refused to leave him with Hamilton, though that officer offered them one hundred pounds sterling for his ransom with no other view than to give the Captain his parole. Boon also acknowledges the kindness of several English gentlemen who offered to supply his wants, and would have pressed many gifts upon him — all of which, however, with the simple pride which formed so large an element of his character, he firmly but thankfully declined. His valour, his fortitude, his skill, his integrity, had all impressed themselves upon the Indians with whom these are the paramount virtues. His fame had evidently reached the remotest parts of the northern British settlements, and his personal deportment, when he was encountered, had justified the golden opinions he had won.

His ten followers were left as prisoners at Detroit, but he was taken back to Chilicothe. Here he was adopted into a family, became a son, and won greatly upon the affection of his new parents, his brothers, sisters, and their friends. He preserved his cheerfulness, and this was a great virtue in their eyes. He had no complaints, no murmurs, put on no evil brows, obeyed their instructions, and grew friendly and familiar with all around him. He won their applause at their shooting matches, though, as it would seem, rather by shooting ill than well. The Indians, vain of their skill, do not like to be beaten, and the good sense and tact of our forester never suffered him to show the superiority which he possessed. "I was careful not to exceed many of them in shooting, for no people are more envious than they in this sport. I could observe in their countenances and gestures the greatest expression of joy when they exceeded me; and when the reverse happened, of envy." The King of the Shawanees treated him with particular favour, and, after awhile, he was suffered to hunt alone, and at liberty, as one in whom they had entire confidence. For a time he maintained his fidelity, and brought in regularly the spoils of his hunting, but he meditated escape the while. They take him to the salt springs on Scioto, where his time, for ten days, is employed either in hunting, or in making salt. When he returns to Chilicothe, he was alarmed by the sight of four hundred and fifty chosen warriors, armed to the teeth, and covered with war paint, preparing to go against Boonsborough. This discovery precipitates his resolves. On the sixteenth of June, circumstances seeming to favour his design, he leaves his tribe before day, and reaches Boonsborough on the twentieth — a distance of one hundred and sixty miles. In this flight he ate but one meal. He found the fortress in bad condition, but immediately proceeded to its repair, strengthening the gates and posterns and forming double bastions. Fortunately, the Indians gave him time for this. His flight had determined them to delay the proposed assault. In the mean time their spies cover the country, and the council house is frequently opened for discussion. The savage tribes are getting more and more anxious, as they view the daily progress of the "Long Knife." They begin to dread his number as they dread his peculiar resources, and to see in the presence of such hunters as Daniel Boon, a fearful augury, against which they cannot shut their eyes — a sign of their own extermination, and of that

> Advancing multitude
> Which soon shall fill these deserts.[8]

They were preparing for a last grand effort, in which they were to make their resources, as they fondly thought, commensurate with their object. But Boon was not intimidated, and while their preparations were yet in progress, he carried the attack into their own country. Meeting with a party of

[8] William Cullen Bryant, "The Prairies," lines 116–117.

thirty near the "Paint Creek Town," on their way to join the Chilicothians, he gave them battle and dispersed them, without losing a man. Eluding the main force of the savages, then on their march for Boonsborough, he reached that post in safety, and in season for its defence. The enemy appeared before it on the eighth of August. They were four hundred and fifty-four in number, under the command of Capt. Duquesne and eleven other Frenchmen, beside their own chiefs. They had British and French flags flying, though the fort was summoned in the name of his Britannic majesty. These were Canadian Frenchmen.

The danger was a threatening one. The force in the garrison was small. The number of the enemy was unusually large for an Indian force, and they were led by European officers. But the hearts of our people did not fail them. They had succeeded in securing their horses and cattle within the pickets, and Boon was soon ready with his answer to the stern summons of the foe. "Death," he says to himself, "is better than captivity!" He had already tasted enough of that bitter draught. "If taken by storm, we are doomed to destruction; but we must prevent that and preserve the fort, if possible." His answer to the enemy, whose chief came himself beneath the walls to receive it, — was after a very plain, but a very manly fashion. "We shall defend our fort while a man of us lives. We laugh at your preparations. We are ready for you, and thank you for the time you gave us. Try your shoulders upon our gates as soon as you please; — they will hardly give you admittance."

They knew Boon's firmness of character, and were discouraged by his answer. They resolved to try the effects of cunning rather than valour. Another interview was obtained, and Boon was assured that, by the special instructions of Governor Hamilton, they were only to take captive, and not to destroy them. But of this they declared themselves hopeless, and would be content to treat for peace, and depart quietly, if nine of the garrison would come forth for this purpose. The artifice did not deceive our borderers, but they prepared to comply with the proposal, relying on their caution, their courage, the vigilance of the garrison, and other circumstances, for their safety. The conference was to be held within sixty yards of the garrison, — within rifle-shot, in short, — and this arranged, Boon, with eight others, advanced from the fortress into the plain. Here, at the given distance, the chiefs of the besiegers were met, — the terms of amnesty agreed on, papers drawn, and regularly signed and delivered. "And now," said the Indians with delightful simplicity, — "it is customary on all such occasions for hands to be shaken, in token of future friendship." It was with a rare confidence in the physical strength, the muscle and activity of himself and men, that Boon agreed to this also; — "for," says he, "we were soon convinced that they sought only to make us prisoners." The gripe of friendship, indeed, became a grapple, and the little party of nine were surrounded by the greater part of the Indian army. But, the confidence of our borderer in the courage and conduct of his men, did not deceive him. They threw off their assailants, broke through the throng, and amidst a heavy but random fire, succeeded in reaching the fortress. But a single man was wounded. Then ensued the battle. The fort was completely environed, and the fight continued with little intermission for nine days. Finding that they made no impression by this mode of warfare, the enemy opened a mine, the shaft advancing from the Kentucky river, which was but sixty yards from the fort. The garrison discovered their object by the discoloration of the river, and proceeded to baffle them in this object by cutting a trench across their subterranean passage. This proceeding became revealed to the besiegers by the clay thrown out of the fort, and effectually served to discourage the further prosecution of their attempt. So far they had gained nothing. They had slain but two of the garrison, and wounded twice that number. They had made no impression upon the firmness of Boon and his companions. Their own losses were very great for an Indian army, — thirty-seven killed, and more than twice that number wounded. Sick of a game so unprofitable, they suddenly disappeared on the 20th of the month, after a leaguer of thirteen days. This was the last attempt upon Boonsborough. It has been asked why the Frenchman who led this force did not attempt escalade. The stockades were but twelve feet high, and every Indian had his tomahawk. The force was five times that of the garrison. But it must be remembered that an Indian army has no men to lose. They will never rush on death. They employ no forlorn hopes. Their policy is never to engage in battle, unless with the chances wholly in their favour. To mount battlements in the teeth of ninety rifles, was a game too hazardous for them to play; and it is scarcely possible that, even if Duquesne counselled the attempt by storm, the savage chiefs listened to him one moment. That they were busy enough in their own way may be guessed from the fact that the garrison picked up one hundred and twenty-five pounds weight of bullets, to say nothing of the greater number that were buried in the logs of the fortress.

During Boon's captivity at Chilicothe, his wife, despairing of seeing him again, returned with her family to "the settlements." — It was thus that our foresters called the abodes of civilization. As soon as Boonsborough was relieved from its leaguer, and there seemed no immediate call for his presence, he followed her thither, and once more removed bag and baggage to the wilderness. In the meantime, the war became scattered over the whole face of Kentucky. The white intruder became the common enemy, and the numerous Indian tribes which had heretofore fought among themselves, now concentrated their arms upon him only. Numberless were the conflicts, bloodless or bloody, which constantly took place, in which new men were making themselves distinguished while they laid the foundation for social securities which they themselves were destined never to enjoy. The return of Boon was not a return to quiet or inactivity. He was forever on the alert, — on the watch to assist the stranger, to rescue the captive, to help the distressed. He was always ranging, now as a hunter, and now as a spy, — no region too wild for his adventure, no danger too threatening for his courage and confidence. He passed from duty to duty with a readiness and promptitude that left him no time for repose, and as little for apprehension. Wonderfully fortunate, he did not always escape with impunity. On the sixth of October, while returning with his brother from a scout, they were fired upon from an Indian ambush. His brother was shot down at the first fire, and Boon was closely pursued for three miles, — the Indians trailing with a dog. Availing himself of the first chance, Boon succeeded in shooting the dog, and thus escaped.

The winter which followed was early and severe. The inhabitants suffered greatly, as the corn of the previous season had been very generally destroyed by the Indians. The people lived chiefly on buffalo flesh. But there was a consolation even in the severities and privations of the season, since it confined the savages to their wigwams. With the spring they reappeared, and obtained some advantages. Captain Ashton, with twenty-five men, was worsted in a fight with a superior number. Ashton was slain, with twelve of his men. Capt. Holden was defeated in like manner with seventeen men, and every day resulted in new disasters. The Shawanees, the Cherokees, Wyandots, Tawas, Delawares, and several others on the northern frontiers, were united against the settlers; and, under the influence of two renegade white men, McKee and Girty, whose deeds have made their names infamously known throughout the West, were inflamed to constant and bloody activity. The prospects of the new colonies were gloomy enough, and it was equally necessary to inspirit the settlers and to check the Indians. On the 18th August, 1782, Boon, with Colonels Todd and Trigg, and Major Harland, collected one hundred and seventy-six men, and took the trail after an army of five hundred Indians, who had but a few days before assailed Byrant's Station, near Lexington, but without success. They pursued this body beyond the Blue Licks, to a remarkable bend of the main fork of Licking river, and overtook them on the 19th. At first the savages gave way. The pursuers, ignorant of their number, passed the river, pressing the pursuit. The enemy rallied, in a good position, formed the line of battle skillfully, and, satisfied of their great superiority, awaited the attack. It began very fiercely and lasted for fifteen minutes, when Boon's party were compelled to retreat with a loss of 67 men, seven of whom were prisoners. Cols. Todd and Trigg, and Major Harland, were all slain. Boon was the sole leader surviving, and he lost his second son. The battle was terribly bloody while it lasted. The Indians, having lost 64 men slain, put to death four of their prisoners, that the number lost on both sides should be equal. Boon says, that the Indians acknowledged that another fire would have caused their dispersion. The fugitives were met by a party led by Col. Logan, but they came too late; a little sooner, and the defeat must have been a victory, and no such loss would have been sustained. The principal slaughter was made during the flight. When the whites gave way, they were pursued with the utmost eagerness. The river was difficult of passage and some were killed as they entered, some as they swam, others as they ascended the opposite cliffs. The melancholy news was brought in a few hours to Lexington, which it left full of widows.

Boon immediately joined another expedition under Gen. Clark, and once more went in pursuit of the same body of

Indians. The pursuit was commenced with great secrecy and promptness, and the savages were overtaken within two miles of their towns, but not before they had received the alarm from two of their runners. They fled in confusion, dispersing on all hands, not waiting the attack, and leaving their villages and all they possessed to the fury of the whites. These hurried, winged with rage and eager for revenge, through many of their towns on the Miami. Nowhere were they withstood. They slew but few of the enemy and took but few prisoners; but they burnt the towns where they came, destroyed their corn, fruits and provisions, and swept the country with desolation. This inroad had its effects. It dispirited the savages, broke up their plans, dissolved their confederacy, and taught them the impossibility of contending, with any hope of success, against the superior resources of the white man. It was Boon's last campaign. But he still remained a wanderer. As Kentucky grew populous, he passed to less crowded regions, removed finally to the Missouri territory, and in upper Louisiana received a grant of 2000 acres of land from the Spanish authorities. He settled at Charette, on the Missouri, some distance from the inhabited parts of the country, and followed the habits of life which delighted his early manhood. He was still the hunter and the trapper, and continued so to the day of his death, which occurred in 1822. A newspaper account represents him as having been found dead in the woods with his rifle in his grasp. Such a finish to such a life, would have been equally appropriate and natural. It is related that, some time before his death, he had his coffin made out of a favourite cherry-tree, upon which, for several years, he bestowed a course of rubbing, which brought it to an exquisite polish. He had reached the mature term of eighty-five years, through vicissitudes, toils and dangers which are apt to abridge greatly the ordinary length of human existence. It will not be thought extravagant, if, in addition to the merits of being a brave and good man, and a great hunter, we consider him a great discoverer also. Standing upon Cumberland mountain, and looking out upon the broad vallies and fertile bottoms of Kentucky, he certainly thought himself so. We have no doubt he felt very much as Columbus did, gazing from his caraval on San Salvador; as Cortés, looking down from the crest of Ahualco, on the valley of Mexico; or Vasco Nunez, standing alone on the peak of Darien, and stretching his eyes over the hitherto undiscovered waters of the Pacific.

Note to the preceding article.[9] — A friend writes us in regard to one item of the preceding article, that we are possibly in error in our description of the physique of Boon. We represent him as a tall man of powerful frame. This description was drawn from various sources which have hitherto been acknowledged as adequate authorities on this subject. Still the point is one which, whatever may be its importance, can scarcely be considered concluded. Our correspondent is not prepared, of his own knowledge, to say that the description is not correct; but he gives a pleasant account of one of his neighbours, on the banks of Pacolet River, in South Carolina — one James Moseley — an old man, truthful, honest, and highly esteemed by all around him, who claimed to have known Boon well, to have frequently slept in his cabin, and been the companion of his wanderings. Moseley died in Union District at the mature term of eighty-four years. He came from the Yadkin to the Pacolet, and lived on the former river, in Boon's neighbourhood, when he made his first trip to Kentucky. Describing him at that period — and he was then in the very fulness of his vigour — Moseley said that he weighed about one hundred and fifty-five, that he was not above five feet eight or nine inches high — was marked by a lively, spark-

<hr>

[9] This material was originally published under the title "Daniel Boone — James Moseley" in the *Southern and Western Magazine*, II (August, 1845), 131–132.

ling blue eye, was very active, a tight, well-made fellow, athletic, and, as we may well suppose, capable of enduring any degree of fatigue within the compass of mortal muscle. We have no reason to suppose that a description so precise, is not in the main correct. Our friendly correspondent answers for Moseley as a witness; — and there is no reason for surprise, when we learn that a great hunter is not a plethoric and over-fed person. Where the labours of the chase are taken on foot, it is but reasonable to suppose that the hunter is a lean man. Such is always the case with the Indians and with our own people, where they attract our attention for their expertness in the woods. Little flesh, a frame rather slight than slender, broad shoulders, narrow hips, and a wiry muscle, are the usual marks of the keen and active hunter. "James Moseley," says our correspondent, "was himself something of a Leather Stocking. He had been a great huntsman in his time, had fought frequently with the Indians, as frequently with the Tories, lived forty years in the same log cabin, was received as a welcome guest by the wealthiest of our people, and died, as he began the world, in poverty, with an unblemished char-acter, and without an enemy. To the last hours of life, he lived upon his own labour, and was indebted for no obligations which he could not and did not recompense." He deserves this record.

ARTICLE V

CORTÉS AND THE CONQUEST
OF MEXICO [1]

I. — The Despatches of Hernando Cortés, the Conqueror of Mexico, addressed to the Emperor Charles V., written during the conquest, and containing a narrative of its events. Now first translated into English, from the original Spanish, with an Introduction and Notes, by George Folsom, one of the Secretaries of the New York Historical Society, Member of the American Antiquarian Society, of the Archaeological Society of Athens, etc. New York: Wiley & Putnam. London: Stationers' Hall Court. 1843.

II. — History of the Conquest of Mexico, with a preliminary view of the ancient Mexican civilization, and the Life of the conqueror, Hernando Cortés. By William H. Prescott, author of the "History of Ferdinand and Isabella." "Victrices aquilas alium laturus in orbem." — Lucan. In three volumes. New York: Harper & Brothers. 1843.

Spain, at the beginning of the fifteenth century, was the great military nation of Europe. She had served a long and painful apprenticeship, very equally marked by triumphs and abasements, in order to arrive at this proud distinction. Her training had been as severe as it was protracted, and it was not until her petty independent and frequently conflicting states, had become united under one rule, in the reign of Ferdinand the Catholic, that this reputation was rendered unquestionable by her complete ascendancy over foes and rivals. In glancing over the long catalogue of events, the long train of causes and their consequences, by which this happy consummation was at length made sure, the historian almost fears lest he should become the romancer. With all his forbearance, unless the reader will travel with him through the venerable

[1] Originally published in the *Southern Quarterly Review*, VI (July, 1844), 163–227.

chronicles, he cannot well escape the imputation of having yielded his convictions to his theme, and embarked on the wide sea of historical speculation, rather with the wing of the imagination than the sober, questioning mood of a conscientious judgment. The temptation to rise above the usual subdued forms of utterance, requisite for history, is equally pressing and peculiar. Never was history, in itself, more thoroughly like romance; never was the narrow boundary between the possible and the certain, more vague, shadowy and subtle. Truth seems to hang forever over the abyss of doubt; — the probable loses itself in a wide empire of uncertainties, in which the historian, trembling always lest he should lose his guide, grasps unscrupulously, at last, upon the nearest forms which promise a refuge for his thought; and is delighted, finally, to lose himself in any faith which will put at rest his incredulity. Well may the reader, as he lingers over the story of wild revenge, chivalrous adventure, and faithless or audacious love, pause and wonder if it be not, indeed, the cunning fiction of the poet, which, through the medium of his fancy, endeavours to beguile his judgment. From the year 712, when Gebel-al-Tarik, — the one-eyed Tarik, — Tarik El Tuerto, — first planted his flag and footstep upon the rocky heights of Calpe, threatening with the pale terrors of the crescent, the fairest regions of the cross, to that day of triumph when Boabdil el Chico, the last and feeblest of the Moorish kings of Spain, turned his back upon the green plains and gave his last sigh [2] to the gay and gorgeous towers of Granada, — her history was a long march of battle, — a fierce and protracted struggle, day by day and year by year, in which her mightiest and meanest mingled with equal ardour; rejoicing, as it were, in a strife which partook in no small degree of the character

[2] [*Simms's note*] "*El ultimo suspiro del Moro*," is the poetical title given by the Spaniards to the rocky eminence from which Boabdil took his last look of that city which he "could weep for as a woman, not having the heart to defend as a man."

of a sacred war, — fought, as it was, against a people who were equally the enemies of their country and religion. The Gothic dynasty, under which the soil of Spain fell into possession of the Moors, though previously long declining, enfeebled by the grossest vices, corrupt by luxury and sloth, and deserving if not ready for a foreign master, did not sink without a noble struggle, — would not have fallen, in all probability, but for the treachery of some of its most trusted captains. The stock, however abused, however forgetful of itself in the hour of prosperity, was a good one, and its virtues survived the nation. In the extinction of the tyranny of Roderick the kingdom perished,[3] but the sacred principle of liberty was saved; and, in the wild recesses of the Asturian mountains, under the patriotic guardianship of native princes, the seeds of a mighty empire were planted, whose dominion, in the end, and for a time, like that of Great Britain in present times, bade fair to overshadow, with its wings of conquest, the remotest regions of the habitable globe. The kingdom which was founded in blood by Pelayo, — the great sire of guerilla warfare in Spain, — could only be maintained by his followers with valour. Fortunate was it for the future that it was sustained and strengthened by necessity. Poverty and privation seemed to purify the souls, while they rendered hardy the sinews of the defeated race. With daily struggle came daily increase of virtue, not less than strength, — vigilant instincts, habitual courage and increasing numbers. Eight centuries of conflict brought its fruits, and the long chronicle of wars between the rival races was gloriously finished in the final conquest which rewarded equally the valour and the virtue of the Christian. This long

[3] Simms wrote a five-act blank verse play on Roderick for the Charleston Theatre in 1825, when he was nineteen years old. Though accepted and put in rehearsal, the play was withdrawn by its author after a quarrel with the theatre manager. Years later Simms refashioned this play into two of his least successful novels, *Pelayo: A Story of the Goth* (2 vols.; New York, 1838) and *Count Julian; or, The Last Days of the Goth* (New York, 1845).

period, distinguished by the most remarkable achievements, whether of masses or of individuals, — achievements in which the stubborn and faithful courage of the Spaniard, was admirably matched by the generous ardour and intrepid spirit of the Moor, — leaving it long a doubt on which banner victory would at last settle with its sunshine, — presents us with one of the grandest romances of military history, second to none of which we read, and fully equal to the Jewish, — from the time of the Kings to the Captivity, — which it somewhat resembles. The empire of Spain, once more rendered unique by the possession of her ancient geographical limits, was prepared, by the training of her sons, for their wide extension. The Moor of Granada sullenly yielded up the lovely regions which he had crowded with the trophies of his peculiar genius, and rendered classic by his peculiar arts and tastes. The Spaniard was at length free to repose from a conflict, which had tried equally his patience and his courage for seven hundred years.

But he had no desire for repose. The labours of his life had not prepared him for the arts of peace. He succeeded to the possessions, but not to the genius of the Moor. He conquered the works, but not the arts, of his accomplished enemy. Skilled in arms, and skilled in little else, his long wars and constant conquests had endowed him with a swelling and elevated spirit. Something of this temperament might also have been caught from the oriental genius of the people he had overcome. Was he, then, to retire from the triumphs of the field to its miserable toils, — from the glorious enterprises of war, to the meaner arts, the insignificant objects of trade, — from the noble task of conquering kingdoms, to the lowly struggle after petty gains? There was not a Spaniard in the army that witnessed the surrender of the keys of Granada, that would not have wept bitter tears, like those of the Macedonian, if told that this was to be the last victory he should behold, —

that he was to have no more triumphs, — that there were no more cities to fall, — no more foes of the faith to overcome, — no more worlds for conquest.

He was destined for better revelations. Happily, as it were, to save a victorious people from the mortification of falling into undignified repose, — at the very moment while their salvos yet rang along the banks of the Xenil from the courts of the Alhambra, announcing the fall of the last fortress which the enemy possessed in Spain, — and while the question might naturally be supposed to address itself to the heart of the ancient veteran, and the bold young cavalier — what next are we to do, — whither shall we now turn, — where seek the foe, — in what quarter achieve the conquest? — even at such a moment, and as if in order to answer these doubts and inquiries, a strange prophet rose up amongst them, — a noble, grey-headed and grey-bearded prophet, after the fashion of the ancient Jewish patriarchs, — a mild and gentle father, sweetly faced, sweetly spoken, who spoke as one filled with a faith, — confident as from heaven, — not to be driven from his purpose, — not to be baffled in the new truths, however disputable, which he came to teach. He preached a new crusade, — he announced new empires yet to be gathered within the blessed fold of Christ, — empires of the sun, of a nameless splendour, such as might well throw into shadow and forgetfulness even the lovely region just rescued from the Moslem grasp. Lucky was the moment, as well for himself as for the conquering army, when Christopher Columbus presented himself, for the last time, before the sovereigns of Leon and Castile. It was, perhaps, quite as much to give employment to restless enterprise, as with the hope of conquests in new lands, that rendered his painful pilgrimages at last successful. Strange as were his promises and predictions, — grossly improbable and evidently imperfect as his theories appeared when examined by the lights, in that early day for science, in the possession of Christian Europe, — there was something in the assurance which it gave of valorous employment, too grateful, too glorious, not to compel a certain degree of credence in the hearts of a military nation. It was to the hope rather than to the faith of Spain, that the great prophet of American discovery addressed himself; and, only half believing, yet yearning to believe, they permitted him to throw open to their arms and eyes, the ponderous and immeasurable gates of the Atlantic. It would be perfectly safe to assume, that, as no nation but Spain could be persuaded to attempt the discovery of the new world, so no people but hers could, at that period, have succeeded in its conquest. Hers alone was the sufficient training for such bold designs, — such a grasp of ambition, such habitual and enduring courage in pursuit. The protracted struggle with the Moors, at which we have briefly glimpsed, had prepared her for the most audacious adventures. It was in consequence of the severe lessons acquired in that school of chivalrous courage and military conduct, that she was able to send forth such a throng of captains, — and such captains, — worthy of her people and of the wondrous empires which they were yet to win. The conquest of America — Peru and Mexico — was only the last act in the conquest of Granada. They were parts of the same great drama, which, compressing epochs into hours, and the events of long ages into a life, we might properly entitle, "The last days of Spanish glory." The spirit which effected the delivery of Spain from the footsteps of the heathen, was the same spirit which impelled her arms against the heathen who was yet unknown. In many instances the performers were the same. The scene was varied, not the action. The heroes, but not the ideal sentiment of heroism which prevailed with both. Had Granada not fallen, Spain would not have dared to take the seal from the unknown waters. The enterprise might have enured to John of Portugal or Henry of England, or might have been left over to the present days of steam and commerce.

It does not affect the propriety of this opinion, that the persons most prominently distinguished in the Spanish wars with the Moors, do not appear in the first enterprises of Columbus. The spirit of an age is something which, happily, survives a generation. It was but natural that the war-worn captain should retire, and yield place to his successor, the page and esquire, who had buckled on his harness. They had been taught by his skill, stimulated by his example, counselled by his precept. With his banner, they caught up his enthusiasm. They were not unworthy of their training. The pupil did rare honour to his master by surpassing him, — carrying his deeds of daring and chivalry to a pitch of splendour, which must preserve the history of both, with the greatest and noblest of the past, to all succeeding times. Spain was one great school of romance and romantic daring. The spirit which had led the crown to conquest was a common possession of the people. Such a possession is not easily extinguished. It goes on, working silently, perhaps, but still working, and still producing fruits. For ages after the extinction of national freedom, this spirit will break out, reviving all the past, and rescuing a people from their thraldom. In Spain, when Columbus preached the new world, and long after, it was a triumphant spirit, working wonders, and every where astonishing the world by its successes. Such captains as Gonzalvo de Cordova, — the Great Captain, as they fondly style him, — then busy in the wars of Italy, — Hernando Cortés, Vasco Nunez de Balboa, the Pizarros, De Soto, Almagro, Ojeda, Ponce de Leon, etc., were all remarkable men, — worthy to take rank in the best military annals of the Roman Republic. Distinguished by rare courage, they were not less so by their great coolness and sagacity. They were no boy-warriors, famous at a charge, but feeble in every other respect. They could think as well as strike — endure as well as inflict, — of admirable judgment in moments of doubt, — of martyr-like firmness in moments of depression. We do not often meet with such men, even singly, in the history of other nations. Here we encounter them in groups, in families, of unequal merit, perhaps, as individuals, yet how distinguished — how superior, even when least prominent. It is usual to ascribe to the sagacity of Ferdinand — himself no warrior — the immense power and height to which Spain arose under his administration, and after it, in the hands of his successors; — but we should be doing great wrong to history, were the concession to be made to the sovereign, without specially referring to these mighty subjects, — if we passed regardlessly their claims, nor yielded to them the high and palmy merit of having done for their master all that the most loyal attachment, seconded by the most liberal endowment, as well of nature as of art, could possibly bring to the support and glory of a sovereign. If the distinguishing test of greatness be held, as it has been, to be the ability, in the worst times, and with the worst means, of achieving the most wonderful results, — then, certainly, it cannot be denied that these Spanish captains, whether the theatre of action be the sierras of Alpuxarra, or the wild passes of Central and of North America, not only proved themselves great, but the very greatest of warriors — distinguished by an audacity which seemed to regard no achievement worthy of attempt, which danger did not absolutely environ, — no danger, as beyond the endeavours and aims of a fortune, which had already plucked its brightest honours from the worst!

Were we in the mood, after the fashion of Mr. Carlyle, to endow a modern Pantheon with Hero-divinities,[4] we should

[4] Simms here refers to Thomas Carlyle's *On Heroes, Hero-Worship, and the Heroic in History* (1841), obviously the model for this essay, as Washington Irving's *Life and Voyages of Christopher Columbus* (1828) and *The Conquest of Granada* (1829) were sources for its early Spanish history.

not hesitate to choose, from the crowd of heroes who might fairly present themselves for this distinction, as ranking honourably with the worthies of the past, the young adventurer from Medellin, Spain, by name Hernando Cortés. In making this selection, however, we must not be misunderstood. We are expressing, by this preference, only that sort of admiration which we yield to military greatness, — to the man of mere performance, — the hero, — in the case of Cortés, we may say, the politician, — the man of iron nerves, of inflexible composure and fortitude, — doing without questioning, — prompt, brave, cruel, — resolute to win the game, once begun, at whatever sacrifice, the prize of which is to be the great and perhaps unenviable distinction of which we have spoken. Our eulogium, therefore, is necessarily qualified. We must not be understood as regarding this species of greatness, as the highest, — as deserving our unmixed acknowledgments, or, as at all comparable with that which arises from moral endeavour, — the achievement of intense thought, — of an original framing and endowing intellect, — the soul, living and labouring only for the benefit and the blessing of mankind. The creative mind must always rank very far above the destructive. We have no purpose of confounding these moral distinctions of fame, upon which the better lessons of Christianity are now beginning very generally to insist. The greatness which we now discuss is that of a class, —

From Macedonia's madman to the Swede, — [5]

whose renown is acquired, and, perhaps, deservedly, in periods of society which need a scourge, an avenger, an executioner; whose claims to renown rest upon the fact that they are themselves superior to the exigencies of their times, make them subservient to their genius, and out of their blind strength and brutal excesses, evolve a power which, in some

[5] Alexander Pope, "Epistle IV," line 209.

degree, contributes to the great cause of human progress. Keeping this distinction and limitation in mind, we do not scruple to declare that the greatest of these modern men was Hernando Cortés, — a man great in a period of great men, — achieving wondrously at a time of wondrous achievement, — displaying the very highest of those mental attributes which give elevation to the brutal deeds of war, at a period when these attributes were numerously possessed by others, — and holding his triumphs with a firmness, and wearing his honours with a meekness, which leaves nothing to be wished for, which sees nothing wanting, in making the comparison of his character, as a whole, with that of any other conqueror, whether of ancient or modern times. Compared with that of Alexander of Macedon, and the career of Cortés will be found to be marked by performances in no respect inferior to those of his predecessor, — in many superior, — in all those, in particular, by which rare endowments are rendered useful and their fruits permanent. Among his virtues, which the other had not, were coolness, modesty, self-restraint and religion. And who shall venture to compare the conquest of a feeble race like the Persian, enervated by the most effeminate luxuries, and emasculated by the most degrading influences of slavery, with the fierce people of Montezuma; — a people by nature warlike, and rendered terribly so by their sanguinary religion, and the constant domestic conflicts which their religious sacrifices and cannibal appetites equally required them to maintain. It was only in the approach of the Macedonian to the wastes of Scythia, that he found an enemy worthy to be mentioned in the same breath with the warriors of Tlascala and Tenochtitlan; and these, if comparable to the Mexican, in mere hardihood and brute courage, were very far inferior to them in the arts, — wanting utterly in those resources of invention and ingenuity which the latter possessed, — upon which valour falls back from defeat, and provides itself anew, by fresh agents and implements, for baffling the progress of a conqueror.

The life of Cortés writes itself. We have long been in possession of its details and of its claims. The works before us scarcely add any thing to our former possessions. They correct small inaccuracies perhaps, they supply some minute deficiencies, they give us a few more details; — but, so far as the achievements and fame of Cortés are interested, they were unnecessary. His name and that of Mexico, are coupled for eternity. They survive together; and the books of his contemporaries, even when written in his studious disparagement, are unavoidably memorials of his greatness. These "letters of Cortés," by Mr. Folsom, are for the first time in an English dress. They are useful, — they facilitate the progress of the student. The translation is neatly and faithfully done. The style is simple, direct and unambitious. The introduction, by which the translator supplies the omission caused by the loss of the first letter of the conqueror, leaves nothing to be desired by the reader. His compilation is equally succinct and comprehensive. The work of Mr. Prescott possesses higher claims to our regard as an original narrative. It is an elegant and eloquent production, rich and copious in expression, yet distinguished by a grace and simplicity worthy of any English historian. It is in the clearness and beauty of his style, and his conscientious and careful analysis of authorities, that Mr. Prescott's chief excellencies lie. We may travel with him confidingly, and yield our faith without hesitation, whenever his conclusions are declared. We have reason to be proud of his production.

Most readers are acquainted with the general facts of this history. The grand outlines of the conquest of Mexico are familiar to all. They are, perhaps, equally well prepared to believe, that it was one of the most remarkable events on record, whether in ancient or in modern annals. As a study, it

cannot be too closely read by him who would learn from example the best lessons of circumspection; of deliberate foresight, governing prudence, and that audacity, which, as if by
inspiration or instinct, discerns, at the proper moment, when
mere habitual courage and ordinary effort will no longer suffice. To the lover of romance, this is one of the most brilliant
— full to overflow, of the very material which his passionate
nature most desires — of those

> ——————— disastrous chances
> Of moving accidents by flood and field;
> Of hair-breadth 'scapes i' the imminent deadly breach;
> Of being taken by the insolent foe,
> And sold to slavery— [6]

Ay, indeed! and something worse than slavery: of being hurried to the highest towers of Moloch, — stretched out on the
bloody stone of sacrifice, and impaled, — head downward,
perhaps, — flayed alive before the most horrid of all blood-
smeared, brutal divinities, — the breast laid bare, — the heart
plucked forth, hot and quivering, and flung to the savage god,
even while the flickering consciousness yet lingers in the
straining eye-balls of the victim. These, and such as these, —
terror-rousing, horror-raising pictures, — are to be read in this
most wondrous history, — a history, we may say again, almost
without a parallel.

Cortés was the born-hero of this history. We have a faith in
this providential adaptation of the agent to the work. We believe that each great man has his mission. We are not now
speaking of great men in the newspaper sense of the term, —
not your little great men, — great on the stump, in the canvass,
in the management of parties and committees. Of the kind of
greatness to which we now allude, the world is never overstocked. Our great men are not men of every day. They arise
once in an age, and are the saviours — at least, the representa-

[6] *Othello*, Act I, scene 3, lines 134–138.

tives of that age. They distinguish it by a mark, and it thence remains unforgotten. They embody its highest virtues, its most eminent characteristics. They do for it what cannot be so well done by any other person — what is done by no other person — and what, until they have shown the contrary, is thought by all other persons to be beyond the reach of performance. They are the people who show, like Alexander, how the knots of Gordius may be untied; like Columbus, how eggs may be made to stand on their own bottoms; like Cortés, how the fierce, gold-loving Spaniard, faithless to all beside, may yet be won to follow the footsteps of one man, in the face of seeming certain death, with almost worshipping fidelity.

Hernando Cortés was the chosen hero of this great conquest. He had all the requisite endowments for the work. The eye of foresight, directing with the most consummate prudence; the deliberate resolve, which never changes its aspect nor swerves from its course when it has once received its impulse from matured reflection; the capacity, so to fathom the souls and resources of the men, his subordinates, as to be able to assign, at a moment, the particular duty to each which he is best able to perform; the nerve, never to falter or suffer surprise; the will, never to recede when taught by deliberate conviction to advance; the courage, which, not shrinking from fearful deed when necessary to be done — when necessary to safety and success — yet never indulges in wanton exercise of power; — yields to no bloody mood, no wild caprice of passion, and is beyond the temptations of levity; great physical powers for performance and endurance; a valour swift as light; a soul as pure as principle; a quickness of thought; a promptitude of perception; a ready ingenuity a comprehensive analysis of difficulties and resources — these, with many other virtues of character, active and passive, might be enumerated, to establish his claims to the high place which we are prepared to assign him. Of the great moral question, whether the conquest itself might not properly have been forborne, — whether it were justified, not merely by the morals of nations — such morals as nations then possessed — but under the intrinsic and inevitable standards of right and religion; — we shall say nothing. This is a question which we need not here discuss. Tried by the moral judgments of our day, and there would be but one opinion upon the Mexican conquest; such an opinion as we are all prepared to pronounce upon the murderous warfare recently pursued by the English among the junks and cities of the Chinese.[7] The mind naturally revolts from the idea that justification can be found for any conqueror, wantonly overthrowing the altars, defiling the homes, and slaughtering thousands of a people who have offered no provocation to hostility, — whose lands lie remote from the invader, — whose interests and objects conflict not with his, and, whose whole career has been, so far as he is concerned, of an equally innocent and inoffensive character. And, when this invasion and butchery occur in the history and at the expense of a people so far advanced in the arts of civilization as the Mexicans, the enormity becomes exaggerated, and — were we not to consider the standards of morality prevalent in the time of the conquest, and the farther apparent justification to be found in the sanguinary and horrible practices of the Mexicans themselves — our sentence would be one of instant and unqualified condemnation. But, discarding this inquiry, and leaving the question open for future moralists, let us pass to a rapid survey of the prominent events in the life of the remarkable man by whom the conquest of Mexico was undertaken and achieved.

Hernando Cortés was born at Medellin, a little town of

[7] Simms is referring to the war between Britain and China which began over the opium trade in 1839 and ended with British victory and possession of Hong Kong in 1842.

Estremadura, in the year 1485. He sprung from the people. When he grew famous, the biographers, as if anxious to show that nature could not be the source of greatness, contrived to discover that he was of noble family and illustrious connections. The probability is that this is mere invention. Enough for us that he was a man. Fortunately for him, he was a poor one. The energies of his original nature were not sapped away by artificial and enfeebling training. He had all the proofs, in his character, of having come from sturdy stocks, with a genius uncramped by sophistication. Nature was left tolerably free to work her own will on her favourite. Happily, if schools and colleges did little to improve, they did as little to impair his genius. At an early period, he gave proof of some of those qualities by which he was finally distinguished. With great ardency of temper, he betrayed a resolute will and an independent judgment, — qualities which, though they may sometimes arise from mere blood, are yet quite as frequently the distinguishing attributes of inherent capacity, which, in the consciousness of its own resources, is anxious for their development and irks at all restraint which delays their exercise. They would make him a student of law at Salamanca, but, though the age and country were decidedly military, Spain was already overstocked with lawyers. Cortés felt no call to this profession, let his parents call never so loudly. He was sent into the world for very different uses. He was a man of action, rather than a wrangler, — of deeds, not of words. His words, however much to the purpose, were usually but few; and the profession of law, in Spain then, as in our day, called for unnatural copiousness. The motives were sufficient for eloquence, then as now, to swarms of hungry seekers; but these motives moved not him. His soul needed a higher stimulus than avarice. He obeyed his destiny, abandoned the pen for the sword, and, at seventeen, we find him preparing to join the army of the great Gonsalvo. But Italy was not to be the theatre of his performance. Fate interfered to keep him from that subordinate position, into which, at his early age, and in the ranks of a warfare filled up with the veterans of the time, he must have fallen. Nay, a farther training was necessary in less arduous employments. His sinews were not yet sufficiently hardened, his frame not sufficiently formed, his temper not enough subdued, for fields of active warfare. Napoleon, in after days, said to the French, "send me no more boys — they only serve to fill the hospitals." The military career of Cortés, the work for which he was wanted, needed more time, more preparation, a better training than had been his. He fell sick, and, before he recovered, the time for marching had gone by. Italy was no longer open to the adventurer, and he turned his eyes upon the Atlantic. Impatient for action, circumstances seem about to favour his desires. His kinsman, Ovando, is made governor of Hispaniola. With him he determines to set sail. All things are in readiness, but his fortune, as if the fruit were not yet ripe for his hands, again interposes, and again, through the medium of suffering, prevents his departure. It is one characteristic of heroism, that it must be doing. The blood of Cortés required to be kept in exercise. Your knight-errant, fierce in conflict, is equally fond in dalliance with the fair. Love seems naturally to supply the intervals of war. Nothing, indeed, would seem more natural than that the ardency of the warrior should be equally great in all fields of combat. It is Mr. Moore who sings —

> 'Tis always the youth who is bravest in war,
> That is fondest and truest in love.[8]

Of the truth of our hero's passion in the present instance, but little need be said. Of its earnestness, we may make the most ample admissions. It must be remembered that he was

[8] Misquoted slightly from Thomas Moore, "Remember the Time" ("The Castilian Maid"), Oxford ed. (1910), p. 315.

still only seventeen. Impetuosity of character is scarcely matter of reproach at such a period. As eager after beauty in that day, as, in after years, in pursuit of less hazardous conquests, we find him incurring, with blind passion, dangers almost as serious. He must serenade his mistress before parting. Nay, there are fond last words to be spoken, — and he attempts to scale her windows. We must not look too austerely on this achievement. The gallantry of Spain was never of a very sensual order. It was so much mingled with pride and romance, that it became elevated with sentiment. The guitar and the serenade, borrowed from the tender and voluptuous Moor, implied, in the practice of the graver Spaniard, little more than a platonic passion. At least, it is but charity, at this late period, and in the case of a person so very young, to prefer such a conclusion. Besides, in the absence of any knowledge on the subject of the damsel, it would be improper to put any scandalous interpretation on the adventure. A last song, a last sigh — nay, a last kiss — may be permitted to the parting lover, about to pass, seeking his fortune, over that wilderness of sea, into that wilderness of savages that lay beyond. Certain it is, that, whether encouraged or not, our hero, hurried by passion beyond propriety, was precipitated from a crumbling wall, and spared more serious injuries at the expense of a broken limb.

The expedition sailed without him, and, tossing with feverish fiery pulses on a bed of sickness, he was compelled to stifle his impatient yearnings for adventure with what composure was at his command. His eager, impetuous nature, drew good from these disappointments. They formed portions of a necessary training for the tasks that were beyond. They taught him to curb his eager soul, to submit to baffling influences, to meditate calmly his resolves, to wait upon events and bide his time. Did the world go smoothly with the boy, he might never

be the man. Rough currents bring out the strength, and teach
the straining muscles of the swimmer.

But Cortés was not always to be baffled. He sailed for Hispaniola in 1504, when but twenty years of age, and reached
the desired port in safety. Here he was well received by his
relation, Ovando, honoured with a public office, with lands
and slaves assigned him. He became a farmer. In this mode of
life we may well ask what becomes of his ambition, — his military passion, — that eager temperament whose tides were per-
petually driving him upon the rocks. The life of agriculture
seems an unperforming one. Its requisitions are grave, subdued
and methodical. A quiet nature, a dogged devotion to the soil,
would seem its chief requisites. And yet, a purely agricultural
people, particularly where they possess slaves, is usually a
martial one, — delighting in exercises of the body, — famous in
the chase, — admirable in the use of weapons. The management of slaves, — such slaves as the Spaniards had to subdue, —
the restless, roving savage of the Mexican archipelago, the
blood-thirsty Caribbean, the revengeful and kidnapped native
of the Combahee, — required the vigilant eye of a master-
spirit. We are not to suppose that the true nature of Cortés
was left unexercised while he clung to the sober tastes of agriculture. For six years he pursued this vocation, showing no
impatience, — none of that feverish, forward temper which
had marked his boyhood. He indulged, as far as we can learn,
in no repinings. That he learnt many good lessons in the management of his subjects, — many useful lessons of government
as well as of patience and forbearance, — schooling into
strength that fiery nature, which, as we have seen, was only
apt to lead him into mischief, — we may not unreasonably imagine. At all events, we may conclude him to be exercising a
necessary nature in all this period, as it is at variance with all
human experience to suppose a great mind to remain satisfied,

for any length of time, with a condition which is uncongenial with its ruling characteristics. In 1511, we find him connected with a military expedition for the conquest of the Island of Cuba, — but not in a military capacity. This duty over, he resumed his farm with a diligence that looked like devotion. He was successful as a planter. He was the first among the Spaniards to stock his plantation with cattle, — to raise sheep, cows and horses, — in the management of which he betrayed equal pains-taking and success. This was showing singular thoughtfulness in one so young; — singular flexibility of the mental nature, which could thus so readily adapt itself to tasks and exercises in which it had never had any training. Strange, too, that one so ardent, so ambitious, so eager, should thus so easily content himself. We are reminded of other great men; — of Scipio, and Cincinnatus, and Washington. The list might be extended. In this very flexibility — in this singular capacity to subdue and keep himself back until the coming of the proper season, — this resolute forbearance of all vain and immature endeavour, — we behold the essential proofs of greatness. He was able to wait — the most difficult duty of the ambitious. He was able to conceal his true desires — without which capacity few succeed in their development, surrounded as they are by a world of rivals. Very like, there was no will of our hero in this forbearance. This passiveness was none of his own. His moods were in abeyance, under the control of influences, moral and social, to which he was ready to submit, and which he might not seek to fathom. It will not lessen the merits of a great man to believe that he is patient under the direction of a destiny which can better determine than himself the true modes and periods for the application of his powers. To submit, while in the full consciousness of his powers, is, in itself, no small proof of superiority.

But agriculture, however successfully conducted, did not furnish the necessary employment for his genius. His will was shaping out another course. He embarked in commerce, — and prospered as he had done in planting. He was a man to prosper. He carried into trade the same keen vigilance, fixed resolve, persevering endeavour, watchful forethought. This field afforded him occasions for enterprise — made him extensively known among the men whom he was to guide, — increased greatly the resources of money and credit, without which, at that time and in that community, the opportunity for great adventure was not easily to be found. He became a man of substance, a capitalist, and was called and considered, accordingly, as he would be now, a very reputable person. So his neighbours thought him. He every where secured their confidence, — his word became an authority, — his word had a significance. He, somehow, compelled their regard and veneration, and his judgment swayed that of older men. That they knew the audacious character of his mood, we may also infer, as we find them choosing him as their representative when a great danger was to be incurred. He did not shrink from the trust, offended Velasquez, the Governor of Cuba, and was honoured with imprisonment in consequence.

From this imprisonment he was soon set free. He was not a man to remain long in any meshes. But this governor of Cuba, who was of a temper equally mean, jealous and vindictive, was of capricious humours, which constantly found cause of annoyance in the character of Cortés. One of these provocations sprang from a cause equally natural and vexing. The constitutional infirmity of our hero — his passion for the sex — does not seem to have suffered much abatement in his farmer and merchant life. An intrigue with Doña Catalina Xuarez de Pacheco, a lady of noble blood — a sister of whom had been married by Velasquez — was revealed to this suspicious dignitary. The governor "was something more than wroth," and the storm which ensued was only hushed by the marriage of Cortés with the lady. This union, which he seems to have been reluctant to approach, he had no reason to regret. Doña Catalina made him a good wife, and followed him to Mexico, where she died some years after the conquest. He was wont to say that he prized her as highly as if she had been the daughter of a Duke.

Though not yet a conqueror, Cortés, as we have seen, has not been living entirely in vain. His career, though comparatively humble, has yet been honourable. It is worthy of remark, that, in all this period — a space of nearly eight years since his arrival in America, — he has not only achieved no military enterprises, but has shown no disposition for arms; a fact sufficiently striking when his previous aspirations are remembered, — doubly so, now that his after career is known, and particularly surprising when we consider how frequent were the examples of military adventure, shown daily by the daring hidalgos of Cuba and Hispaniola. The singular avidity with which, in that day, Spaniards of all classes embarked in schemes, however wild and visionary, which involved peril, stimulated avarice and gave provocation to valour, might well, we may suppose, awaken that impatient temper which we have seen breaking away from academic walks in eager desire for fields of war, — scaling walls in obedience to the working passions of youth — and, altogether, betraying that forward impetuosity of character which seldom desires weightier suggestion to action than what springs from its own inner tendencies. It would be idle, at this late moment, to seek to account for this remarkable forbearance, or to endeavour to reconcile those seeming caprices of temper, which, were we more familiar with the moral influences acting on his moods, might show them all, however apparently in contradiction, to be working harmoniously together. It is the superficial judgment that finds inconsistencies in character, simply because it never looks below the surface. The restraints on the mind of Cortés, arising from his duties, his interests, or, it may be, and probably was, from a real conviction of his own temporary deficiencies, — compelling patience, must naturally have brought him wisdom. He saw, from the numerous failures and baffling defeats of the cavaliers around him, that the day had not yet arrived, — that the fruit was not ripe, — that there was an accepted season of action, for which courage must be patient. To know "when," is quite as important to achievement as to know "how." Every day sent forth its novel armament from Hispaniola and Cuba. Brave preparations distinguished each adventure, — worthy and valiant cavaliers led the enterprise, — yet how few attained the goal, — how many perished in sad defeat, — how many more came back with ruined health, fame and fortune. The keen, vigilant eye of Cortés, took counsel of strength for the future, as he beheld the weakness of those who went before him. He saw that the hour was yet to come, — they had shown that they were not the men for the hour. May we not suppose, knowing as we do his career, that, at such moments, with such reflections, a fond but secret emotion in his soul informed him, that the hour and the man were destined to cooperate hereafter in his own patiently-abiding self!

It is said by some of the historians that his greatness, in spite of the generosity which he showed, or seemed to show, to his companions, was tainted by the miserable vice of avarice, — perhaps the meanest and least manly of all vices. To this passion, they allege, are we to ascribe his persevering devotion to his agricultural and commercial pursuits. His liberality to his companons, say they, was only a superior sort of policy, by which he attached them to his person, making them the subservient creatures of his ambition. But the statement involves many contradictions, and assumes for Cortés a variety of passions, all earnest and in action, such as we rarely discover in any person, and which, if in possession of the mind of any man, would be apt to leave him unperforming, a constant victim to the most momentary caprices. Ambition and avarice seldom work together. We are not satisfied that there is not some great mistake in the usually received biography of Marlborough, who is on record for a rare union of these natures, so at conflict, — the one soaring to the summit, the other grovelling at the base of all human appetites and aims. The passions are foes, not twins. There is no affinity between them. The frank, impulsive nature of that sort of ambition which seeks for renown through the medium of arms, is hardly capable of that cold consideration of small gains, — that petty, slavish, matter-of-detail spirit, which is for realizing the pounds by a constant concern for the pence. Ambition is a thing of large generalization, which usually scorns details, and shrinks, with a sort of disgust, from all servile literalnesses. It looks upward, and not, as Mammon, that "least exalted spirit of heaven," [9] upon the gold of the pavement beneath his feet. If its glance is ever cast below, it is only because, perched like the eagle on some sky-uplifting eminence, there is nothing farther to be sought or seen above.

It would be more easy to believe, in the case of Cortés, that he was not understood by his neighbours. As nobody at this period suspected the great military and statesman-like genius which he possessed, so no one could reasonably determine upon those proceedings in his career, the objects of which were latent, and only determinable by the grand results. It is not easy to look back, after the grand march of a conqueror, and sit in just judgment on his first beginnings. It would not, perhaps, be easy for himself to do so, and determine accurately upon his own motives. We are all so much the creatures of circumstances, — so much led by our own instincts, — that we seem motiveless in a thousand movements, when, in fact, we have been impelled by a secret nature, su-

[9] A paraphrase of *Paradise Lost*, Book I, lines 679–680: "Mammon, the least erected Spirit that fell/From heav'n."

perior to mere worldly deliberation, — a nature which op-
erates like an instinct, with all the energies, and, seemingly,
with all the prescience of a god. Doubtless, Cortés worked
under some such influences, without well knowing why he
worked and wondering sometimes at his own passivity. Supposing that he conjectured something of his future career, it
is natural he should seek the acquisition of fortune, — nay, that
he should hoard and secure it with all prudential care, in contemplation of the wondrous enterprises which lay before him.
We find him, when the time for these enterprises arrived,
frankly embarking all of his fortune in their prosecution.
Keeping this fact in mind, there will be no difficulty in ac-
counting for the two-fold desire which he showed, at once to
accumulate money, and by the generous use of it, at times, to
attach his companions to his arms. There is yet another consideration which needs only to be entertained for an instant,
to make it doubtful whether he is justly liable, at any time, to
the charge of withholding his resources, or betraying any uncommon or close regard to acquisition. Liberality of mood,
like most objects of moral analysis, is a thing of relative respect. Among one set of people, a person shall be held selfish
whom another class will esteem as generous in a high degree.
Cortés, differing largely from the usual profligacy of Spanish
cavaliers, — men reckless equally of past, present and to come,
— might naturally enough suffer from their denunciations, yet
deserve no reproach of avarice in any justly-minded community. He certainly differed from themselves, — he was no
profligate, — he respected laws which they despised, — he was
prudent when they were profligate, — sober when they were
intoxicated, — firm when they were wild, — and, consequently, triumphant when they failed.

The circumstance that strikes us, over all, and as wonderfully significant of his character, is the calm, unchanging quiet
of his life, during the long period of — as we must regard it —

his probation. Believing as we do that every great mind has not only some partial knowledge of its own endowments, but some strong presentiments of what are to be its future performances, we are half disposed to ascribe this seeming lethargy, in his career, to a deliberate purpose of self-training and self-preparation, for the work which was before him. No great mind is entirely without a knowledge of its deficiencies. The greatest minds are those who first and most fully discover them. Cortés felt his infirmities of temper. His nature was originally too fierce and intractable. His blood needed schooling. His impetuosity — and this was the disease of Spanish heroism — would have been the greatest impediment to his conquest of Tenochtitlan. It was only by restraining and subjecting his own, that he could hope to subdue the minds of others to his will. Will is not yielded in the attainment of patience. It is strengthened, made consistent, and doubly intense from its habitual compression. If there were no secret suggestions of his own nature, counselling him to this result, the observant thought of Cortés would have received the lesson from instances hourly before his eyes. It was in consequence of this deficient training, that the brave and gallant cavaliers who preceded him in the march of discovery, and helped to prepare his way, suffered all their disasters. He saw them daily returning in poverty and mortification, who had set forth in all the pride and insolence of spirit which characterized the Spanish chivalry at that wondrous period. He saw that it was not from want of skill or deficient courage, or inferior numbers in the field, that they failed, — but of the proper temper, of the adequate reflection, of the decisive judgment, all of which, operating equally upon the minds of one's followers and foes, make victory inevitable, and reap certainly its fruits.

There were yet other considerations, natural enough to an intellect so well balanced and so greatly endowed as that of Cortés, by which his patience was induced and his career influenced. Conscious that his extreme youth was unfavourable to his claims to command and lead, and unwilling to go upon great enterprises in a subordinate capacity to those by whom they were most likely to be rendered futile, he preferred to wait upon time, and prepare for the more favourable progress of events. The born-leader of men is always thus content to wait, conscious that his mission cannot be wrested from his hands. It is only your spirit, doubtful of itself and destiny, that is forever forestalling time and hurrying prematurely into the field, for the real dangers of which it has made no preparation. In truth, Cortés had been in the field from the beginning, even as the race horse is already master of the prize, whose previous training and exercise has made him sure of it, the moment that the time of trial has arrived. In his seclusion he had been at work. In his retirement he had been making the preliminary conquests which were to secure the greater. His regular habits of industry, his stability of character, his uniform good sense, had secured him friends among the cooler, the more sober and reflective of the population of Cuba and Hispaniola, — so that they were all ready to say, when a man was needed for man-work — *this* is our man! His generosity to his companions, admitted even by those who dwell upon his avarice, had won him other affections among the ardent. He himself was ardent without being insane. Frank in his deportment, easy of address, ready in his intercourse, unassuming even when firmest, and gracious even when unfamiliar, he had contrived to win golden opinions from all sorts of people. Besides, though as yet quite unknown in a military capacity, he had yet, strange to say, acquired the popular confidence in his self-possession, fortitude and courage. His conversation, though animated, was always sensible, and one trait, given by Solis,[10]

---

[10] Antonio de Solís y Ribadeneira (1610–1686), Spanish historian, wrote *Historia de la Conquista de Méjico, Población, y Progresos de la América Septentrional* (1684).

is worthy of being remembered: "He always spoke well of
the absent." With a vigorous constitution, unimpaired by dis-
sipation or disease, he was possessed of great physical strength,
and accomplished in all martial exercises. His stature was
good and well proportioned, active and robust. His chest was
broad and prominent, — his countenance clear, bright and intelligent, — his beard strong and black, — the expression of his
eyes lively and amorous, — and, to conclude in a word, and to
show the fruits of that period of probation, which, to the careless mind, would seem to have been utterly without fruits, —
he was a general favourite with both sexes. Verily, we may
begin to conclude, that our farmer and merchant-hero, so far,
has not been working entirely in vain. Let the future speak
for itself. We are not to forget, however, among the essential
and important qualities in the moral constitution of Cortés,
that he entertained an abiding sense of the presence of the
Deity in all the concerns and workings of humanity. He was
of that earnest, concentrative nature, that all operations of his
thoughts were impressed with the serious influences of a deep
and still dependent faith. The Deity was always present to
his imagination as a constituent motive in his own proceedings.
Like Columbus, even when he wrought in error, he flattered
himself that he wrought for truth; and it was in some sort a
holy sense of indignation at the atrocities which he beheld
among the pagan nations, in their loathsome worship, that
reconciled him on some occasions to his own savage excesses.
These were occasional only. Cortés was among the most indulgent of the captains of the time. He was merciful beyond
his age, and could forbear to claim its sanction for crime, even
when his own performances would seem to have required it.
This religious faith which he possssed, it may be remarked,
was one of the chief sources of the audacity of his courage.
How should he doubt of the result, who, adopting the banner
of Constantine, sees, ever visible in its awful folds, the inscrip-

tion which pious zeal may well assume to embody an encouraging assurance from Christ himself, — "Amici, Crucem sequamur, et in hoc signo vincemus." [11]

Such was Hernan Cortés, — thus prepared and thus encouraged — when it became his part to enter actively upon that theatre of performance for which his whole nature had been craving. He was called into action at a period most opportune for his ambition. Hitherto, the result of Spanish discovery in the new world, had failed of its expected fruits. The predictions and hopes of Columbus had been verified in part only. The ocean had been disarmed of its terrors, — the gates of the Atlantic had been rolled back, never again to close, — a new world had been given to the empires of Castile and Leon — but the more worldly appetites of the discoverers remained in a great degree ungratified. The fruits of adventure had not recompensed the voyagers. The crown had not realized its outfit. The possessions were barren. Instead of the precious metals and minerals, the drugs and spices, the gems and treasures of the golden Chersonesus, which had been liberally promised by the hopeful imagination of Columbus, a few small and comparatively unproductive islands, in a waste ocean, dependencies of sea and sky alone, were all that he yielded, in confirmation of his dreams and theirs, to the royal sovereigns whom he represented. He took from the gold of the sceptre in the extension of its sway. He himself never knew the extent and importance of his own discoveries. Within a stone's throw of Yucatan, he veered about capriciously, as if under the wing of a mocking fortune, like another prophet, not permitted to set foot in the Canaan to which he had pointed out the way for his people. Some

[11] Constantine the Great (c. 288–337), Roman emperor, was said to have seen a cross in the sky bearing the words *In hoc signo vinces* ("By this sign you shall conquer"). He used the cross as a symbol on his armor, standards, and banners. Simms's longer sentence, "Friends, follow the Cross, and by this sign we conquer," has no historical authority.

glimpses of the wonders of Mexican civilization were all that was vouchsafed him, in his last disastrous voyage. He picked up a canoe of unusual size, while on the upper coast of Guatemala, in which were found cotton coverlets, tunics without sleeves, mantles, coverings for the loins, — garments of happy fashion and exquisite texture, wrought with nice skill and delicately dyed in various colours. There were other commodities, weapons of war, choice viands, wines and fruits, and instruments of copper. The great results enured to other men. They penetrated the same waters, and finally made the discovery of Yucatan, — a realm of immense population, filled with cities of equal wealth and pomp and magnitude. But their discoveries bore no fruits corresponding with the promise which they held out to enterprise. The eager avarice, the yearning ambition of the Spaniard, groans with the very impatience of desire at the new prospect. Diego Velasquez, the Governor of Cuba, a man of whom we have already spoken, as mean, avaricious and inconstant, dazzled with the golden and other ornaments which had been plucked from the shrines of false gods in Yucatan, prepared to attempt the conquest of that country. A small armament was sent forth which did not succeed to his desires. His captains did not obey his wishes. Another was prepared, and the command of it was finally given, though slowly and with many misgivings, to his brother-in-law, our farmer, merchant-hero, *Hernan Cortés*. Appointed to this command, Cortés entered upon his tasks with all the energies of his nature. He yielded his whole fortune to the adventure, — he contracted debt in the more earnest prosecution of his work. The enterprise in his hands became popular. Men flocked from the standards of other and long-practised leaders, to follow under his. The dignity, resolution, skill, judgment, with which he proceeded, now alarmed the fears and suspicious of Velasquez. The popularity which he suddenly seemed to acquire, was itself an annoyance. Even the employment of his own wealth in the adventure prompted the capricious governor to apprehend that Cortés designed to make it entirely his own, and cut him off from his share of the profits. The admirable energies put in requisition by our hero, confirmed this fear; and there were not wanting those to whisper in his ears such doubts and suspicions of his captain, as strengthened all his own. Besides, it was remarked that a wonderful change of air and manner had suddenly taken place in our hero. It seemed as though his soul had risen into the consciousness of a new strength. There was a serious elevation of bearing, — a massive and noble-looking loftiness, now distinguishing his deportment — that amply spoke for high and hopeful purposes. Whatever might have been the levities and frivolities of his character before, these immediately gave way to a conduct such as might well become a consciousness of the great achievements which he was about to execute. He was no longer the mere tradesman, chaffering in the thoroughfare, — no longer the plodding farmer, tenacious of his petty cares and sovereignty. Velasquez saw in his newly-assumed carriage, a spirit too strong for his control, — too independent and too inflexible to submit patiently to the will of an inferior. Weak and irresolute himself, he trembled for his share in the enterprise, and heartily repenting of the trust confided to Cortés, he determined to withdraw from him its command. But this was not so easy of execution as resolve. While yet he hesitated, not daring to proceed openly, dreading a rupture with a person equally adroit and popular, Cortés saw into the secret misgivings and purpose of his narrow and apprehensive spirit. He was, perhaps, apprized of it by others, for he had friends on every side. His resolves were prompt and decisive of his character. He suddenly set sail for the port of St. Iago, contenting himself with a courteous but distant salute to the governor, who watched his progress at some distance from the shore. The latter had not anticipated this proceeding, or his own might have been more prompt. He knew that the preparations of Cortés were far from complete, and fancied that he should have sufficient time at any moment to arrest him. But the jealousy which waits upon time, is apt always to lose the occasion, and he who deals with rival or suspects him, must never postpone performance till the sunlight. Of the various attempts made by Velasquez to defeat the enterprise, or, at least, to deprive Cortés of all participation in it, details are unnecessary. They were equally ungenerous and unsuccessful, and Cortés seems to be wholly justified in the opinions of the moralist, in finally throwing off all connection with his brother-in-law. His keen vigilance, resolute character, and, we may add, his favouring fortune, enabled him to baffle all the efforts of his enemy, and these were continued with equal pertinacity and spite long after our hero had won his way to the city of Montezuma. Some of these efforts may command our more particular notice hereafter. Enough, however, that, in defiance of strifes on shore and storms at sea, we find the fleet of Cortés, early in the year 1519, safely moored at the appointed rendezvous at the island of Cozumel. Of this place, which is now deserted, the reader will find some interesting particulars, in the late work of Mr. Stephens on the antiquities of Yucatan.[12]

Thus, then, at the age of thirty-three, Cortés stood on the threshold of his great career. We have spoken of his physique and personal appearance, — of his great vigour and elasticity of frame, — of his pleasing countenance, and the general attractiveness of his bearing. It remains to say, that he excelled in fencing, horsemanship, and all other of the military and chivalrous exercises of the age. He was temperate, indifferent to what he ate, regardless of privation, capable of enduring

---

[12] John Lloyd Stephens (1805–1852), American traveler and author of *Travel in Central America, Chiapas, and Yucatán* (1838) and *Travel in Yucatán* (1843).

any toils in common with the meanest foot-soldier. He was not heedless of the impression produced by fitting costume, and wore ornaments, which were usually more remarkable for their richness and value than their show.

His armament consisted of eleven ships, under as many captains. On the 10th February, 1519, he reviewed his forces at Cape St. Antonio. "They amounted to one hundred and ten mariners, five hundred and fifty-three soldiers, including thirty-two cross-bowmen, and thirteen arquebusiers, besides two hundred Indians of the island, and a few Indian women for menial offices. He was provided with ten heavy guns, four lighter pieces called falconets, and a good supply of ammunition. He had besides sixteen horses." [13] With this force did this great man enter upon the conquest of the magnificent, the strong, the warlike and numerous people of Tenochtitlan, and the contiguous nations. His review was closed with a speech, almost the only speech on record of a great warrior, the promises of which were amply verified by the result. He told them, just as if he had himself beheld it all, of the extent, the danger, the glory of the enterprise in which they were about to engage. He was about to lead them, he said, to countries more vast and opulent than any they had known, and the conquest of which must make them famous to all succeeding ages. "But," said he, "these are to be won only by incessant toil. Great things are achieved only by great exertions. Glory was never the reward of sloth. If I have laboured hard and staked my all in this undertaking, it is for that renown which is the noblest recompense of man. But, if any among you court riches more, be but true to me, as I will be to you and to the occasion, and I will make you masters of more than Spain has ever dreamed of. You are few in number, but strong in resolution. If this does not falter, doubt not that God, who has never

[13] William H. Prescott, *History of the Conquest of Mexico* and *History of the Conquest of Peru* (Modern Library Giant, New York, n.d.), p. 144.

failed the Spaniard in his battle with the infidel, will shield you, though encompassed by a cloud of enemies. Your cause is just — you fight under the banner of the Cross. On, then, with alacrity and confidence, and carry to a glorious issue the work so auspiciously begun." [14]

At Cozumel, Cortés soon proved to his soldiers, that, while he disdained to follow in the steps of other cavaliers, so also did he reject many of their practices. One of his captains, arriving at the island first, displayed the red hand to the natives, drove them from their homes, and despoiled their temples. Cortés rebuked his follower, restored the spoils, and succeeded in recalling the Indians to their homes, and converting them, after the fashion of the time, to the faith of Christ. Their uncouth idols, tumbled from their teocallis, made way for the Virgin and the Child. Here, Cortés was fortunate in recovering a Spaniard who had been captured by the Indians in a previous expedition, who had acquired the Maya language, and was thus of great importance to the intercourse carried on with the natives of Yucatan. He had been eight years in captivity. Cortés proceeded from Cozumel, by water, to Campeachy, in the neighbourhood of which he found one of his ships which had been missing. He then proceeded to the river Tabasco, which had been penetrated by Grijalva, one of his predecessors. This river he ascended with a considerable force in boats and brigantines, until he discovered a town, built of bricks, and surrounded by a wall of timber, through loopholes in which it could be defended by missiles. Failing, after entreaty, to procure the supplies of water and provisions which he required, and defied by the savages, he dispersed his troops in several divisions and succeeded in storming the place, which was gallantly defended. The savages fought with equal skill and bravery, and, singling out Cortés, who particularly distinguished himself in the conflict, they addressed themselves

[14] Prescott, p. 145.

with special ferocity to his destruction. "Strike at the chief," was their cry — which drew upon him attentions equally honourable and dangerous. He lost his sandals in the struggle, and fought barefoot in the mud. A second battle followed in the plains of Ceutla. The Indians marshalled their legions, — legions indeed, — stretching out in dusk array to the very edge of the horizon. The fight which followed was a terrible one, but, in the most trying moment of the encounter, the eye of faith, among the more superstitious Spaniards, discovered a sacred ally from heaven fighting in their ranks, — no other than the blessed St. James, the patron saint of Spain, — who, mounted on a grey horse, conducted, to the shame of all other captains, to the final overthrow of the infidel. As far as we can see, Cortés himself wrought as effectually to this consummation, as the blessed saint whose business it does not seem to have been. He contented himself with victory, and forbore unnecessary slaughter. His mercy had its effect, not less than his valour. The savages felt their inferiority to the strange invader. Their chiefs sent in their submission, and appeared with the usual tribute of gold, slaves, and garments of feathers and cotton. Among the female slaves thus tendered, was one, the possession of whom, by the Spaniards, was soon ascribed to the particular interposition of heaven. She proved to be a native Mexican, taken by the Yucatanese when young, who still preserved her own language, and was capable of translating for the conqueror, where his recovered Spaniard failed, — namely, when they came in contact with those who spoke the Aztec dialect. She was baptized at Tabasco, and took the name of Marina. The Spaniards afterwards called her Doña Marina, and the Mexicans Malinche. We are compelled to state, moreover, that she soon attained a closer personal relationship to the captain-general than good morals will justify. The amorous nature of our hero was not more subdued by trade and agriculture than his military ambition. Marina was beautiful and attractive of person. Her temper is described as generous and gentle. She was equally faithful to the chief and useful to the expedition. She had a quick mind, and soon acquired the Castilian. Love may have helped greatly to facilitate the study of the language. The Spaniards held her name in high veneration. She bore a son to Cortés, of whom the historian remarks, that he was "less distinguished by his birth than his unmerited persecutions." [15]

From the conquered people of Tabasco, Cortés received his first intimations of that great empire which he was destined to conquer. His yearning spirit suffered no delay. A day of solemn festivity was spent among the conquered savages, to whom he gave the rites of the Catholic faith. The breeze favoured, and, re-embarking, he held his way along the coast until he reached the island of San Juan de Ullao; and here the Aztec dialect succeeded to that of the Mayan, and Doña Marina as interpreter to Aguilar. Here, something more was learned of Mexico, and of Montezuma, its potent sovereign. Cortés was pleased with the country, and landed on the very spot which is occupied by the modern city of Vera Cruz. At this place he founded a settlement and opened an intercourse with the natives. To the chief of these he declared his purpose of meeting their monarch, — a resolution which provoked the scorn of the savage who had no notion that the world could contain a prince so powerful as his own. Of the Aztec civilization at this period, Mr. Prescott has given us an elaborate and interesting picture, to which we commend the reader. It would too greatly expand our article, were we to attempt to say any thing on this subject, or on the kindred topic which involves the history of those wondrous ruins of civilization which make conspicuous and curious the whole face of the adjoining country. Enough for us that Mexico was, in one sense, the mistress of the neighbouring nations. Montezuma was a

[15] Prescott, p. 163.

sovereign of considerable ability and acknowledged bravery. But his reign was troubled. Cortés arrived at a happy juncture. The internal condition of Mexico was not one of repose. The elements of discord were at work. She was surrounded by enemies, who hated as they feared her power; and discontents within the kingdom were the natural consequence of a condition of unexampled prosperity, — of an iron-browed despotism, and of nobles, haughty and aspiring, who possessed equal motives and facilities for revolt. The success of the Spaniards was necessarily facilitated by these influences, and the superstitions of the Mexican monarch were of a kind particularly to favour the progress of the invader. Venerable predictions taught him to fear the presence of a white and bearded people, and numerous omens occurring at the period of their arrival on the coast, quickened the apprehensions of a monarch, whose nature seems to have been morbidly alive to such influences. How he strove, — by what arts, falsehoods and open violence, — to retard the approach of the Spaniards to his capital, must be sought in the elaborate histories before us. But the resolution of Cortés was no less fixed in the attainment of that object. He pressed forward with a will as absolute as that of death, and the Aztec monarch, beholding in him the very fate that he feared, ceased, of a sudden, to exercise those qualities of courage, prudence and decisions by which he had made himself feared of other foes, and by which the present might have been baffled. We see him yielding, hour by hour, and step by step, to the progress of a power, the very glance of which seems to have paralyzed all his own, as that of the serpent is said to paralyze the faculties of the trembling song-bird upon whom he fastens the fascinating terrors of his eye. Great were the mistakes which he made in his futile endeavours to arrest the approach of the Spaniards. The very presents by which he revealed the wealth of his kingdom, furnished an irresistible impulse to the object which they were meant to divert and to dissuade. His expressed wish that the invaders should not advance, betrayed his terrors; and his terrors, seen not less by the surrounding natives than by the Spaniards, while they encouraged the revolt of the one, stimulated the audacity of the other. The reader has a sufficient idea of the splendour of the presents sent by Montezuma to Cortés, the survey of which did not lessen the resolution of the latter to see the other in person, and express his acknowledgments. Other gifts followed, with a renewal of the refusal of the Aztec monarch to suffer the Spaniards to penetrate his empire. But the very terms of the refusal betrayed his timidity, and it was unavailing with the invader. As well might the puny fawn in the jaws of the carcajou, deny that he should finish the repast the flavour of which is already on his palate.

While Cortés hesitated to advance, rather in consequence of some discontents among his troops than because of any doubts or apprehensions of his own, he became aware, by certain ambassadors from the Totonacs, of the domestic relation of Mexico with the surrounding nations. Taught that the conquered and ill-used people who had been brought by force of arms beneath the rule of Montezuma, were prepared to avail themselves of the first opportunity for throwing off the yoke, he at once grasped the grand idea of using them against their conquerors, of fighting the one people against the other, and thus economizing, for final issues, the strength and valour of his own. Ingeniously suppressing the discontents in his camp, occasioned by the fears of some, and, in part, by the machinations of certain friends of Velasquez, he founded a city to which was given the name of Villa Rica de Vera Cruz. A magistracy was set over it. To this magistracy he surrendered the powers obtained from the Governor of Cuba, and received from them, in return, in the name of the sovereign, a similar authority. The more violent of the friends of Velasquez were put in irons and sent on ship-board, where they soon learned to moderate their hostility, and join with their comrades in the common cause. It was no hollow peace. The wonderful address of Cortés secured their affections, and they were ever afterwards faithful to his fortunes.

We hurry over, as unnecessary to our narrative, the minor events which followed. He passed into the territories of the Totonacs, estimated to contain a hundred thousand warriors, with the Cacique of whom he formed an alliance, and from whom he obtained four hundred *tamanes*, or burden bearers. Passing from the city of Cempoalla to that of Chiahuitzla — both Totonac — he found frequent occasion to display his admirable judgment and sagacious policy. In the latter city, an adroit movement committed this people to his cause, in such a manner as to make him very sure of their fidelity. At Cempoalla, as at Cozumel, he overturned the idolatrous and blood-smeared altars of the Indians, even though at the worst hazards of insurrection, and set up the gentler images of the virgin and child in their place. The savages seized their arms to prevent the indignity, but Cortés, with his wonted decision, having arrested the Cacique and principal inhabitants, subdued the tumult without bloodshed, and the fact that the divinities lately held so potent, did not avenge their own dishonour, tended, very naturally, to lose for them, in the eyes of their worshippers, the odour of their sanctity. It is to be remarked that, wherever he came, our hero seemed to have shown himself quite as solicitous for the diffusion of the true faith, as for the extension of his own conquests; and he sometimes pursued this object, at risks which, as a mere leader of armies, he would never have incurred.

His "City of the True Cross" fairly built, or rather begun, he prepared for his great movement. Despatches were sent to Spain containing his proceedings. His first letter is not now to be found. But Cortés wrote well, in a frank and direct manner, with a good natural style, forcibly, fluently, and sometimes with eloquence. With this letter he sent the treasures which he had obtained, the rare stuffs, sundry Mexican manuscripts, specimens of their picture writing, and four Indians, who had been rescued from cages where they had been kept for sacrifice to the bloody divinities of Aztec worship. Thus assuring himself, as well as he might, that the record of his discoveries, so far, was rendered safe, he proceeded to the performance of one of those daring acts by which the character of the man is at once stamped, with the signet of greatness, for the wonder of his age. He destroyed his shipping, and thus deprived himself and followers of all means of escape. There was now no possibility of retreating from the work. Triumph now was necessary to safety — the conquest of Mexico to life itself. Not to advance would be to revive the courage of Montezuma, to impair that of his allies, and to bring upon his little colony the united forces of both, by which he must be overwhelmed or driven into the sea. Terrible was the consternation, and wild the rage of his followers, when the ships were sunk. But one small vessel remained. Their mutinous arms were lifted against him — he had led them, they cried, to the shambles — to butchery! But he quieted them, even as the waters subside from storm, after a breath from heaven passes over them. But one small vessel was suffered to remain, and this he yielded to the irresolute who were willing to depart. "As for me," said he, "my part is chosen. I remain here while there is one to bear me company. For those who shrink from the dangers of our glorious enterprise, let them go in God's name. Let them take the one vessel and depart for Cuba. There, they can relate where they left their commander and their comrades." "To Mexico!" was the unanimous answer to this speech.[16] The proper chords were touched. The enthusiasm of the soldiery responded to their chief, and all their confidence in his skill and in his star at once revived in

16 Prescott, p. 202.

their bosoms. The destruction of his fleet was an act, not only of wondrous courage, but of admirable forethought. The fortunes of all were now staked upon the same cast, and a death-blow was given to the faction of Velasquez. In the absence of all means of escape, the inferior mind at once turned in hopeless dependence upon the master spirit of the company.

On the 16th of August, 1519, Cortés commenced his march for Mexico. His force amounted to four hundred foot, and fifteen horse. Thirteen hundred Totonac warriors and a thousand *tamanes*, accompanied the expedition. The latter were employed to transport the cannon, seven in number, and the baggage of the army. Forty of the chief citizens attended his march as guides and counsellors, not to say hostages. The garrison at Vera Cruz, was left in charge of Juan de Escalante, an officer at once prudent and skilful, and warmly attached to his commander. The advance of Cortés was marked by great vigilance. He was always guarded against surprise. His maxim, to his soldiers, was, "We are few against many, my comrades — be prepared, then, not as if you are going into battle, but as if actually in the midst of it." [17] His course was first for Xalapa, a city which has given its name to a valuable medicine [18] — thence for the martial republic of Tlascala — a people who still preserved their independence in the face of continual conflict with the greater power of Mexico. To this people Cortés sent despatches. They were important to his enterprise. His object was to use them against their neighbours, to employ their understood hate of the Mexicans as a means of his own progress. The Senate of Tlascala was divided in its opinion as to the reception to be given to the Spaniards. A party was favourable to their application, but another opposed it; and it was first determined to try the strength of the Spaniards before making any concessions. Twice, thrice did the brave

[17] *Ibid.*, pp. 211–212.
[18] *Ibid.*, pp. 212–213. The medicine is Jalap, *convolvulus jalape*, a purgative.

savages meet him, without any decisive results. The Tlascalans were beaten on all occasions, but they were still unsatisfied. Thousands fell, but they always left the field in good order, ready to resume the struggle next day. On the 5th September, 1519, a terrible battle was fought, giving the Spaniards a conclusive victory. But the conflict had been marked with such vicissitudes, as more than once moved the invaders to despair. Numbers nearly reconciled the inequality of weapons. Masses almost succeeded in overpowering individual prowess. Faction in the Tlascalan ranks helped the Spaniards; and the failure of a last hope and effort, in which, according to the advice of their priesthood, they had substituted cunning and artifice for arms, subdued their hostility. They became firm allies and fast friends of the Spaniards, and one of the greatest obstacles to the great conquest was finally overcome.

But the followers of Cortés began to despond. If they had met such enemies in the people of Tlascala, what might they not fear in the Mexican. Our hero had his answer to their fears, and it was again successful. He showed them that their only hope was in progress. They must go forward to find safety. Flight and fear would only bring upon them Mexican, Tlascalan, Totonac, the numerous herds of foes which covered the face of the country, all united, and all against the common enemy.

Their successes against Tlascala, that formidable foe whom he himself had never been able to conquer, increased the apprehensions of Montezuma. He saw, in Cortés, the creature of destiny — his own fate — appointed to realize all the vague terrors of the old tradition. Feeble and trembling still, he despatched new embassies and other presents to the advancing chieftain — congratulated him upon his victories — and concluded, as before, by regretting that it was not possible to receive him in his capital. But Cortés was just the man to overcome the impossible. What was not possible for Montezuma

was easy for him. He said as much in his reply — and the devoted Mexican now saw that his fate was unrelenting. The
issue was no longer to be avoided, and he strove to make a
merit of the necessity. Another Aztec embassy soon followed
the preceding. It spoke a different language. The sovereign
now declared his wish to see the strangers, and his ambassadors
were instructed to conduct them to the capital. His policy,
still insincere and vascillating, was yet rendered somewhat
bolder from his necessities. Other suggestions had spoken to
his fears. His purpose now, in urging their coming, was two-
fold — not only to get the Spaniards more completely into his
power, but to prevent them from forming any alliance with
his Tlascalan enemies. He was too late for the latter object.
In prosecuting the former, he suggested their route by the
city of Cholula, and there made his arrangements for their destruction. The Tlascalans exhorted Cortés against compliance
with this suggestion. But his will was stronger than their fears.
He was quite as much the creature of his destiny as Montezuma. He must go onward by that very route, by Cholula,
and it was at the peril of the Aztec monarch if he played him
false. It proved so.

Cholula was the sacred city of the Mexicans as Mecca is of
the Mohammedans. It was under the particular protection of
Quetzalcoatl, their god of air, whose mystic attributes embodied unexampled powers. There was a superstitious hope,
entertained by the Aztec monarch, that this deity would contribute to free him from the man of destiny whose iron hand
was lifted over his empire. His altars were raised upon the
loftiest mound of the place, and thousands of human victims
annually bled upon his shrines. The city, embosomed among
volcanic mountains, lifted four hundred sacred towers in their
emulation. The population was one hundred and fifty thousand. These were warlike, inured to arms, fierce and fanatic.
To these, add thousands more, trained soldiers, concealed

within and without the city, sent by Montezuma to make sure
the cruel purpose of his mind. Yet, into this city, thus provided for his reception, thus strengthened within and without,
hating and fearing him, and sworn vassals to the will of their
sovereign, the resolute conqueror threw himself, with his little
band of Spaniards. Six thousand Tlascalans attended him,
whom, however, as their presence seemed to offend the
Cholulans, he left without the walls.

The reception was glorious and without a cloud. Admirably
could these cunning enemies disguise their hate. Their faces
were wreathed in smiles. They covered the Spaniards with
garlands, even as the lamb is dressed for the slaughter. The
Spaniards were no lambs, true, but they were welcomed as
victims, and conducted, as in a sort of triumphal procession,
with every show of ostentatious honour and affection, to their
appointed quarters.

But a few days changed the aspect of affairs, and the deportment of the Cholulans. They were now ready for the
destruction of the strangers. Their plans were ripe for execution. The city was filled with armed men. The streets were
barricaded, stones were carried to the house tops, missiles ac-
cumulated, and vast cavities dug in the thoroughfares and
planted with upright and pointed stakes, the better to defeat
the movement of the cavalry. To crown and complete all, a
great sacrifice of children was made to propitiate the favour
of their cruel gods!

The star of Cortés prevailed! His own suspicions excited,
were confirmed by tidings afforded by his mistress, who had
wormed the secret from an indiscreet Cholulan woman. Great
were his anxieties in consequence, but he was equal to the exigency. He dissembled with the Caciques, and got them into
his power. His plans were laid with equal skill and secrecy,
and the event was a massacre rather than a conflict. The Holy
City was sacked, and in the flames of its ruined temples, and

the blood of three thousand worshippers, the imbecility of their false deity was fully shown to the wretched conspirators. Cortés seems to have stayed the havoc the moment he conceived the safety of his people to be certain. He suffered no women to be slain, and prevailed upon his Tlascalan allies, who had joined him at the first sounds of danger, to liberate their captives. How far his conduct deserves reproach — in how much it may be justified by the necessity of the case — is not a question for us. The first step of Cortés was the true offence. The attempt at conquest, not a crime in his day, is one in ours. Once within the walls of Cholula, as a guest, he had the most perfect right to anticipate the treachery of those who had sought only to make him the victim of his confidence.

The fall of Cholula carried a terrible fear to the heart of Montezuma. If he was in doubt before, he trembled now. Despondency took the place of fear in his soul, and the oracles of his gods, whose altars were made to smoke hourly with the blood of their human victims, yielded no encouraging response. Another embassy to the Spaniards disavowed any share in the conspiracy of the Cholulans. Cortés, meanwhile, was acquiring newer strength. Terrified by the vengeance inflicted on Cholula, other cities sent in their submission. To treat with these, to purify the *teocallis* of the conquered city, and establish Christian, upon the ruins of the pagan, churches, employed the conqueror a few weeks, and he then led his army on the route to Mexico.

What plains he passed, — what mountains he overcame, — what toils he suffered, — what snares he escaped, — these must be read in the more copious histories. Suffice it, they were such as might well have discouraged any ordinary valour, — might well have baffled a common genius, and set at nought every ambition less honoured with the favouring smiles of fortune. But the star of Cortés prevailed. His followers had learned, even as those of another mighty spirit of modern periods, to confide in his destiny. No fatigues made them weary, — no dangers appalled. Their hopes grew with their toils, — their courage with the difficulties in their progress. The very wonders by which their dangers were attended, seemed to expand their souls with sentiments of daring, which rendered progress itself something superior to triumph. At length, passing an angle of the sierra of Ahualco, they suddenly beheld the beautiful valley of Tenochtitlan unbosomed before their delighted eyes.

The sight compensated for all their toils. Never was prospect more beautiful. Woods, waters and cultivated plains — glowing, glorious cities, girdled by shadowy hills, gathered, in picturesque dependency, lovely in tint and hue, and exquisitely imposing in distinct and noble outline. Immense plains of forest stretched away beneath their feet in a wondrous circle, spanning the slopes that led downward to the valley. Within this circle, another, of cultivated fields — maize and maguey, tracts of luscious fruits and realms of delicious flowers, — seemed alone sufficient to reward the human sense for all human privation. In the centre of this great basin lay the wondrous lakes and lakelets of Anahuac, their borders "studded with towns and hamlets, and in the midst — like some Indian empress, with her coronal of pearls, — the fair city of Mexico, with her white towers and pyramidal temples, reposing as it were upon the bosom of the waters." [19]

We know, from the days of Cæsar, that, with a great genius, to come and see, is to secure the conquest. Cortés looked down upon the lovely realm before him, and his eagle eye at once marked it for his own. While he gazed upon his prey from the slopes of Ahualco, where was the sovereign of Tenochtitlan? — where was Montezuma? — with what thoughts, what last hopes, what final purposes? Sacrificing before his impotent deities elbow-deep in human blood, — summoning

[19] Prescott, p. 286.

them in vain to his rescue, — and groaning over the approaching cloud, from whose awful bosom the thunders of fate were about to vomit ruin on his kingdom. Never did brave monarch more completely cower beneath the arm of that destiny to which he was yet most reluctant to submit. Cortés is at length in Mexico — within the palaces of her kings, — a sovereign over the very soul of her sovereign. "The gods have declared against us," said Montezuma mournfully, to those who counselled resistance; "the gods have declared against us, — we should only fight in vain." [20] In the advent of superior divinities, the savage deities might well be silent. Milton embodies the idea very nobly, in his hymn on the Nativity:

> The oracles are dumb,
> No voice or hideous hum,
> Runs through the archéd roof in words deceiving,
> Apollo from his shrine
> Can no more divine,
> With hollow shriek the steep of Delphos leaving.[21]

The genius of the Christian faith had as effectually cowed that of the Aztec religion, as that of Cortés had overcome the spirit of their otherwise brave and despotic sovereign.

For the description of Mexico itself, — for the details of its wondrous magnificence, — the reader must be referred to the glowing narrative of Mr. Prescott. We can say as little of the modes of life, — the manners and customs of its people. As in a drama, we must confine ourselves to the action, the development of the leading characters, and the several prominent events which conduct to the catastrophe. Montezuma received his guests with a lofty hospitality. But he disguised the suffering, and, perhaps, the evil passions, at his heart. He was munificent, indulgent, conciliatory, — but these were only so many proofs of the awe which he entertained of these mys-

[20] *Ibid.*, p. 289.
[21] "On the Morning of Christ's Nativity," stanza xix.

terious strangers, of whom ancient prophecy had taught him to apprehend so much. They had shown themselves heedless of his power; they were in his palaces, self-invited guests; and what he beheld of them in personal interview, — their strange and wondrous music, their horses, their artillery belching forth such thunders as shook the walls of his temples, — were all significant of attributes, with which, in all his wealth and magnificence, he felt it would be idle to contend. Unwilling to submit, yet not daring to defy, the unhappy monarch sunk,[22] no less in his own, than in the sight of his people. The indiscretions of his troops precipitated events, and gave a colour to the more decisive proceedings of Cortés. An Aztec chief had ventured to murder two Spaniards near Vera Cruz, under circumstances of particular atrocity. This brought on a pitched battle between the Mexicans in that neighbourhood, and Juan de Escalante who had been left in charge of Vera Cruz. The former were defeated, and the prisoners referred the whole proceeding to the instigation of Montezuma himself. One of the Spaniards had been taken captive. His head, cut off, was sent to the Aztec emperor, no doubt as a decisive proof of the mortality of the invaders, — a matter about which the Indians were naturally doubtful. Cortés received this information very nearly as soon as Montezuma. He resolved on the boldest measures. His own safety required it. He was in the midst of powerful foes. He was in the palace of a subtle and deceitful prince, — one of great power and matchless cruelty. His followers were few. There was no possibility of flight. It was equally impossible that he should remain long in Mexico, unperforming, a dependent on the doubtful fidelity of its monarch. Neither his genius nor his policy was prepared for this. His plan was soon conceived, but it was one to task all his courage and resolution. His design was to seize upon the per-

[22] This form for the past tense was common for this class of weak verbs in America in the nineteenth century.

son of Montezuma, and hold him as a hostage for the good conduct of his people. A day was appointed for this purpose. The night preceding, we are told by the historian, "he was heard pacing his apartment to and fro, like a man oppressed by thought, or agitated by strong emotion." [23] He might well feel the struggle with himself. What might the morrow not bring forth, of tremendous struggle with his fate!

Mass was heard by Cortés and his soldiers in the morning. It was quite as well that the saints should be on their side. An audience was asked of Montezuma, and Cortés, with five chosen cavaliers, all in armour, appeared in the palace of the monarch. Small armed parties of the Spaniards, were also ordered to drop in, as if by accident, while the conference was in progress. When all seemed ripe for the development, the Spanish chieftain, changing his tone, abruptly accused the Aztec monarch with his treachery. Cortés required that the cacique, with his accomplices, by whom the Spaniards were murdered, should be brought to justice. The king consented, and the messenger was despatched with the royal signet. The next demand of Cortés, that Montezuma should take up his abode in his quarters, found less ready compliance. "When was it ever heard that a great prince, like myself, voluntarily left his own palace to become a prisoner in the hands of strangers." Cortés assured him it was but a change of residence, not imprisonment. "If I should consent to such a degradation," replied the monarch, "my subjects never would." He offered his sons and daughters as hostages, but the Spaniards were inflexible. The conference lasted two hours. Vexed at the fruitless discussion, an impatient cavalier, Velasquez de Leon, cried out, — "Why waste more words on the barbarian. If he resists us, we have but to plunge our swords through his body." [24] The unhappy monarch submitted. His hour was

[23] Prescott, *Conquest of Mexico*, p. 343.
[24] *Ibid.*, pp. 344–345.

come. The hand of destiny was upon his forehead. He left the palace with his conqueror, drooping in behavior, dejected and downcast in visage, — a sovereign in name only, and fully conscious of the cruel dishonour which his cowed spirit left him no power to resent. His people would have rushed to arms for his rescue, but the pusillanimous monarch quieted the tumult which his more noble ancestors would have directed. The proceeding of Cortés is justified on the score of policy, — but he was guilty, subsequently, of one seeming inhumanity, the justification of which may be as complete in this case as in the other, but which has not come down to us. When the criminal cacique by whom the Spaniards had been murdered, was brought to execution, fetters were put upon the wrists of the captive sovereign. This indignity completed the terribly humbling lesson which he had undergone. He wept unmanly tears which were only less unbecoming than the gratitude he expressed — the undignified joy — when the fetters were at length removed by his conqueror.

But the indignity to which Montezuma submitted, aroused a different feeling among his people. His caciques and lords were a high spirited and valiant race. They looked on the Spaniards with detestation, and longed to resent the shame which they had brought upon the kingdom. Their first movements to insurrection were promptly suppressed by Cortés, aided by Montezuma himself. Several chiefs were placed in confinement, and the threatened commotions happily subdued. Meanwhile, the Spaniards had covered the lakes of Mexico with their vessels, were in the receipt of the public revenues, and Montezuma had sworn fealty to the crown of Spain. But one thing yet remained to be done, which the wild and inconsistent fanaticism of the Spaniards conceived to be absolutely essential to the completion of a conquest undertaken in the name of God. This was the overthrow of the Aztec worship, and the substitution for it of that of Jesus. It was in vain that Montezuma pleaded against the innovation, — urging the strongest arguments of policy against it. Cortés was unyielding, and one of the *teocallis* was purified and converted into a Christian temple. The discontents of the Aztecs increased, and Montezuma formally announced to Cortés the necessity for his departure. An insurrection was preparing which he could not control, — in which the whole spirit of the people, wrought upon at once by patriotism and the priesthood, was about to declare itself by a final resort to arms. There was no repose for the invaders. Their conquest was insecure. By day they grasped, by night they slept upon, their weapons!

While such was the relation of Cortés to the Mexicans, he was troubled with other tidings from his own countrymen. His emissaries, sent to Spain, had not been successful in procuring a sanction for his proceedings; and Velasquez, Governor of Cuba, furious at his exclusion from enterprises which had already borne such famous fruits, fitted out a new expedition, the command of which was entrusted to a brave but rash cavalier, named Pànfilo de Narvaez. This person was to supersede Cortés, to deprive him of his command, and proceed against him as a rebel. But Narvaez, lax in discipline, shallow in judgment and arrogantly confident of himself, was not the man to cope with Cortés. Yet he was provided with an overwhelming force; his squadron consisted of eighteen vessels, carried a thousand Spaniards, and as many Indians: eighty of the former were cavalry, eighty arquebusiers, and one hundred and fifty cross-bowmen. The expedition was amply supplied with heavy guns, military stores and ammunition. It was one of the bravest armaments that had ever ridden in the Indian seas.

Cortés was seasonably apprized of his dangers. His people were true to him, and he had friends, or soon made them, among the followers of Narvaez. Conscious that he risked all that had been gained in leaving Mexico, he was yet equally aware of the necessity of meeting his new enemy. His precautions and preparations for all events, the details of which must be sought in the history, were all singularly admirable and effective. Under Alvarado, one of his best captains, he left one hundred and forty men in the capital — two-thirds of his whole force. With these he left his artillery, and the greater part of his horse and arquebusiers. He took with him but seventy soldiers, but they were picked men, — veterans, whose sterling mettle had been tried in a thousand dangers. Six months after his entry into Mexico, about the Middle of May, 1520, he went forth, the master of an Indian empire, to save it from the rapacious hands of his own countrymen. His march was rapid. In celerity lay his safety. On his way he was joined by Sandoval, another of his captains, with a body of soldiers from the garrison of Vera Cruz, and several deserters from Narvaez. His force was now increased to two hundred and sixty-six men. Frequent embassies had passed between himself and his enemy. The latter was reported to be puffed up with conceit, and unpopular with his soldiers. Cortés declared himself willing to submit, if he could produce a royal commission. But that of Velasquez, he was not prepared to recognize. The parties could not be reconciled. Arrived at the *Rio de Canoas*, Cortés was but a league distant from the camp of Narvaez, which was at Cempoalla. The river was swollen by recent rains. The storm had not spent its fury. He paused for a while, and suffered his men to rest till night. Then, he resumed his march, and, crossing the river with difficulty, in the very highest of the tempest, he penetrated the camp of his unconscious foe. No sound was made, no drum beaten, no trumpet sounded, until each division of his little force had reached the point assigned it. Then came the storm of men and weapons with that of the elements. Stupified by sleep, blinded by the tempest, uncertain where to go, or whom to strike, the soldiers of Narvaez rose from their repose only to be overcome. The fight was not of long duration. Narvaez was struck down by the thrust of a spear which deprived him of an eye, and his cry of pain and terror was followed by the triumphant shout of Cortés, which announced the easy victory. The proud Narvaez, in chains, suffering from the mortification of defeat and wounds, said to Cortés when they met, — "You have great reason to thank fortune for having given you the day so easily, and put me in your power." "I have much to be thankful for," said Cortés in reply, "but, for my victory over you, I esteem it as one of the least of my achievements since my coming into this country." [25] The truth embodied in the repartee, gave peculiar force to its sting. The affair, notwithstanding the modest pride in the answer of Cortés, was a most brilliant piece of generalship.

The conquered troops became his own, and in good season. Mexico was in revolt. The Spaniards were assaulted in their quarters, — the brigantines burnt upon the lakes, — several of the garrison were killed, and many wounded. The work of conquest was to be begun anew. The forces of Cortés, on reaching Tlascala, were a thousand foot and one hundred horse. He obtained two thousand soldiers from the Tlascalans. With these he advanced upon Mexico. His garrison there was closely besieged. His presence relieved it. Mexico was re-entered by the Spanish chieftain, without fighting, on the 24th June, 1520. The rashness, if not the cupidity, of Alvarado, had occasioned the outbreak. But the Aztecs were ripe for it before. A massacre of the people took place, by the Spaniards, at one of their public festivals, in which many of their nobility were slain. Alvarado excused himself by alleging that he had proofs that this festival was to be made an occasion for insurrection. He had simply anticipated their purpose. In all probability there were mixed motives at work, producing the event. Cupidity on the one hand, provocation on the other, and the

[25] Prescott, p. 395.

natural jealousy of two rival races, so closely in contact, yet entertaining such sentiments of mutual distrust and hate. The judgment of Cortés upon Alvarado, may be recognized as just. "You have done badly," said he, after he had heard his explanation. "You have been false to your trust. Your conduct has been that of a madman." [26] Vexed with himself, and at the unhappy choice which he had made in the captain of his garrison, Cortés was betrayed into unusual impatience of manner and remark. The dangers were accumulating around him, — among them that of famine. The Mexicans no longer supplied their markets; and when he spoke angrily and contemptuously on the subject to the attendants of Montezuma, they disappeared only to make the matter worse. The next day the city was in rebellion, — the drawbridges were raised, — the great avenues leading to the capital were swarming with warriors, — the terraces and *azoteas*, or flat roofs, in the neighbourhood of the quarters of the Spaniards, covered with combatants, watchful of every opportunity to wing a shaft or missile. The whole immense population of the valley of Tenochtitlan was in arms for the expulsion of the invader.

We cannot linger for details. The war was begun with all the energies of a vast military nation thoroughly excited, — a proud people, wounded to the quick in all their sensibilities, — pride of character, religious sentiment, reverence for their kings and for their deities, — affection and patriotism. Mexico alone contained a population of three hundred thousand souls, and the cities by which she was encircled, though greatly inferior, were also greatly populous. They were all united for the common object. Generalship there was none. The masses swarmed around the Spanish quarters, and were mowed down in battalions by the musketry and cannon. It was the old contest of the naked man against the armed — the highest form of European civilization against the untaught savage. But num-

[26] Prescott, pp. 407–408.

bers reconciled this inequality. Thousands perished, but the Mexicans were undismayed, and strove against death at the very muzzles of the blazing guns. The conflict only ended with the night. With dawn the battle was renewed, and ended with the day, to be resumed again with the morrow. The Spaniards were again victorious, but the Mexicans were not to be defeated. Cortés sallied forth with his horse, exhibited prodigious valour, committed immense havoc, and, with a chivalrous disregard of himself, encountered the greatest dangers in defending the meanest of his men, which endeared him the more deeply to their affections. He was severely wounded; but his reflections after the fight occasioned sufferings more severe. His eyes at once opened upon all his dangers. He felt how much his impatience had erred — how much he had mistaken the Aztec character; and he resolved to conciliate their monarch whom he had rather avoided since his return. When, therefore, the return of the ensuing day showed that the fight was to be renewed, Montezuma was required to interpose between the invaders and his subjects. He consented with reluctance, declaring his belief that the effort would be in vain — that the Mexicans would not give ear to his entreaties. Surrounded by a guard of Spaniards, and several Aztec nobles, clothed in the imperial robes, with a diadem upon his head, he ascended the central turret of the palace. As he advanced along the battlements, a change like that of magic, overspread the combatants. The strife ceased, the cries of battle were silenced, many prostrated themselves upon their faces before a monarch, once, and still, so much venerated. But when he spoke for peace, and for the strangers, a murmur ran through the multitude. Their furious passions were not to be restrained — overleapt all barriers, and the cries of scorn and bitterness which replied to his address, were followed by a cloud of missiles. The Spanish guards interposed their bucklers, but too late. Three of the missiles took effect upon the monarch, and he fell to the ground from a stone, which struck him on the temple, and left him senseless. Shocked at their own passionate deed, the Mexicans dispersed in terror from the spot. The last scene in the destiny of Montezuma, followed soon. He died, rather of a broken heart, than of his injuries. These might have been cured but he refused help — tore way the bandages from his wounds, and declared his anxiety to die, as the only means of escaping from disgrace. He rejected the proffered rites of Christian salvation, saying — "I have but a few moments to live, and will not, at this hour, desert the faith of my fathers." [27] He was the victim of a fate which a less superstitious mind must easily have baffled.

The hours that he yet lingered, after his injuries, were employed by the Spaniards in fighting. The panic of the Mexicans was of short duration. They had returned to the conflict. Opposite to the Spanish quarters, at the distance of a few rods only, there stood the great *teocalli* of an Aztec god. The mound, with the sanctuaries that crowned it, completely commanded the palace occupied by the Spaniards. This position was taken by a select body of Mexicans, five or six hundred in number, directed by many of their nobles, and warriors of the highest distinction. From this elevation they hurled their missiles upon the Christians, with equal certainty and profusion. It was necessary to dislodge them. Cortés assigned this duty to Escobar, with a hundred men. But he was thrice repulsed. It was necessary that he should himself undertake the enterprise. His left hand was badly wounded, but he fastened his buckler upon the arm and thus made it useful. We cannot narrate the particulars of the conflict which ensued. Enough that, fighting step by step, he gained the summit of the teocalli, one hundred and fifty feet in air. Here, in the sight of the whole city, Cortés and his comrades met in deadly and close combat with the best warriors of Mexico. The hostile parties

[27] Prescott, p. 435.

forbore the struggle below, to gaze, terrified and anxious, upon that above. The area was large enough for the meeting of a thousand combatants. It was paved with broad flat stones. The edge of the area was without parapet or battlement. "Quarter was neither asked nor given; and to fly was impossible. The least slip would be fatal; and the combatants, as they struggled in mortal agony, were sometimes seen to roll over the steep sides of the precipice together." [28] Cortés himself narrowly escaped this dreadful fate. Two of the Aztec warriors had devoted themselves to his destruction. They were willing to perish for this object. They were men of great muscle and vigour, and, simultaneously seizing upon him, they dragged him towards the brink of the precipice. But Cortés was a man of wonderful strength and agility. The struggle was one of giants — of life and death. By an earnest concentration of all his vigour, at the happy moment, he succeeded in releasing himself from his assailants, one of whom he hurled, with his own arm, into the terrible abyss. The battle lasted three hours. The teocalli remained in the hands of the Spaniards. The gods and shrines of the Aztecs were delivered to the flames in their fight. But they were unsubdued, unshaken, and a new day only opened upon newer conflicts. We cannot pursue these issues, the result of which was that Cortés must abandon his conquest for the time. But if ever mortal genius warred valiantly against necessity, it was his. There is a point beyond which human strength may not prevail, and this only did the Spanish General forbear. Mind and body strove, equally strong, against the iron fate which impelled his departure, and it was with the composure of a mighty spirit that he at length resigned himself to a necessity which he was no longer able to avert. Compelled to fly from Mexico, every precaution was taken to render flight successful, and, on the night of the first of July, 1520, the gates of the Spanish quarters were

[28] *Ibid.*, pp. 425-426.

silently thrown open, and the Christian army set forth amid clouds and rain, only too happy if, in the gloom which covered earth and sky, they should escape the keen eyes of their vigilant enemies. But they were not fortunate in this hope. Their flight was discovered, and the huge drum in the temple of the Aztec war god, announced to the exulting Mexicans the departure of the hated strangers. Rising at the signal, the masses poured forth from street, and house, and citadel — from lake and suburb, like a forest of hungry wolves, infuriate in winter for their prey. The horrors of that night, to this day known in Spanish chronicle as "the melancholy night" — *Noche Triste* — who shall describe? We are reminded but of one parallel to its terrors in the wide pages of modern history — the passage of the Beresina — the flight from Moscow! The details alone, copious, peculiar, full of wondrous struggles of man for life, man against his deadly enemy, man maddened by desperate fear and by a hate as desperate — would suffice for its proper comprehension. We shall attempt no particulars. The history, itself, will but imperfectly describe the dreadful character of that night-long conflict, ended not with dawn, and arrested only by the sheer exhaustion of the Aztecs. Freed, at length, from the press of enemies, Cortés could look about him and comprehend the full extent of his disaster. He wept at the survey, but his tears were those of manhood, that weeps only the irreparable. His soul was still unyielding. His depression never impaired the hope that looked forward to the raising of the curtain which kept the wondrous drama from its glorious dénouëment. Already he meditated the means for the re-conquest of the great city which he had been just compelled to abandon. And yet his present escape was still doubtful. The Mexicans, in small bodies, hung upon his steps, assailed his flanks, and vaunted his destruction as an approaching event. "Go on," they cried, "go on! You go to your doom." [29]

[29] Paraphrase of Prescott, *Conquest of Mexico*, p. 457.

Their meaning was soon read as the weary Spaniards reached the heights that looked down on the valley of Otumba. The whole force of Mexico awaited him in this spot. Far as the eye could reach were to be seen the white garments, the waving banners, the shining helmets and shaking spears, of the Aztec chivalry. They had gathered, in confident hope, as the eagles to their prey. Perilous, indeed, was the prospect for the weary and dispirited Christians. But Cortés addressed himself to the danger, with all the manhood of his most hopeful hours. A few words to his followers, and a short prayer to God — commending himself and people to His protection and the care of the Virgin — and the fearless captain led his small battalions into the very heart of the enemy's array. The day went against him. Slaying was not conquering. Where hundreds of the Aztecs fell, thousands rushed to fill the ranks. The Spaniards were engulphed by the myriads with whom they fought. Most of them were wounded — Cortés, himself, twice, and upon the head. His horse, wounded also, was abandoned for another. The field seemed no longer doubtful. The event was almost decided against him, when the keen eye of the Christian chief distinguished, by the peculiarity of his decorations, the commander of the Aztec forces. A body of young warriors — the flower of the Indian nobles — guarded his person and the sacred emblem of Aztec sovereignty which he bore. The value of this badge was known to our hero. A single glance sufficed, and the instant mind of Cortés conceived the mode of extrication. Turning quickly to a select number of his cavaliers, he exclaimed — "There is our mark! Follow me!" His war cry rose again above the clamour, and, striking his iron heel into his steed, he plunged into the thickest array, solicitous only of the one object. He attained it! The ferocity of his attack was successful. His lance struck the Mexican commander to the ground, and, in the loss of their sacred banner, the Mexicans lost the victory. All was panic in their ranks. They fled in the blindest terror, and, wondering at their own unlooked for successes, the Spaniards remained to reap the rich spoils with the glory of the field. They reached the friendly city of Tlascala without farther annoyance.

Of the subsequent jealousies of the Tlascalans, of the discontents among the Spaniards, it needs not that we should say more than that the genius and the star of Cortés, succeeded in soothing the one and subduing the other. He himself was prostrated on a bed of sickness, and the events around him, and the tidings from abroad, seemed to work adversely to his fortunes. But, let not the brave mind tremble in adversity. Great men are strengthened by trials, as muscle is made by toil. It is the pressure upon the soul that makes it speak and work, and bound and glow, in the consciousness of the resources that might else rest in inglorious repose within. The mind of Cortés rose above its difficulties. His good star was not to be baffled. "Fortune," says he, in a letter to Charles the Fifth, "favours the brave. The Spaniards are the followers of the cross. Trusting in the mercy of God, I cannot believe that HE will suffer them and His own good cause to perish among them. I am resolved not to descend to the coast, but, at all hazards, to retrace my steps, and once more beard the foe in his capital." [30] How admirably does ambition deceive itself with the words of piety. If Cortés was not a Christian, he certainly believed that he was doing the work of one. And who shall say that he was not? Who shall say that a less determined warrior, a less sanguinary people, could have succeeded in the overthrow of those bloody superstitions which daily immolated thousands of God-made men, on the shrines of the horrid Moloch of Aztec superstition!

We pass over subordinate events, including his conquest over certain of the Aztec allies and tributaries, in which his followers regained their former confidence in the superiority

[30] Prescott, *Conquest of Mexico*, pp. 470–471.

of their arms. The details are replete with proofs of the wonderful sagacity and resource of their leader. It is not the least remarkable feature in the history of a great conqueror, that the tribes which submit to his arms, are always made faithful by his moderation and justice. His men were recovered from their wounds. They had regained their courage. Fortune had brought unlooked for reinforcements to their strength, and, confident of support from the Tlascalan and other neighbouring people, and taught by experience in what manner to avoid former errors, Cortés prepared to resume his design against Mexico. But the boldest conception of purpose, as essential to his object, was that of framing vessels at Tlascala, to be taken in pieces, on the shoulders of the *tamanes,* to the lakes of Mexico. A fleet was to be borne on the shoulders of naked men, across forest and mountain, for a distance of sixty miles, before it could be launched upon its destined waters. The conception was worthy of the genius of a great captain. It is not surpassed in history. Yet, what a proof of the prescience of Cortés, that he should, when commanding the destruction of the fleet at Vera Cruz, have insisted upon the preservation of the iron, the bolts, and sails and cordage. Without this fleet, he could not have succeeded against the capital. While his workmen were busy in its preparation, he commenced his march. His force of Spaniards fell little short of six hundred men. He had been fortunate in adding to his strength by the acquisition of more than one small body of adventurers, who, cast upon the shores at Vera Cruz, readily agreed to follow his superior fortunes. Forty of his men were horse, eighty arquebusiers and crossbow men — the rest were armed with sword and target, and with a long copperheaded pike which Cortés had borrowed from the people of Chinantla. He had nine pieces of cannon, but his supply of powder was small. To this force was added a multitude of native warriors, from Tlascala, Cholula, Tepeaca, and other territories. Before setting out on his expedition, he published a code of ordinances for his army which remarkably display his character. These insist upon order as the great law, equally divine and human — upon the conversion of the heathen as the great object of the expedition — prohibit blasphemy and gambling, brawls, and private combats, with other laws of a like nature equally calculated to promote discipline, general propriety, temperance and honesty, and to elevate the character of the common soldiery. The ordinances, we may add, were enforced with undeviating severity. The march took place in December. It was tedious and painful, rather than dangerous. Clouds of dusky warriors hung upon his footsteps, but afforded no serious obstacle. His cavalry brushed them from his path in a few resolute charges. The policy of the Mexicans does not seem to have designed meeting their powerful enemies in open field. Their present sovereign was Guatemozin, a nephew to the last monarch, but very much his superior. His superstitions did not maim his courage. He was young, not more than twenty-five, "elegant," says Bernal Diaz, "in his person, for an Indian, valiant, and so terrible, that his followers trembled in his presence." [31] He had considerable military genius, great sagacity, and if any Aztec could have retrieved the fortunes of his country, and remedied the disasters of the preceding reign, he was the man. He had distinguished himself in battle, and, hating the Spaniards with the sort of religious hate which Hannibal is said to have had against Rome, he accepted the sovereignty of his country at a time when its perilous honours might well have discouraged the ambition of any common spirit. He was not unworthy to oppose the genius and the arms of Cortés.

On the 31st December, 1520, the Spaniards once more entered the venerable city of Tezcuco, once the rival capital to Mexico, eminent upon one of the lakes which occupy the

---

[31] Prescott, pp. 489–490.

basin of Tenochtitlan. The place was comparatively deserted.
Its lord had fled, and Cortés elevated another to the throne.
His next movement was upon the city of Iztapalapan, which
he took after a desperate resistance. But the fierce resolve of
the savages almost converted his victory into a defeat. While
the soldiers were engaged in the sack and destruction of the
city, the Aztecs had broken down the mole which fenced out
the waters of Lake Tezcuco. The country was laid under
water, and the Spaniards, loaded with booty, and struggling
waist deep in the lake, were assailed by their enemies, who,
swarming the basin with their canoes, assailed them with
deadly missiles. Their escape was difficult, and their Indian
allies suffered prodigious loss. It was evident to Cortés, not
only that the Aztecs were counselled by captains of great
character and spirit, but that they had come into the field
with that self-sacrificing spirit of patriotism from which it is
scarcely possible to expect too much. It was equally necessary
that he should be wary as well as brave.

The fate of Iztapalapan helped his progress. It struck terror
to the hearts of the other cities, and gained him allies among
the contiguous tribes. Other battles followed, and the town of
Chalco was added to his conquests. The war had no respite,
and the progress of the Spaniards was continual. Every day
gave them new victories and new allies. The policy of Cortés
conciliated friends quite as rapidly as his arms overthrew enemies. He extinguished the hereditary feuds of ages, and united
tribes in a common object, which had been at variance a thousand years. In the full tide of his successes, he sent an embassy
of captive nobles to Mexico, proposing favourable terms for
its surrender, — proposing the confirmation of Guatemozin in
his authority, if the city would return to its allegiance. To
this the brave Aztec deigned no answer. His determination
was made to defend the empire to the last.

With the arrival of the brigantines from Tlascala, Cortés

prepared to prosecute the conquest. There were thirteen vessels of different sizes. They were yet to be put together, rigged, equipped and made ready for service. A canal was to be dug for the purpose, — a work of immense labour; and, while thousands of the allies, and a select body of Spaniards, were assigned these duties at Tezcuco, Cortés resolved on reconnoitering the capital. Early in the spring, he left Tezcuco, with three hundred and fifty Spaniards, and the main strength of his allies. He had advanced but a few leagues, when he was compelled to skirmish with a considerable body of Mexicans. These he drove before him. At the insular town of Xaltocan, a fierce battle took place, in which he was again successful. Other towns were abandoned at his approach, — the enemy hovering in dark masses in sight of his advance. After two fierce conflicts, he occupied the town of Tacuba, a portion of which was burnt by his wild allies. Every day, during his halt in this place, was employed in fighting with the unwearied Aztecs. In one of these combats, which almost uniformly terminated in favour of the Spaniards, the courage of Cortés had nearly led to his destruction. Heated with the ardour of pursuit, he followed the flying foe upon the great causeway which had once been so fatal to his army. He was led into an ambuscade. When far advanced, the Aztecs, strengthened by fresh troops, turned upon him, and swarms of boats suddenly covered the waters on either hand. A storm of missiles, from lake and causeway, rained upon the Spaniards. Nothing but their coolness and indomitable courage saved them in the retreat. Cortés received, in this affair, another intimation of the superior military conduct of the Aztec warriors. While at Tacuba, he made a second attempt at accommodation with the Indian emperor, but without avail. He was told by the chiefs that Mexico was not now governed by Montezuma! That city was now in a good state of defence. The havoc which had swept its streets was not apparent, — its injuries had been repaired, and the taunts of their warriors invited him once more to penetrate its dangerous passages. He needed no exhortation on this subject. But the time for his battle was not come, and, constantly busy in coercing the towns around, and controlling the avenues to the capital, he waited, with the patience of resolve, the launching of his brigantines. His deeds, meanwhile, were securing him all the results of fame. His name, and the reputation of his armies, had penetrated the whole country. Ambassadors from Indian States on the remotest shores of the Gulf of Mexico, tendered their allegiance, and sought his protection; and reinforcements of Spaniards — a more important acquisition — reached him from Vera Cruz. Cortés employed himself and men in a second reconnoitering expedition, marked by constant conflicts with the savages, in most of which he was successful. These conflicts were no child's play. They were marked by indomitable courage on the part of the enemy, and dangers to the Spaniards which tasked all their own courage and the genius of their leader. But their march was onward, and conquest followed their footsteps. Cuernavaca, a mountain city, was taken, after great labour and a sanguinary conflict. A battle followed at Xochimilco, or "the field of flowers," in which Cortés made another narrow escape. In the thick of battle his horse lost footing and fell. Before he could rise, he received a severe blow on his head. It was with difficulty, assisted by a Tlascalan and two of his servants, that he could regain his feet, shake off his enemies, recover his saddle, and brandish his lance in the face of his enemy. But for the desire of the Aztecs to make him prisoner, he could not have escaped. His life was in their hands. The result of the affair was, as usual, a victory to the Europeans.

This battle was followed by others. Guatemozin made strenuous efforts to recover Xochimilco from the conqueror. His policy was to send detachment after detachment against the Spaniards, so that, even though victorious, they might be wearied out by the war. But he gained nothing by this policy.

The successive defeats only served to dispirit his warriors, and confirm them in their belief of Spanish invincibility. Not caring to continue this warfare, Cortés set fire to the captured city, and returned, though not without frequent fighting, to Tacuba, where he found the canal completed, and his brigantines rigged and equipped, and ready to descend upon the lake. But, before this event could take place, another, of less grateful character, was in progress. Cortés returned to Tacuba to discover conspiracy in his army. A dangerous design was set on foot, menacing his authority and life. It was headed by one Villafana, a common soldier. We need not ask his motives. They may be conjectured. The good star of Cortés prevailed for his safety. One of the conspirators, touched with compunction, betrayed the secret. Without losing a moment, — with that decision which marked his character, — Cortés, attended by a few of his favourite officers, proceeded at once to the quarters of Villafana. The criminal, confounded at the sudden apparition of his commander, and confused by his guilt, endeavoured to swallow a paper which he snatched from his bosom. The prompt grasp of Cortés arrested the movement. Looking over the fatal list, it was with equal surprise and mortification that he read the names of several in whom he had every confidence. But his sagacious mind instantly comprehended the necessity of keeping this discovery to himself. He destroyed the scroll, and contented himself with the execution of the one ringleader. The conspirators trembled, but without cause. The magnanimous judgment of Cortés forbore farther inquiry. In an address to his troops he told them that the guilty man had made no confession. His admirable policy never once suffered them to suppose that he had any suspicion of the guilty parties; but his vigilant eye watched them nevertheless, — they were never permitted to see how closely.

At length, the curtain rose upon the last act in the great

drama of the conquest. On the 28th of April, 1521, the brigantines were borne through the canal upon the lake. The event was marked by due solemnity. Mass was said, and the whole army received the sacrament; prayers were offered up, and a benediction invoked upon the little navy, the first ever launched by Europeans upon the waters of America. It was a proud moment for Cortés. It was the triumph of his peculiar genius, — the harbinger of its final triumph over fortune and Tenochtitlan. His forces numbered more than a thousand men. His material and appointments were superior to what they had ever been before. Three hundred of his men were assigned to the vessels, each of which carried a heavy piece of ordnance. His Indian confederates were summoned to the siege. Fifty thousand of these came from Tlascala. But, we hurry over the preparations, — over numerous events, highly interesting in themselves, but too much calculated to crowd our pages and distract the single interest which is our object. The first opposition which the Spaniards met from the Aztecs, was when they attempted to "cut off the pipes that conducted the water from the royal streams of Chapoltipec to feed the numerous tanks and fountains of the capital." The Aztecs knew the importance of this work, and fought desperately to save it, but the Spaniards prevailed. A part of the aqueduct was demolished, and water, from this source, no longer found its way to the capital. The flotilla of Cortés, commanded by himself, was soon environed by clouds of canoes; but there was no fight. The frail vessels of the savages were overswept by the advancing brigantines, and such a slaughter followed, as to leave the Spaniards forever after in full possession of the Aztec Sea. This afforded them vast advantages in every conflict along the causeways leading to the capital. But the courage of the Indians seemed to increase with their disasters. The fighting was incessant, by night as well as day. The two principal avenues to Mexico were soon in the hands of the assailants. There yet remained a third, by which the besieged could still maintain their communications with the country, and effect their escape. This was finally taken possession of by the Christians, and, with these avenues in their power, and in full command of the lakes, the blockade of the capital was complete.

But Cortés was not the man to carry on the war by blockade merely. His warfare was active also. His vessels on the lake were made to co-operate with his troops upon the causeway, until, step by step, the Aztecs were driven from every position along the avenues. The breaches which they had left by tearing away the bridges, were filled up, and, securing a solid and secure passage for his horse and artillery, Cortés at length confined his opponents to the limits of the city, into which he penetrated, destroying the dwellings as he advanced, that they might give no shelter to his numerous enemies. In this way, the Spaniards reached the old quarters which they had held in the time of Montezuma. The Mexicans fled for refuge into the sacred enclosure of the *teocalli*. Here the priests, from the terraces, in their wild and bloody vestments, chanted to their gods, and shouted encouragement to their warriors. The Spaniards poured into the area, and a party, rushing up the winding steps of the *teocalli* to its summit, hurled the priests headlong down the sides of the pyramid, and stripped the horrid image of the Aztec war-god of its gorgeous decorations. This profanation aroused the fury of the Aztec warriors, and reinvigorated their courage. A dreadful fight ensued, in which their reckless desperation proved more than a match for Spanish discipline. A rout ensued. The voice of Cortés was no longer heeded by his men in the eagerness of their apprehensions. Nothing saved them but the sudden appearance of a small body of cavalry, by which they were rescued. The horse and rider were still objects of terror to the Mexicans. Cortés beheld their hesitation, availed himself of the movement, and drove them back to the enclosure, while he ordered a retreat.

A second attack upon the capital soon followed, distinguished, like the former, by a struggle, step by step, in which the immense numbers and dogged valour of the foe, atoned for their inferior capacity for war. This time, however, in penetrating into the city as he had done before, Cortés resolved upon a measure by which the more completely to intimidate, and perhaps impress the superstitious feelings of the Aztecs. He fired the venerable abode of their monarchs, — the House of Birds, — and other fabrics equally dear to the eyes and imaginations of their people. The result was not what he expected. It made them desperate rather than desponding; and the task of extrication, that night, from their thronging myriads, was equally difficult as on the day before. Day by day, in the same manner, was the assault continued, and each day brought him nearer to his object.

Guatemozin, meanwhile, was doing all within the province of Indian warfare to save his empire. We cannot detail the process by which he contrived to relieve the labours and maintain the valour of his men. His conduct was conspicuous in all their efforts, and his adroitness enabled him even to capture one of the Spanish brigantines, and render another useless. The contest was waged at the same time on the lake, on the causeways and in the city. The Aztec monarch was true to himself and empire. But famine began to press upon his people. Deserted by their allies, hemmed round by hostile legions, unsuccessful in the fight and unable to escape, they yet betrayed no terrors. Their spirits were unbroken, even though pestilence began to show itself among them — the most terrible of all the allies of famine.

Cortés strove vainly to save them. He offered to spare their lives and city. He implored them, by means of captives whom he dismissed, to be merciful to themselves, and, by timely concession, to avoid their own and the destruction of their country. But they heard his proffers with scorn — they had no thought of submission.

Impatient of this obstinacy, the high-mettled cavaliers of the Spanish army urged their General to a *coup-de-main*. To this he was opposed. The time had not come. He allowed himself, however, to be overruled, and the result confirmed his opinions. The army entered to the assault in three divisions — one of which he led in person. The others were entrusted to brave, but hot-headed officers, who rushed head-long into a cunning snare laid for them by the Aztecs. The division led by Cortés, himself, was successful in its objects; but terrible was the result to the others. His whole efforts were now addressed to saving them from the destruction by which they were threatened. "I will die rather than desert my poor followers in extremity!" And narrow, indeed, was his escape in this magnanimous endeavour. He became a conspicuous mark for his enemies. "Malinche! Malinche!" was their cry, as they hurled their missiles and darts, their stones and arrows, at his person. Six of their most athletic warriors rushed upon him at the same instant, striving to drag him into their boats by which the causeway was environed. He was disabled by a severe wound in the leg, and, prostrate, was only saved by the desperate exertions of two devoted followers. These baffled the enemy for a moment, and gained time for the approach of the captain of his guard, who, with several others, succeeded in tearing him from the grasp of the enemy who were struggling with him in the water. He was once more raised upon the causeway. One of his pages, leading him a horse, was struck down with a javelin. Guzman, his chamberlain, seized the bridle, but as Cortés mounted, the faithful attendant was snatched away by the Aztecs, and dragged to their canoes. While the General lingered, unwilling to leave the spot, his bridle was seized by a faithful follower, who hurried him away from a conflict in which no skill or valour could well prevail against the immense numbers which opposed them. The danger was not even then over, nor the escape easy. Cortés, at length, regaining firm ground, rallied his broken squadrons under the fire of his artillery, and, charging at the head of a body of horse, which had not been in the action, beat off the infuriate enemy. Speaking comparatively, the Spaniards had suffered a terrible defeat. "It is for my sins," said Cortés, "that it has befallen me!" [32] That night the war drum in the great temple of the Mexicans was heard. It denoted some solemn ceremonial, — and as the Spaniards looked out they could behold a long procession, winding up the steps of the great pyramid — and could detect among the figures, the white skins of their brother Christians — captives taken in the dreadful conflict of the day — stripped to the waist, and decorated for the horrid sacrifice of the Aztec Moloch.

The Mexicans, elated by these events, gave themselves up to unmeasured exultation. The priests assured them that the wrath of their offended deities was appeased. They predicted that, before the end of eight days, all their enemies should be delivered into their hands. This prediction had an equal effect upon the Mexicans themselves, and upon the superstitious allies of the Spaniards. Company after company deserted. But a few faithful chiefs, with their followers, remained, and these were not wholly uninfluenced by the prediction. Cortés was firm under this defection. He treated the prophecy with scorn, and simply requested the retreating squadrons to halt upon the road until its falsehood should be shown by the lapse of the appointed time. The Spaniards themselves, encouraged by the constancy of their General, were undismayed. They yielded none of their resolution, relaxed in no degree the severity of the blockade, and still, with prompt carnage, of musketry and cannon, swept away the long files of the Aztecs

[32] Prescott, *Conquest of Mexico*, p. 580.

at every fresh assault. The brigantines, still in possession of the lake, made effectual the *cordon* about the beleaguered city.

That great triumph of Guatemozin was his last. His priests had blundered in fixing the time of their prediction. Supplies of ammunition and military stores came from Vera Cruz. The war was to be resumed with new resolve. The determination of Cortés, now, was to advance no step without securing the safety of the army. Every breach in the causeway, every canal, was to be filled up as soon as it was gained. The buildings were to be pulled down for this purpose. Palace, temple, hut — all were to be demolished in his path. The cavalry and artillery must have room for exercise. This was a painful necessity which Cortés was slow to admit. He wished to spare the city, which he styles "the most beautiful thing in the world," but this desire was inconsistent with its conquest. His losses and defeats had arisen only from this anxiety, which, springing from a moral emotion — the love of the beautiful — is one that should escape the censure, even of the mere man of policy. The war was renewed. The work of desolation advanced. The Mexicans struggled on, in spite of famine and other woes. Their provisions were exhausted. They lived on rats and reptiles, on the mucilaginous weeds and scum which floated upon the lake. Verily, their resolution was worthy of that ancient Spanish town, which, in the wars of Rome, opposed itself, through like perils and necessities, to the conquests of the great Scipio.[33] One more effort was made by Cortés to subdue the resolution of Guatemozin. But in vain. The stubborn Prince forbade that any of his followers should hereafter, on pain of death, speak of surrender. The answer of the Mexicans, for which the Spaniards waited two days, was spoken with their weapons in a general sortie. Their strength was not equal to their fury. The attempt betrayed their im-

[33] Humantia, a Spanish city razed by Scipio Aemilianus in 133 B.C. after fourteen months of siege.

potence — they recoiled from the dreadful fire of artillery and musketry from causeway and brigantine, which received their columns — recoiled and shrunk back into the yet secure quarters of the capital, wearied and fainting with their futile endeavours.

These were not destined long to be secure. The work of demolition went forward. Cortés, with all the inflexibility of a destroying angel, steadily pursued his plan for making sure his footsteps. The citadel whence he drove the savages, was immediately cast down by his pioneers. Palace, and temple, and dwelling, shared the same fate. Daily, with this labour before them, the several divisions of the Spanish entered the departments of the city which were assigned them for destruction. Their progress was slow, but terribly certain. The very slowness of the operation, as it betrayed the patience of the invader, declared his unyielding determination. Vainly did the Aztecs rage from their high places where they yet lingered. Their lordly edifices were tumbled into the canals before their eyes. Dry land occupied the place of water. Ruin raised his mutilated front where stood the consecrated tower. There was fighting still, daily and continued struggles, but it was without effects, save where it helped on the invader. Weeks were consumed in these struggles and these labours, and the Aztecs were as unyielding as the Spaniards. We should occupy too much space to attempt the description of even the most terrible of their conflicts. Devoted as they were to death, they might well fight to desperation. The ordinary means of subsistence had long since failed them. They gnawed the bark of trees, the roots of the earth — they drank brackish water from the lakes. Pestilence followed in the train of famine. They sickened and died in the highways, their bodies lying, unburied and putrifying, in court yard and canal. The famishing survivors looked like spectres, but without the power to affright. Their dwellings presented yet more appalling sights.

While some were struggling in the agonies of death, others were festering in corruption. Women and children perishing of hunger, men mangled in battle, and crawling from sight, on the approach of the invader, as it were, in the very mockery of life. But, impotent as they were, and amidst all this suffering, the Aztecs breathed nothing of submission. They had imbibed the indomitable spirit of their monarch, and the people were as one man. The women shared their spirit, and standing by their feeble warriors in battle, prepared their slings, supplied their stones and arrows, and confronted all danger at their sides, with the constantcy of a temper that already knew the worst.

At length, the invaders reached the market-place of Mexico, a vast inclosure covering many an acre. They had gained it after a dreadful struggle. They had passed the single canal which lay in their way. They had won the huge teocalli of the Aztec war god, and consigned its sanctuary to the flames. These successes were not of easy achievement. The defence of these shrines called forth all the spirit of superstition and patriotism. They fought as in the best days of their valour: but they fought against the fates. The genius of the invader mocked their struggles, as impotent against his fortune. They could only howl in piteous lamentations, as, baffling their skill and valour, and defying their deities, they beheld the conquerors firing the consecrated dwellings of gods to whom they had vainly given their faith and confidence.

The young Emperor of the Aztecs, meanwhile, remained courageous and immovable. His capital was in ruin before his eyes. His nobles and subjects were dying around him. The limits of his reign were so narrowed that he might stretch forth his hand, and on every side feel the superior presence of the foe. But he was still unconquered. When Cortés, in the hope that his extremities might induce his submission, persuaded one of his noble captives to bear to Guatemozin pro-

posals to that effect, the stern young monarch, at once commanded the sacrifice of the messenger. Thus baffled in his
desire to save and to spare what remained of the city and its
defenders, Cortés resolved upon a general assault. The fleet
and army prepared to co-operate. While the latter penetrated
the city, the brigantines were ordered to batter the houses near
the water. At this moment some overtures were made by the
Aztecs for accommodation. "Why," said some of the chiefs,
stretching forth their emaciated arms to him as he entered
their precincts — "Why," said they, "are you slow. Why not
put an end to our miseries!" Cortés, moved by the piteous appeal, replied, "I wish not to destroy but save you. Why is
your master obstinate? Why will he not treat with me? I wish
for this — a single hour will suffice for me to crush him and
his people." [34] But the fierce young monarch could not be
persuaded to a conference. He remembered the fate of Montezuma, and distrusted the faith of the Spaniards. Chagrined at
an obstinacy which at once baffled his humanity and policy,
Cortés ordered the assault. His confederate tribes were un-
leashed for the conflict, and he penetrated the last hold of the
Aztec warriors. They were ready to receive him — their most
able bodied warriors in the van, covering their feeble and
crippled comrades. The women mingled in their ranks, in the
streets, and on the house tops, looking a fury in their eyes,
which, it was lucky for the Spaniards, could be declared in no
more formidable manner. The fury of men and women was
alike impotent. In vain did they rain their arrows — in vain did
they hurl their missiles upon the invader. They were sent by
feeble sinews. Famine, which had failed to subdue their souls,
had most effectually sapped the vigour of their arms. But
when did men fight more valiantly, and with so little loss of
resolution, from the conviction of its fruitlessness? The inequality of power was too great between themselves and the

[34] Prescott, *Conquest of Mexico*, p. 600.

invaders. While the Spanish arquebusiers poured in their deadly fire on one hand, the brigantines replied by successive vollies on another. The besieged, hemmed in on every side, girt by death, opposed themselves in vain to the torrent. The carnage was horrible; the ground was heaped with slain, and the maddened combatants could only meet in conflict by climbing over the mortal mounds which havoc had raised between them. The narrative, as given by Mr. Prescott, is a terrible one. We had marked it for extract, as a fair specimen of his writing, but our space will not suffer its insertion. Enough that, when sated with slaughter, the Spanish retreat was sounded. Forty thousand men are said to have perished in the work of that one dreadful day.

Such conflicts must soon terminate. No courage, no resolve or resource, can stand them long. The next day, which was the 13th of August, 1521, a day memorable as the close of this dreadful struggle, Cortés prepared to renew the assault. But, willing to afford one more chance of escape to the wretched Aztecs, he sent another message to Guatemozin. The answer was, "Guatemozin is ready to die where he is — he will hold no interview with the Spaniard. It is for him to work his pleasure." "Away, then," said the stern conqueror, "away to your countrymen, and let them prepare for death. The hour is come!" [35] He nevertheless postponed the assault for several hours, in the hope that some change might be induced in the inflexible spirit of the Indian. He seemed reluctant to urge the last desperate measures against so brave an enemy. But his troops murmured at the delay. Rumours were spread that the Aztec monarch was preparing to escape across the lake, and the Spanish General reluctantly gave the signal for the assault. This was, in other words, the signal for massacre. Cortés placed himself upon an *azotea*, which commanded the scene of operations. The Spaniards found their enemy hud-

[35] Prescott, p. 604.

dled together in a confused crowd of all ages and sexes, in masses so dense as to seem designed less for the purpose of combat, than to facilitate the expected carnage. The causeways were crowded to the water. Some had climbed the terraces; others feebly supported themselves against the walls of the buildings. Their garments were squalid and tattered, and the famine glaring from their eyes, only served to heighten the spectral ferocity of their expression. They possessed the ancient spirit but not its strength, and met the assailants with a flight of arrows. But these feebly seconded their hate. They fell ineffectual from the padded coats of the Spaniards. Then followed the crash of more potent implements of war — the peals of cannon, the sharp, rattling discharge of fire arms, and the shouts, hellish and infuriate, of the herds of Spanish allies, exulting in the near accomplishment of their long contemplated hope of vengeance. Why attempt the description of the horrible scene that followed. Why show the last hopeless struggle of the Aztecs, butchered on the causeways, or gasping in the overwhelming waters in which they sunk on either hand. The battle raged equally on lake and land. The last hope of the lordly race of Tenochtitlan, was extinguished in the bloody horrors of that day. It was at its close when Gautemozin was taken. Bravely, indeed, with a stern resolution worthy of the greatest times and people, had this gallant Indian clung to the falling fortunes of his country. He had done all that man could do in the circumstances under which he stood. He was no mere savage; — but, with the indomitable obstinacy of one, he united large resources of civilization, and superior powers of intellect and observation. His defence of the capital had been singularly adapted, in most respects, to his own and the condition of his enemy. As we have seen, it was unavailing. It was only then that he attempted flight, and this attempt may have contemplated the safety of his wife and followers rather than his own — may have contemplated nothing less than future struggles with the invader, in other places of security and strength. He was not the Roman fool,

> To die by his own sword,[36]

so long as there were hopes of good battle, yet in reserve for his countrymen. In the moment of danger and captivity, he betrayed no apprehension. His surrender was much more dignified than that of Santa Anna at Jacinto. When his piragua was encountered by the brigantine of Garci Holguin, and the Spaniards were about to fire, he was the first to rise, armed with buckler and *maquahuitl*, in defiance to the assailants. But the cry of his followers declared him to be their lord. They could implore mercy for him, having no prayer for themselves. The Spanish captain arrested the fire of his soldiers. At this command, the young monarch lowered his weapons. "I am Guatemozin," he exclaimed, "lead me to Malinche, (Cortés.) I am his prisoner. Let no harm come to my wife and followers." When Holguin told him to command the people in the other canoes to surrender, he replied, with a dejected air, — "It is not necessary. They will fight no longer, when they see that their prince is taken." [37] The fight ceased from that moment. In the conquest of Guatemozin, that of Tenochtitlan was complete. He had been the soul of his empire. It was now a corse, at the mercy of the Spaniard.

When brought into the presence of Cortés, Guatemozin betrayed no sort of apprehension. Emotion he must have shown. His deportment was dignified and modest. As Cortés came forward to receive him, he broke the silence by saying, "I have done all that I could for the defence of my people. I am your prisoner. Deal with me as you list. Dispatch me with this" — laying his hand upon the hilt of a poinard in the General's belt — "and rid me of life at once." Cortés could appre-

---

[36] Paraphrase, *Macbeth*, Act V, scene 8, lines 1–2.
[37] Prescott, *Conquest of Mexico*, p. 606.

ciate the noble character of his captive. "Fear nothing," he replied; "you shall be treated with honour. You have defended your capital like a brave warrior. A Spaniard knows how to respect the valour of his enemy!" [38]

This assurance was unhappily forfeited in the sequel. It is the reproach of Cortés that his noble captive fell a victim to suspicions which do not seem to have been justly founded. He was kept, in a sort of honourable captivity, for some time after the conquest. But, insurrections among his countrymen were laid to his charge. He was put to the torture, and subsequently executed, professing his innocence, reproaching Cortés for his perfidy, and dying like a Prince. Whether the charge were true or not, the better nature of Cortés, when time was allowed for reflection, recoiled at the cruel severity of his proceedings. His conscience smote him for the too ready credence he had given to the accusation, — for the too stern penalty with which he had visited the supposed criminal. He suffered bitterly from a natural remorse, which, while it testifies to his consciousness of crime, at least equally declares the acuteness and justness of his sensibilities, and, we trust, the merit of his repentance.

Thus fell the wondrous empire of the Aztecs, — an empire of the greatest magnificence, great numbers, and immense resources, — an empire upheld by crime, and maintained by cruel wars, — stained by the most shocking rites and governed by the most relentless tyranny, — the wonder of its own people, — the terror of its neighbours, — the admiration of the European. Its destiny was fulfilled by the stranger, as shadowed out by its own traditions. The great drama which began with the fall of Montezuma, by the hands of his subjects, was carried out to stern completion by the sacrifice of the nobler Guatemozin, to the suspicions of the conqueror. And here our narrative might properly conclude. The triumph of our hero

[38] *Ibid.*, p. 607.

is complete. The object of the grand action which makes the glory of his career, is attained. He is at the summit of his conquests. There is no point of elevation, yet beyond, attainable, which is desirable for him to reach. The further survey presents him in less favourable lights, — shows him struggling against injustice, and finally its victim. The last days of a great man, "fallen from his high estate," have something mournful in them, particularly if he shall have been one accustomed to command. Yet, a biographical propriety hurries us forward. A few paragraphs must suffice to close a history, the leading events of which have been already absorbed in the narrative.

Of the subsequent career of Cortés, in fixing the civil power of Mexico and in extending and making sure his conquests, it will be enough in this place to say, that they prove his resources as a statesman to have been quite as remarkable as those which he had shown in the character of the conqueror. He secured the submission of the country, suppressed insurrection, rebuilt the capital, and, by well conceived expeditions, explored its remotest provinces. When this difficult work was all complete, he returned to Spain, where he found a most brilliant reception. His presence confirmed his conquest over his enemies, who were numerous in that quarter. All jealousy of his designs was set at rest. The Emperor ennobled him, and with the title of "Marquess of the Valley of Oaxaca," conferred upon him a princely domain in Mexico. But the future government of the country he had won, was not confided to his hands. In his respect, the suspicious policy of Spain differed in no particular from what it had been in the case of Columbus. Greatness is very apt to be distrusted the moment it ceases to be necessary to conquest, — the moment its achievements and discoveries are sure. A military command was given him. He was named Captain-General of New Spain and of the coasts of the South Sea, — a dignity which simply conferred up on him the privilege of making new conquests — if he could. He subsequently married into a noble house and returned to Mexico, where he was regarded with distrust by the authorities. His eager and proud spirit did not suffer him to remain long in unperformance. He fitted out new expeditions, which were only partially successful. He returned to Castile, where he was received with coldness by the Emperor. His offence was two-fold. He had claims upon the crown, and he was no longer fortunate. We pass over the melancholy history of entreaty met with indifference, and complaint answered with impatience. The fate of Cortés, in seeking justice, is a story which is often read. The aged veteran was thrust aside to make way for younger spirits. The monarch found it easier not to acknowledge obligations which he could not recompense; and, after a fruitless prosecution of his claims for three years, Cortés determined to abandon them and return once more to Mexico. But mortification and disappointment had impaired his health. He was not permitted to re-visit the scene of his conquests, but, taken with a mortal illness, while making preparations for his voyage, he died near Seville, on the 2d December, 1547, in the sixty-third year of his age. He met his end with the same composure with which he had gone into battle, — he made his will, a remarkable document, — confessed his sins, received the holy sacrament, and yielded himself meekly, and with humble confidence, into the hands of his Maker. We read his character in his story. It has been our purpose to make this speak for itself, — to select and bring out the prominent performances of his life, and educe the moral of his life from its successive scenes and performances. What is wanting to our analysis must be supplied by that of Mr. Prescott, to whose delightful history, we trust, we have shown the way to numerous readers.

ARTICLE VI
THE WRITINGS OF
JAMES FENIMORE COOPER [1]

The Two Admirals. A Tale. By the Author of the Pilot, &c. Philadelphia; Lea & Blanchard. 1842.

W<small>E</small> are among those who regard Mr. Cooper as a wronged and persecuted man. We conceive that his countrymen have done him gross injustice — that they have not only shown themselves ungenerous but ungrateful, and that, in lending a greedy ear to the numerous malicious aspersions which have assailed his person and his reputation, they have only given confirmation and strength to the proverbial reproach, of irreverence and ingratitude, to which countries, distinguished by popular governments, have usually been thought obnoxious. [2] We do not mean to regard him as wholly faultless — on the contrary, we look upon Mr. Cooper as a very imprudent person; one whose determined will, impetuous temperament, and great self-esteem, continually hurry forward into acts and expressions of error and impatience. We

[1] Originally published as "Cooper, His Genius and Writings," *Magnolia*, n.s., I (September, 1842), 129–139. Simms's style of referring to titles of works by Cooper and others has been left unchanged.

[2] After his return to America from Europe in 1833, Cooper's growing distaste for certain aspects of the manners and morals of his countrymen and of their abuse (as he saw it) of the democratic system found expression in *A Letter to His Countrymen* (1834); a satire, *The Monikins* (1835); *The American Democrat* (1838); and two fictional attacks, *Homeward Bound* (1838) and *Home As Found* (1838). The newspapers supporting the Whig party bitterly attacked Cooper's character and his works; he retaliated with libel suits in which he was regularly victorious. Simms's defense here is undoubtedly motivated both by his admiration for Cooper and by his desire to defend a fellow anti-Whig. The best studies of this aspect of Cooper's career are Ethel R. Outland, *The "Effingham" Libels on Cooper* (University of Wisconsin Studies in Language and Literature, No. 28, 1929) and Dorothy Waples, *The Whig Myth of Fenimore Cooper* (New Haven, 1938).

propose to compare sides in this question: — to put the case fairly between himself and countrymen, and show where the balance of justice lies.

Of Mr. Cooper, little or nothing was known, by the American people at large, until the publication of "the Spy." [3] To a few, perhaps, the novel of "Precaution" [4] had brought him acquainted. That was a very feeble work — coldly correct, elaborately tame — a second or third rate imitation of a very inferior school of writings, known as the social life novel. In works of this class, the imagination can have little play. The exercise of the creative faculty is almost entirely denied. The field of speculation is limited; and the analysis of minute shades of character, is all the privilege which taste and philosophy possess, for lifting the narrative above the province of mere lively dialogue, and sweet and fanciful sentiment. The ordinary events of the household, or of the snug family circle, suggest the only materials; and a large gathering of the set, at ball or dinner, affords incident of which the novelist is required to make the highest use. Writers of much earnestness of mood, originality of thought, or intensity of imagination, seldom engage in this class of writing. Scott attempted it in St. Ronan's Well, and failed; — rising only into the rank of Scott, in such portions of the story as, by a very violent transition, brought him once more into the bolder displays of wild and stirring romance. He consoled himself with the reflection that male writers were not good at these things. His conclusion, that such writings were best handled by the other sex, may be, or not, construed into a sarcasm.

Mr. Cooper failed egregiously in "Precaution." So far as we know, and as we believe, that work fell still-born from the press. But for the success of "the Spy," and the succeeding works, it never would have been heard of. But "the Spy" was

[3] *The Spy*, published 1821.
[4] *Precaution*, published 1820.

an event. It was the boldest and best attempt at the historical
romance which had ever been made in America. It is somewhat the practice, at this day, to disparage that story. This is
in very bad taste. The book is a good one, — full of faults,
perhaps, and blunders; but full also of decided merits, and
marked by a boldness of conception, and a courage in progress, which clearly showed the confidence of genius in its own
resources. The conception of the Spy, as a character, was a
very noble one. A patriot in the humblest condition of life,
— almost wholly motiveless unless for his country — enduring
the persecutions of friends, the hate of enemies — the doomed
by both parties to the gallows — enduring all in secret, without a murmur, — without a word, when a word might have
saved him, — all for his country; and all, under the palsying
conviction, not only that his country never could reward him,
but that, in all probability, the secret of his patriotism must
perish with him, and nothing survive but that obloquy under
which he was still content to live and labour.

It does not lessen the value of such a novel, nor the ideal
truth of such a conception, that such a character is not often
to be found. It is sufficiently true if it wins our sympathies and
commands our respect. This is always the purpose of the ideal,
which, if it can effect such results, becomes at once a model
and a reality. The character of the "Spy" was not the only
good one of the book. Lawton and Sitgreaves were both good
conceptions, though rather exaggerated ones. Lawton was a
somewhat too burly Virginian; and his appetite was too strong
an ingredient in his chivalry. But, as his origin was British,
this may have been due to the truthfulness of portraiture.

The defect of the story was rather in its action than its characters. This is the usual and grand defect in all Mr. Cooper's
stories. In truth, there is very little story. He seems to exercise none of his genius in the invention of his fable. There is
none of that careful grouping of means to ends, and all, to

the one end of the dénouëment, which so remarkably distinguished the genius of Scott, and made all the parts of his story
fit as compactly as the work of the joiner, — but he seems to
hurry forward in the delineation of scene after scene, as if
wholly indifferent to the catastrophe. The consequence is,
that his catastrophe is usually forced and unsatisfactory. He
is, for this reason, compelled frequently, at the close, to begin
the work of invention; — to bring out some latent matter, —
to make unlooked for discoveries, and prove his hero, be he
hunter or pirate, to have been the son of somebody of unexpected importance; — a discovery which, it is fancied, will
secure him a greater degree of the reader's favour, than he
could have before commanded. Mr. Cooper seems to rely
wholly on the spirit and success of certain scenes. Take, for
example, the work before us. Analyze the parts of the Two
Admirals. The action of the several fleets in the several prog-
resses of the sea, is, in truth, the only portion of the work on
which Mr. Cooper has exercised himself. We may see, also,
in the purposeless career of young Wychecombe, the true,
and Wychecombe, the pretender, how little pains the author
has taken, either in determining, from the first, what they
shall severally be and do, or by what performances their conduct, respectively, shall be distinguished. It is very evident,
from the first introduction of the American Wychecombe,
that he was to become a person of some importance — the
hero, in fact; and, for this, the mind of the reader is insensibly
prepared by the first chapters of the story. Had Mr. Cooper
planned any story at all, this young man must have been the
hero — must have maintained throughout, and concentrated
within himself, the chief interest of the performance. So, on
the other hand, the false Wychecombe, the bastard, was to
be his foil — the villain of the piece — and the conflict between
the two for mastery, is the great issue for which the reader of
the book prepares himself. But, unwilling to give himself the

trouble of inventing situations, by which this issue could be made up or carried on, Mr. Cooper surrenders himself to the progress of events. He leaves to one to beget and occasion the other. Hence the desultory character of his writings; the violence of transition; the strange neglect to which certain of his characters are destined, in whom he at first strives to interest us; and the hard scramble, which the persons of the drama are compelled to make, each to get into his proper place, for the *tableau vivant*, at the falling of the curtain. This young man, Wychecombe, the American, is nothing, and does nothing; and what a poor devil is his foil or shadow, Tom, the *nullus* — "*nullus*" indeed. These persons, brought in with much care, and elaborately portrayed to the reader, are yet — so far as the valuable portions of the story are concerned — left entirely unemployed. The despatching of Wycherley Wychecombe in the Druid, by Admiral Bluewater, to Admiral Oakes, was one of those simple schemes by which the author still endeavoured to maintain an interest in the youth, in whom he felt that he had, at the beginning, too greatly awakened the interest of the readers. The whole machinery here is feeble, and a writer of romance cannot more greatly err than when he subjects his hero to the continual influence of events. We have no respect for heroes placed always in subordinate positions — sent hither and thither — baffled by every breath of circumstance — creatures without will, and constantly governed by the caprices of other persons. This was the enfeebling characteristic in Scott's heroes. Hence it was that the true interest seldom settled on the person whom he chose to be his hero. Look, for example, at his Waverly, — who, contrasted with Claverhouse, or the brother of Flora MacIvor, shrunk into a very petty person. How small a person is his Wilfrid of Ivanhoe, in comparison with Brian de Bois Guilbert; — his Morton with his Burley; his Roland Græme, his Quentin Durward, and, indeed, most of his chosen

heroes, in comparison with numerous other characters employed as their companions and opposites. This defect, which
would be fatal always to purely dramatic composition, must
be equally injurious to works of romance, in which, to a certain extent, all the standards are dramatic, and from the somewhat dramatic development of which, by continual action, the
chief interest and anxiety of the reader are maintained. Availing ourselves of the dramatic *aside,* we may remark *en-passant,*
that the conception of situation in which the two admirals are
placed, in the progress of this story, is particularly admirable
and touching. — Their respective characteristics are fairly
drawn and nicely elaborated, and whenever they have anything to do with the action, they appear to advantage, and
operate in a manner equally characteristic and effective. It is,
perhaps, the great fault of Mr. Cooper, that, conceiving some
few scenes, or even a single one, with great beauty and boldness, he discards from his mind all serious concern for the rest
— for all those by which they are introduced and finished.
These scenes, in consequence, rise up abruptly — and so far
imposingly — like an isolated mountain wall from the dead
level of a plain. We are astonished when we see them, — we
wonder and admire, — but our feet have grown weary in the
search for them, — we have had a long journey, — and the
querulous will be apt to ask, as now they do — "fine sight, indeed, very lofty and imposing, but, was it worth while to
come so far in search of it?" An equal care in the invention of
the fable, at the beginning, would obviate this question. The
traveller would start, as it were, in the morning of the day —
— a cheering sunshine above him — the green woods around
him, and some merry songbirds, inviting his forward progress
with the most seductive notes. Watchful when he is about to
grow weary, his conductor (the novelist) suddenly points his
eye to a sweet stream, which glides, like a silvery serpent,
through the forest, — seen only at moments, and stealing from

sight with a slow sounding but musical murmur which insensibly invites to follow. Easily beguiled, the wayfarer turns aside for an instant, and makes other discoveries. Step by step he is won along — now ravished by flowers, now startled by dreary caverns, wild precipices, and mysterious shadows of rock and forest: Now he passes rivers, and anon the cultivated fields; now he looks on lake or prairie, and now he starts with the sudden rush and tumble of the cataract. At length, towards the close of the day, he arrives at the object of his quest. The desired spectacle, whether grand and terrible, or simply beautiful and sweet, unfolds itself before him. The awful mountain, towering in forbidding grandeur before his eye, or the snow white cottage, smiling in imploring sweetness, at his feet. Around him are the companions of the day — the persons of his story — those who have joyed and those who have wept — the noble hero who led, and the envious rival who would have destroyed — the venerable form that counselled wisdom, or the dear woman that, with greater success, counselled only love. The dénouëment, whether grave or gay, has taken place, and we rejoice in a progress which has warmed our sentiments, inspired just and generous thoughts, informed our affections, and raised our minds in the contemplation of the noblest images of intellect and feelings. Such were Scott's stories. In the gradual progress of the reader, as of a traveller through a new country, the tale carried us on, step by step, from beauty to beauty, from event to event, each beauty becoming brighter and dearer, each event more exciting and interesting, until we reach the crowning event of all; completing, in a fitting manner, and with appropriate superiority, the whole continuous and marvellous history. There was no violence done to the reader's judgment — his sense of propriety or of justice. So insensible was the progress, so natural the transitions, that we gave ready faith to all his wonders, and the eyes became filled with tears, and the breathing suspended, as the events thickened and strove together; generating in our souls, hope and fear, anxious apprehensions, and those emotions, equally exciting and honourable to our nature, which awaken, in unavoidable testimony, to the skill of the consummate artist. This is the harmonious achievement. It is a tolerably easy thing to write a spirited sketch — a startling event — a hurried and passionate delineation of an action, which, in itself, involves, necessarily, strife and hate, and the wilder phrenzies of the human heart and feeling. But the perfecting of the wondrous whole — the admirable adaptation of means to ends — the fitness of parts, — the propriety of the action — the employment of the right materials, — and the fine architectural proportions of the fabric, — these are the essentials which determine the claim of the writer to be the BUILDER! — by whose standard other artists are to model, — by whose labours other labourers are to learn.

The success of the "Spy" was very great, and it at once gave Mr. Cooper reputation in Europe. It may be said to have occasioned a greater sensation in Europe than at home; — and there were good reasons for this. At that period America had no literature. Just before this time, or about this time, it was the favourite sarcasm of the British Reviewers that such a thing as an American book was never read.[5] Mr. Irving, it is true, was writing his sweet and delicate essays; but he was not accounted in England an American writer, and he himself, — no doubt with a sufficient policy — his own fortunes alone being the subject of consideration — took no pains to assert his paternity. The publication of the "Spy" may be assumed to have been the first practical reply to a sarcasm, which, since that day, has found its ample refutation. It was immediately republished in England, and soon after, we believe, found its way into half the languages of Europe. Its farther and more

[5] Sidney Smith, in the *Edinburgh Review*, XXXIII (January, 1820), 79, had asked, "In the four quarters of the globe, who reads an American book?"

important effect was upon the intellect of our own country. It at once opened the eyes of our people to their own resources. It was something of a wonder, to ourselves, that we should be able — (strange, self-destroying humility in a people springing directly from the Anglo-Norman stock) — to produce a writer who should so suddenly, and in his very first work ("Precaution" was not known and scarcely named in that day) rise to such an eminence — equalling most, excelling most, and second to but one, of the great historical romance writers of Britain. This itself was an important achievement — a step gained, without which, no other step could possibly have been taken. It need scarcely be said, that the efforts of a nation at performance, — particularly in letters and the arts, — must first be preceded by a certain consciousness of the necessary resources. This consciousness, in the case of America, was wanting. Our colonial relation to Great Britain had filled us with a feeling of intellectual dependence, of which our success in shaking off her political dominion had in no respect relieved us. We had not then, and, indeed, have not entirely to this day, arrived at any just idea of the inevitable connexion between an ability to maintain ourselves in arts as well as in arms — the ability in both cases arising only from our intellectual resources, and a manly reliance upon the just origin of national strength, — Self-dependence! To Mr. Cooper the merit is due, of having first awakened us to this self-reference, — to this consciousness of mental resources, of which our provincialism dealt, not only in constant doubts, but in constant denials. The first step is half the march, as in ordinary cases, the first blow is half the battle. With what rapidity after that did the American press operate. How many new writers rose up suddenly, the moment that their neighbours had made the discovery that there were such writers — that such writers should be. Every form of fiction, the legend, tale, novel and romance — the poem, narrative and dramatic — were poured out with a prolific abundance, which proved the possession, not only of large resources of thought, but of fancy, and of an imagination equal to every department of creative fiction. It will not matter to show that a great deal of this was crude, faulty, undigested — contracted and narrow in design, and spasmodic in execution. The demand of the country called for no more. The wonder was that, so suddenly, and at such short notice, such resources could be found as had not before been imagined. The sudden rise and progress of German literature seems to have been equally surprising and sudden — equally the result of a national impulse, newly moved in a novel and unexpected direction. The wonderful birth and progress of American letters in the last twenty years — and in every department of thought, art and science, so far from discouraging, because of its imperfections, holds forth the most signal encouragement to industry and hope — showing most clearly, that the deficiency was not in the resource but in the demand, not in the inferior quality, or limited quantity, but in the utter indifference of our people to the possession of the material.

Having struck the vein, and convinced the people not only that there was gold in the land, but that the gold of the land was good, Mr. Cooper proceeded with proper industry to supply the demand which his own genius had occasioned in the markets, as well of Europe as his own country, for his productions. "The Spy" was followed by Lionel Lincoln, the Pioneers, the Last of the Mohicans, the Pilot, Red Rover, Prairie, Water Witch, &c.[6] We speak from memory — we are not so sure that we name these writings in their proper order, nor is this important to us in the plan of this paper, which does not contemplate their examination in detail. All these works were more or less interesting. In most of them, the im-

[6] *Lionel Lincoln,* published 1825; *The Pioneers,* 1823; *The Last of the Mohicans,* 1826; *The Pilot,* 1824; *Red Rover,* 1827; *The Prairie,* 1827; *The Water-Witch,* 1830.

provement in style, continuity of narrative, propriety of incident, &c., was obvious. In all of them were obvious, in greater or less degree, the characteristics of the author. The plots were generally simple, not always coherent, and proving either an incapacity for, or an indifference to the exercise of much invention. The reader was led through long and dead levels of dialogue — sensible enough, — sometimes smart, sarcastic or playful, — occasionally marked by depth or originality of thought, and occasionally exhibiting resources of study and reflection in the departments of law and morals, which are not common to the ordinary novel writer. But these things kept us from the story, — to which they were sometimes foreign, and always in some degree, unnecessary. His characters were not often felicitous, and, as in the case of most writers, Mr. Cooper had hobbies on which he rode too often, to the great disquiet of his friends and companions. He rang the changes on words, as Scott once suffered himself to do, in the "Prodigious" of Dominie Sampson, until readers sickened of the stupidity; and occasionally, as in the case of David Gamut, mistaking his own powers of the humorous, he afflicted us with the dispensation of a bore,[7] which qualified seriously the really meritorious in his performance. But, to compensate us for these trials of our tastes and tempers, he gave us the most exquisite scenes of minute artifice, as in his Indian stories, — in which the events were elaborated with a nicety and patience, reminding us of the spider at his web, that curious and complicated spinner, which may well be employed to illustrate by his own labours and ingenuity the subtle frame-work of Indian cunning — the labyrinth of his artifice, — his wily traps and pitfalls, and indomitable perseverance. In these details of Indian art and resource, Mr. Cooper was inimitable. In

[7] Dominie Sampson, one of Scott's loquacious bores, is in *Guy Mannering*. David Gamut is a psalm-singing bore in Cooper's *The Last of the Mohicans*. Simms created a notorious example of the type in the talkative but cowardly Doctor Nichols in *The Yemassee*.

Indian Woodcraft praised

his pursuits, flights, captures, — in his encounters, — cunning opposed to cunning, — man to man — the trapper and the hunter, against the red man whose life he envies and emulates, — Mr. Cooper has no superior as he has had no master. His conception of the frontier white man, if less true than picturesque, is also not less happy as an artistical conception of great originality and effect. In him, the author embodied his ideal of the philosopher of the foremast — Hawkeye is a sailor in a hunting shirt — and in this respect he committed no error in propriety. The sailor and the forester both derive their philosophies and character from the same sources, — though the one disdains the land, and the other trembles at the sight of the sea. They both think and feel, with a highly individual nature, that has been taught, by constant contemplation, in scenes of solitude. The vast unbroken ranges of forest, to its one lonely occupant, press upon the mind with the same sort of solemnity which one feels condemned to a life of partial isolation upon the ocean. Both are permitted that degree of commerce with their fellow beings, which suffice to maintain in strength the sweet and sacred sources of their humanity. It is through these that they are commended to our sympathies, and it is through the same medium that they acquire that habit of moral musing and meditation which expresses itself finely in the most delightful of all human philosophies. The very isolation to which, in the most successful of his stories, Mr. Cooper subjects his favourite personages, is, alone, a proof of his strength and genius. While the ordinary writer, the man of mere talent, is compelled to look around him among masses for his material, he contents himself with one man, and flings him upon the wilderness. The picture then, which follows, must be one of intense individuality. Out of this one man's nature, his moods and fortunes, he spins his story. The agencies and dependencies are few. With the self-reliance which is only found in true genius, he goes forward into the wilderness, whether of land or ocean; and the vicissitudes of either region, acting upon the natural resources of one man's mind, furnish the whole material of his work-shop. This mode of performance is highly dramatic, and thus it is that his scout, his trapper, his hunter, his pilot, all live to our eyes and thoughts, the perfect ideals of moral individuality. For this we admire them — love them we do not — they are objects not made to love — they do not appeal to our affections so much as to our minds. We admire their progress through sea and forest — their strange ingenuity, the skill with which they provide against human and savage enemies, against cold and hunger, with the same sort of admiration which we feel at watching any novel progress in arts or arms — a noble ship darting like a bird over the deep, unshivering, though the storm threatens to shiver every thing else around it — a splendid piece of machinery which works to the most consummate ends by a *modus operandi,* which we yet fail to detect — any curious and complex invention which dazzles our eyes, confounds our judgment, and mocks the search which would discover its secret principles. Take, for example, the character of the "Pilot," in the rapid and exciting story of that name. Here is a remarkable instance of the sort of interest which Mr. Cooper's writings are chiefly calculated to inspire. Marble could not be more inflexible than this cold, immovable, pulseless personage. He says nothing, shows nothing, promises nothing. Yet we are interested in his very first appearance. Why and how? Naturally enough by the anxiety with which he is sought and looked for; — by the fact that he promises nothing, yet goes to work, without a word, in a manner that promises every thing. We feel, at a glance, that if any mortal man can save the ship, he is the man. Why is this? Simply because he goes to work, without a word, as if it was in him to do so; — as if a calm consciousness of power was his possession; as if he knew just where to lay his hands, and in what direction to expend his strength. He shows *the capacity for work*, and this constitutes the sort of manhood upon which all men rely in moments of doubt or danger. Yet he gives you no process of reasoning — he has no word save that which commands obedience, — he neither storms, implores, nor threatens — he has no books, — he deals in no declamation. He is the ideal of an abstract but innate power, which we acknowledge and perhaps fear, but cannot fathom. All is hidden within himself, and, except when at work, he is nothing — he might as well be stone. Yet, around him, — such a man — a wonderful interest gathers like a halo — bright and inscrutable, — which fills us with equal curiosity and reverence. With him, a man of whom we know nothing, — whom we see now for the first time, — whom we may never see again, — whom we cannot love — whom we should never seek; and with his ship, — timbers, tackle, ropes, spars and cordage, — a frail fabric, such as goes to and fro along our shores, in our daily sight, without awakening a single thought or feeling; — with ship and man we grow fascinated beyond all measure of ordinary attraction. In his hands the ship becomes a being, instinct with life, beauty, sentiment — in danger, and to be saved; — and our interest in her fate, grows from our anxiety to behold the issue, in which human skill, courage and ingenuity, are to contend with storm and sea, rocks and tempest — as it were, man against omnipotence. Our interest springs from our curiosity rather than from our affections. We do not care a straw for the inmates of the vessel. They are very ordinary persons, that one man excepted — and *he* will not suffer us to love him. But *manhood*, true manhood, is a sight, always, of wondrous beauty and magnificence. The courage that looks steadily on the danger, however terrible; the composure that never swerves from its centre under the pressure of unexpected misfortune; — the knowledge that can properly apply its strength, and the adroitness and energy, which, feeling the force of a manly will, flies to their task, in instant and hearty obedience; — these form a picture of singular beauty, and must always rivet the admiration of the spectator. We regard Mr. Cooper's "Pilot" — breasting the storm, tried by, and finally baffling all its powers, as the Prometheus in action — inflexible, ready to endure, — isolated, but still human in a fond loyalty to all the great hopes and interests of humanity.

Hawkeye, the land sailor of Mr. Cooper, is, with certain suitable modifications, the same personage. We see and admire, in him, the qualities of hardihood and endurance, coolness, readiness of resource, keen, clear sighted observation, just reflection, and a sincere, direct, honest heart. He is more human than the other, since, naturally of gentler temperament, the life-conflict has not left upon his mind so many traces of its volcanic fires. He has had more patience, been more easily persuaded; has endured with less struggle if not more fortitude, and, in his greater pliancy, has escaped the greater force of the tempest. But he is, in all substantial respects, the same personage, and inspires us with like feelings. In the hour of danger, — at midnight, — in the green camp of the hunter, — trembling women, timid men, and weeping children, grouped together in doubt, — all eyes turn to him, as, on the sea, in storm, all eyes address themselves to the "Pilot." If any one can save them he is the man. Meanwhile, the shouts of savages are heard on every side, — the fearful whoop of slaughter; — as, on the sea, the wind howls through the ship's cordage, and the storm shrieks a requiem, in anticipation of ultimate triumph, around the shivering inmates. It is only upon true manhood that man can rely, and these are genuine men — not blocks, not feathers — neither dull, nor light of brain, — neither the stubbornly stupid, nor the frothily shallow. Now, as nothing in nature is more noble than a noble-minded, whole-souled man, — however ignorant, however poor, however deficient in imposing costume or imposing person, — so nothing, in nature, is better calculated to win the homage and command the obedience of men, than the presence of such a person in their moments of doubt and danger. It is inevitable, most usually, that such a man will save them, if they are to be saved by human agency. To Mr. Cooper we owe several specimens of this sort of moral manhood. It does not qualify our obligation to him, that they have their little defects, — that he has sometimes failed to hit the true line that divides the simplicity of nature, from the puerility of ignorance or childhood. His pictures are as perfect, of their kind, as the artist of fiction has ever given us. We say this after due reflection.

The Sea and American Forest Tales of Mr. Cooper, were at length superseded, when this gentleman visited Europe, by others of a very different class. Travelling on the continent, with objects of interest and novelty continually before his eyes, it was very natural that he should desire to try his hand at objects of foreign mould and material. The institutions of Europe, where they differed from our own, were also subjects provoking curiosity and calling for examination. These might be discussed in story; — the old traditions and institutions of a country naturally go together, either in connexion or contrast; — and the genius of our countryman conceived the novel idea of so framing his narrative, as to make it illustrate the radical differences, in operation and effect, of the policy of the new world, in opposition to that of the old. There was yet another reason for this change of scene and material. Mr. Cooper entertained a notion, expressed in some one or more of his prefaces, that the literary material of his own country was too limited and too deficient in variety, to admit of frequent employment. He thought it too easily exhausted, and though he did not say so, it was very evident, at that time, that he thought he himself had already exhausted it. We need scarcely say that we think all this a very great error. In Mr. Cooper's

hands, no doubt, there would be a want of variety; not because of any deficiency in the material, but, simply, because
the mind of Mr. Cooper is limited in its grasp. It is too individual in its aims and agencies, — does not often vary, but
rather multiplies the same forms, characters, images and objects, through different media — now enlarging and now de-
pressing them — now throwing them into greater shadow, and
now bringing them out into stronger light — seldom entirely
discarding them for others, and we should think not easily
capable of doing so. His characters are uniformly the same,
his incidents are seldom varied; — the whole change which he
effects in his story, consists in new combinations of the same
circumstances, heightened, now and then, by auxiliary events,
which are seldom of much additional importance. In Indian
life and sailor life, he was almost uniformly successful — for
the simple reason, that such stories called simply for the display of individual character. They enabled him to devote his
genius, as would be always the desire of his mind, to a single
object. He took a single captive, after the manner of Sterne,
and drew from him, whether in success or suffering, the whole
interest of his story. Whenever it became necessary to deal
with groups, as in Lionel Lincoln, he failed. To manage the
progress of one leading personage, and to concentrate in his
portraiture his whole powers, has been the invariable secret
of Mr. Cooper's success. We very soon lose all interest in his
subordinates. Take away from his stories one or two of the
personages, and the rest are the merest puppets. The Spy contained the best specimens of his grouping, but a large portion
of it depended entirely on Harvey Birch, and, to so great a
degree was this disparity carried, in the use of his dramatis
personæ, that, in some of the scenes between the Spy and
Henry Wharton, the latter almost sinks into contempt, in consequence of his strange feebleness or deficiencies of character.
Mr. Cooper possesses some of the mental and physical char-

acteristics of Lord Byron, in similar degree. He is equally a person of strong will, great impetuosity of character, and intense self-esteem. Such persons inevitably concentrate themselves upon a few objects of interest; and to these they devote themselves with a gush of enthusiasm, which, to minds of less *one-sidedness,* is either amusing or astonishing. So in their social characteristics, — so in their loves and hates, — the one object of regard, for the time being, driving out of sight every other. This is caused by a peculiar organization. It is the preponderance of blood, which, not preventing or baffling the mind, yet impels its exercise in one direction, and confers upon it a marvelous strength in doing so. Such writers — and Milton partook of this — and hence his tragedy of Paradise Lost became a poem — and hence his dramas are all monologues — such writers throw their whole souls into one or more characters, and make all the rest subordinate. Such was particularly the case with Lord Byron. His Harold and Giaour, and Lara, and Manfred, and Selim, are all, in greater or less degree, modifications of the same character. His Sardanapalus and Juan,[8] are the same persons also, though in a rather better humour, possibly, from the better digestion of the author at the time of writing. It would not be difficult to trace Mr. Cooper's one ideal through all his novels. Even in the Bravo,[9] one of his European works, we find the Pilot and Natty Bumppo, where we should least look for them, in the person of Jacopo, the assassin of Venice.

The writer of European romance, unquestionably, possesses greater resources in history than he who confines himself to what is purely American. Time, which hallows all that he touches, had there laid away precious stores for centuries,

[8] Harold is the protagonist of Byron's *Childe Harold's Pilgrimage;* Giaour of his *The Giaour;* Lara of his *Lara;* Manfred of his *Manfred;* Selim of his *Bride of Abydos;* Sardanapalus of his *Sardanapalus;* and Juan of his *Don Juan.*

[9] *The Bravo,* published 1831.

long before the new world was opened to the eye of European day. The antiquities of the old world are so many treasures of fiction, to attain which, the critic of the American story, must task his invention. But this privilege is left him — this cannot be denied; and, possessed of the requisite resources of imagination, he needs but a slender skein of raw material — a solitary item — a fragmentary fact — a word — an action, — and his mind instantly conceives the plan and purpose, out of which he fabricates the divine, and most enduring forms of art.

Persuaded of the inadequacy of native resource, — struck with the novelty of European customs and superstitions, — and, most probably, anxious to measure lances, on their own ground, with the great masters of the art in Europe, Mr. Cooper followed up his American stories, with a series which were wholly foreign. The first and best of these was the Bravo. This was succeeded by the Heidenmauer, the Headsman, &c.[10] It is doubtful whether these works maintained the reputation of Mr. Cooper abroad. They certainly failed to do so at home. Yet they were not failures. They contained many beautiful scenes, — some fine moral and dramatic pictures — occasionally a touching, and sometimes, a thrilling incident, managed with great art, and of excelling beauty — such, for example, as was the murder of the Fisherman by the Venetian Police on the lagune at midnight, contained in the Romance of the Bravo. In some respects these works were an improvement on the American. Their style was better, the plots more intricate, and, though still inartistical, showed more painstaking and better management. Their stories, however — overlaid with discussion and remarks on the effect of laws and institutions upon countries, men and manners — were inferior in interest — there was less felicitous display of scenery, and, as the author was less confident of his knowledge, much of the de-

[10] *The Heidenmauer*, published 1832; *The Headsman*, 1833.

scription was vague, and the characters, framed under hurried glimpses and imperfect observation, were necessarily formal and frigid, wanting in earnestness and life, slow in action, and feeble in will and purpose.

To these succeeded a satirical work entitled the Monikins, which was followed by a "Letter to his Countrymen." [11] These performances, which are among the least popular of the numerous writings of our author, are among those which have contributed in latter days to lessen his popularity and subtract, whether justly or not, from his well earned claims to pre-eminence, as among the first writers of his age. For the proper understanding of Mr. C.'s position we must rise to a consideration of other subjects.

Mr. Cooper is a man, as we have already indicated, very much given to intensify every subject which affects his mind; — a man of that earnest, and not easily satisfied temper, who resolutely perseveres in what he undertakes, and in the prosecution of inquiry or argument, is very apt to probe a matter to the bottom, without giving much heed to the sensibility he wounds. Such men are necessary in every age for the progress of truth, and they incur always the penalties of the reformer. If not crucified or stoned, they are pelted by missiles of one sort or another, the principal of which, in our day, are defamation and slander. In Europe, Mr. Cooper was soon made aware of the humble, and even contemptuous estimate, which was every where put upon the American character. We, at home, urged by our own vanities, and miserably bemocked by the spurious flatteries of false prophets, — school-boy orators and selfish demagogues, — are really of opinion that we not only are, but are universally regarded as, one of the greatest people on the face of the earth. Of this folly and falsehood, Mr. Cooper undertakes to disabuse us. He discovered, very

[11] *The Monikins*, published 1835; *A Letter to His Countrymen*, 1834. Simms again errs in his chronology of Cooper's works.

soon after being in Europe, that we were thought a very small people. Our national and narrow economy seldom permitted any proper displays abroad of our national power, and such as were made were supposed to be rather discreditable than otherwise. The people of the Continent knew us chiefly by British opinions, which were, usually, not merely unfavourable, but scornful in the last degree. This opinion found its expression in a thousand ways. It was the habitual language of the Englishman when the name of American was spoken; and Mr. Cooper records it as a fact, known to himself as to every body that ever travelled on the Continent, that nothing was more common than the practice of the British traveller, to write, on the books kept at the public houses in the chief cities, the most contemptuous comments, on himself and country, in connection with the recorded name of every American. The people of the Continent could easily believe the propriety and justice of this scorn; for, as the Englishman himself was odious among them, by reason of his bad manners, and as they just knew enough of our history to know that we are sprung from the same stocks with him, it was not difficult to arrive at the conclusion, that, what he himself said of his descendant was likely to be true enough. There were other reasons why they should be easy of faith on this subject. Certain young Americans had been behaving badly among them; thrusting themselves by various arts upon society; begging and borrowing money, and indulging in other practices, scarcely less dishonourable, which naturally cast a stigma upon the nation with which they were identified. Mr. Cooper, a proud man, felt this condition of things like a pang: — an impetuous man, he undertook, in some measure, to correct them. He spoke out his defiance to the English, by whom his nation was slandered; and freely denounced the spurious Americans, by whom the country was disgraced. After this, it did not need that he should publish satirical books in order to make enemies

and meet denunciation. His hostility to the English secured it
to him in sufficient abundance from the British press; and his
unsparing reproof of the young Americans, provoking not
only their anger, but that of their friends, was quite enough to
engage against him the active hostility of numberless enemies
among the newspapers, and even the literary journals, in this
country. Our readers need not be told, that, in such a torrent
of news and literary papers (so called) with which the American world is flooded, it is not possible for many among them
to possess a tone or character of their own. In opinion, as in
action, a few lead the way and the rest follow. It was enough
that the British press denounced Mr. Cooper, for the American press, very generally, to denounce him likewise. It would
be a day of independence, truly, when we should throw off
our servile faith in the justice of British judgment, and the superiority of British opinion. To this, the virulence of personal
and party antipathy gave additional tongues, and the consequence was, that, while Mr. Cooper was most busy in asserting our character and defending our institutions abroad, the
press at home was equally busy in denouncing him for his
pains.

It might have been an easy part for an ordinary American
writer to have played in Great Britain. It is so still. You have
but to frame your books so as to flatter English nobility —
conciliate their prejudices, — show the most habitual deference for their preposterous claims to controlling dignity —
studiously forbear all freedom of opinion — all independence
of thought — and let them see that you value a breakfast with
Mr. Rogers,[12] as a matter of too serious importance to be fore-
gone for the pitiful object of proving that you are at once a
man and an American. If you can wholly suppress the latter

---

[12] Samuel Rogers (1763–1855), an English poet, was the virtual literary
dictator of England during the first half of the nineteenth century. His house
was considered the literary center of London.

fact, it is all the better for you — for your success, at least, in getting your breakfast with Rogers or Christopher North,[13] and partaking of the splendid enjoyments of Almacks,[14] under the auspices of Lady Jersey.

Mr. Cooper was not the man for this. He was not the man to make improper and unbecoming concessions, either on his own part, or on the part of his country. His nature led him to defiance, to resistance, to the unmeasured language of his resentment. We do not say that he was altogether wise in this. It is one thing to submit to indignity — it is another to be forever on the look-out, as if expecting to meet it. We are not so sure that Mr. Cooper was not wrong sometimes in his impetuosity — in his violence of tone and manner. There are some things in his deportment, as shown in his own travels, which we are constrained to disapprove and censure; and we are apprehensive that he sometimes mistook the burly defiance of the backwoodsman for the calm, manly tone of gentlemanly independence. This charge has been made against him. We do not make it. We are afraid, however, that the inference may be drawn fairly from some passages of his own writings, in his book of travels in England. His game, while in that country, for the proper defence of his own, was to " carry the war into Africa." To retort upon them their own charges, — to show them the mirror for self-reflection, — and to prove that they, too, were made of penetrable stuff. Mr. Cooper, of all our literary men abroad, seems to have been almost the only one who did not sink his Americanism — who strove to maintain it, and employed his cudgel, whenever his country was defamed, with the able hand and the hearty good-will and courage of a sailor. Whatever his errors may have been, they

[13] "Christopher North" was the pseudonym of John Wilson (1785–1854), one of the principal contributors to *Blackwood's Magazine*.

[14] Almack's, famous assembly rooms in King Street, St. James, London, was popular in the first half of the nineteenth century for gatherings and balls.

are more than redeemed in our eyes by his sturdy, uncompromising attachment to his country. And who can prescribe to the wronged and the indignant, what shall be the measure of his anger? — who shall say, in such and such terms only shall you speak out your feelings? It is for the greatly injured to determine for themselves what shall be their measure of redress. At all events, it was the unkindest fortune, that, while Mr. Cooper was thus doing battle for his countrymen, abroad, — whatever may have been the propriety of his course, — he should not only not find sympathy at home, but, on the contrary, rebuke. At that time, several of our newspapers were either wholly, or in part, conducted by foreigners. These naturally had sympathies only with the countries from which they came. They naturally watched the progress of the foreign controversy, and took sides with their own countrymen. Communications from abroad appeared in our literary and other journals, furnishing accounts of the affair, as may be supposed, hostile to Mr. Cooper. Among a class of our literary papers, such communications were particularly acceptable. No matter whom they disparaged, in what degree of defamation — no matter what prurient displays of vice were made, — what morals suffered here, or what character was defamed or slandered in Europe. It was taken for granted — and was, indeed, a truth too little to be questioned — that there was a morbid hungering, on the part of a large class of American pretenders, to be duly apprized of the doings abroad, particularly of the excesses of the English fashionable world; and some of the most atrocious revelations, fatal to female character, and garnished with the most brutal details of vice, were made by anonymous foreign correspondents, in publicaions which were especially addressed to American ladies. With foreign editors and foreign correspondents, each having, it would seem, *carte blanche*, Mr. Cooper, like every other subject of notoriety or distinction, had the usual risk of defamation to encounter. To these, in his case, is to be added the hostility of party, which he had provoked by an imprudent pamphlet, the " Letter to his Countrymen." This performance took the republican or democratic side with the Jackson dynasty, at the time of its fierce conflict with the old United States Bank. It was not wanting in ability. Some portions of the writer's argument were new and ingenious, and much of it was interesting. But the performance, as a whole, was in bad taste. It lacked congruity. It mixed up various matters of examination and complaint, — an olla podrida of literary, personal and political grievance; which, however well enough discussed, if separate, were yet oddly put together, in such a manner as to impair the value and the force of all. The superior egotism of one which pervaded it, was not its least misfortune and defect. This brought into the field a new and more bitter host of enemies — unscrupulous as the first, and with interests more actively involved in the pressing concerns of party, — such as never suffer any restraints of justice or veneration to impede them in their utterance. Nobody thought much of combating Mr. Cooper's opinions, but all seemed at once impressed with the impertinence of a literary man presuming to entertain a political opinion at all. Even those who concurred with the views of Mr. Cooper, seemed equally to concur with his assailants, in the absurd notion that his literary pursuits effectually excluded him from any right to give them utterance. Of his prudence in doing so, as a selfish man, thinking only of the success of his forthcoming publication, we, of course, offer no opinion. Enough, in this place, to add, that it is to be regretted, not that our literary men do not more frequently engage in politics, but that our politicians are not more generally literary men — at all events, not so very illiterate. Some increase of political decency might be the fruit of their improvement in this respect.

The warfare waged against Mr. Cooper was neither just

nor generous. Envy loves always a shining mark. Dulness hates
distinction. He had offended party, which is the most brutal
of all assailants — a gross, blind savage, equally curbless, piti-
less and conscienceless. He had offended some small Americans abroad, who were eager, under the cover of patriotism,
or any other cover, to revenge their petty personal grievances.
Besides, he had reached that eminence, which, making his
name a familiar and accepted word, was the sufficient reason
with the envious and the mean for passing upon him the sentence of ostracism. He must be voted into banishment. This,
perhaps, is the ordinary penalty of distinction. It is the fate
of all superiority. The lot of genius is most commonly isolation. It is not a charge which can be peculiarly addressed to
the American people, that they leave their own prophets to
disesteem. But Mr. Cooper, lacking the humility of the
prophet, was necessarily exposed to that greater odium with
which injustice resents every effort to disparage or deny its
judgments. His egotism of character left him particularly exposed to the missiles of their ridicule. He had conceived the
notion that foreign governments were concerned and busy in
putting him down; and that, to this cause, he was indebted for
the daily assaults to which he was subjected. But for the intense self-esteem which distinguishes his mind, this notion
never would have troubled it. He would have known, in the
first place, that politicians generally have been of that mole-
breed, which knows nothing of the above-ground workings
of literature. They annex too little importance, for their own
and the good of the country, to the makers of books and ballads — though these build up and overturn empires. Motives
much more reasonable, and sufficiently numerous, were not
wanting for these attacks. We have, in part, already assigned
them. But malice, envy, vanity and party, are never in want
of motives for the destruction of those who stand in their sunshine, or obstruct their performances; and with their victim

pointed out, the "little dogs and all, Tray, Blanche and Sweetheart," were soon in full cry after their distinguished and common enemy. The little dogs of literature needed but to be set on. It was quite an event, calculated to raise them vastly in their own eyes and that of their neighbours, to be seen engaged in the noble business of worrying any more majestic form; and half the two-penny sheets, of dirty yellow, from Squam Beach to Little Harkaway Swamp, on the elbow of Oregon, were eager in squirting out their small supplies of storm, from the tubs in which they churned it, as the weekly periodical supply was demanded. The impatience of Mr. Cooper, which would not suffer him to wait, and his self-esteem, which would not suffer him to place a just estimate on his assailants, hurried him still farther into this unwise controversy. When we use the word controversy, we do not employ it in a very literal acceptation. He did not challenge them to, or meet them in, any direct discussion. But he put them into his books, and this was quite a compliment, which, however unintended by him, was very undeserved by them. Besides, of what avail to show up one of these creatures in his proper light, when the country is so full of them, that they are sufficiently numerous and strong to give one another support and countenance. This, by the way, is one of the greatest evils to which our American literature is exposed. The pretender-critics are so numerous and so noisy, that it is no wonder they succeed so frequently, and for so long a time, in imposing false standards upon the several circles which look to the current press for all the supplies of literary aliment which they crave. It is a question with many on which side to look for their authorities. With a poor people, now for the first time beginning to have a hankering after letters, nothing can be more natural than that they should turn to those who, while selling their wares at the most moderate price, are, at the same time, the most clamorous on the subject of their merits. Quack literature resorts to the same arts with quack medicine, and quacks of all sorts have been, from all times, the most pompous and presuming. They making up in mouthing what they lack in merit; in insolence what they lack in strength; and are hostile to the really honest and intellectual, in due degree with the consciousness of their own lamentable deficiencies. It did not diminish the rancour of this tribe, in regard to Mr. Cooper, that he singled out one of their number as a victim. His Mr. Editor Dodge,[15] making some small allowances for the usual exaggerations of satire, was a very just portrait. There are many such scattered broad-cast over our country — living on its vices — its gross appetites, its base passions, and numerous irregularities; and pandering to tastes and desires, which are equally shocking to manhood and morality. The prying presumption of this person; his utter want of principle; his arrogance at one moment, and sycophancy at another; his blind allegiance to majorities; and the ignorance which keeps equal pace with, and affords at all times the happiest commentary on, his pretension, — all these characteristics were well hit off, and happily illustrated, in the example selected by Mr. Cooper. This character, as a character, has been loudly denied *vraisemblance* by all those who must have felt its truth. It is an exaggeration, certainly, but in all substantial respects it is true. The exaggerations were only such as were necessary to raise the relief, and bring out the person into that pillory sort of prominence which was desirable for the purposes of satire. But the books in which this character was made to play so notorious a part, were unwise and improper books. In writing them, Mr. Cooper proved that he was angry — in publishing them, he proved that he was unjust. The satire which was deserved by his editor, and the sarcasm which was justly due to a particular set, or entire sets, in his

[15] Steadfast Dodge, a newspaper editor in *Homeward Bound,* is a bitingly satiric portrait.

own neighbourhood, was a slander upon the country at large. Mr. Cooper committed the precise error which is so much the error and offence of British travellers among us, that of confounding the commercial metropolis with the country. We protest, again and again, against the false assumption, that the city of New York is to be taken as a fair sample of the characteristics of the United States. Will Boston suffer the comparison, or Baltimore? Sure are we that there is nothing of the same local and moral influences predominating in Charleston and Savannah; and that the sturdy and simple agricultural population of our vast interior, — a sincere and manly people — generous and just — incapable of fraud and falsehood — ignorant of any of the arts by which these are made successful and maintained without discredit — that these should be supposed guilty of the rank vices and excesses, and miserable vanities, which lead to worse vices and excesses in city life, is beyond all doubt a calumny, and beyond all measure an injustice.[16] True it is, that, in the smaller cities, a class will be found always, who, ignorant of any other means of acquiring distinction, emulate the gaudy follies of the metropolis, — and seek by queer equipage and dress — by monstrous fashions, and affectations, which discredit decency and sense, — to draw upon themselves attention. But this notice is generally contempt. The great body of the people go on their way, and smile, if scorn will let them, at the miserable vanities which betray a man into a monster, — a god into the fashion and appearance of an ape. Such persons, in all the smaller communi-

[16] Simms is here stating the "agrarian" view, which has been standard with Southern writers since Jefferson and John Taylor of Caroline (1753–1824). Jefferson gave it perhaps its most emphatic statement when he wrote: "Those who labour in the earth are the chosen people of God, if ever he had a chosen people, whose breasts he has made his pecular deposit for substantial and genuine virtue. . . . let our workshops remain in Europe. It is better to carry provisions and materials to workmen there, than bring them to the provisions and materials, and with them their manners and principles," in *Notes on the State of Virginia* (Chapel Hill, 1955), p. 165.

ties, are few in number, and totally without influence. They neither control in society, in morals or in politics, and live apart, keeping each other in heart and company, by that sympathy and support which they could never derive from any other quarter. Their insignificance should secure a community from any general sarcasm and discredit which their doings may have provoked.

It may be urged that Mr. Cooper had no design in "Home as Found," to make his satire general, — that his home, as found, was meant to be the small province in which his domestic gods were set up; and that his satire was purely local, instead of general. Unhappily, then, he has so managed his work, that his censure sweeps every thing before it. This is the great danger in the preparation of such works. It is difficult to say where the line is to be drawn which limits the application of the satire. One is scarcely prepared, in the first place, to believe that a man of genius and judgment is willing to expend so much thunder on so diminutive an object. The foreigner certainly does not believe it; and for us at home, we are apprehensive that, in the hurry of Mr. Cooper's indignation, and the warmth of his anger, he confounded with his particular enemies the whole American people, and made common war against them. It is in the nature of such a mind as Mr. Cooper's to do heartily, as well as hurriedly, whatever he undertakes. He is apt to generalize too much from small beginnings. His "Traveling Bachelor" was full of proofs to this effect. That was published as "Notions of the Americans." [17] It was very evident that the work should have been called, "Notions of the New Yorkers and New Englanders." It showed very little acquaintance with the South and West. "Homeward Bound" and "Home as Found," were no doubt true to a certain extent. We do not speak of them now as sto-

[17] *Notions of the Americans: Picked up by a Travelling Bachelor*, published 1828.

ries. We presume the author never considered them as such. They were truthful, so far as the satire was confined to certain classes and circles. They were false, so far as they were made to apply to the characteristics of the American people. It was Mr. Cooper's error to have written these books in a moment of great personal feeling — when the freshness of provocation was stirring in his mind, —. when, suffering from injustice, his anger was naturally without measure. There was unquestionably much that deserved the keenest satire and the severest censure. The chief cities were diseased to an enormous extent. Their evil influences were spreading to the country. The rankness of trade and speculation had overrun the land; its vices were fast usurping the place of virtues — fraud was a bold politician, prescribing laws for the people, and matters for government, as if the propriety of his existence were no longer matter of dispute; — bankruptcy was the most profitable of all pursuits — labour was every where driven out of sight as too base for toleration; and sleight-of-hand was the great principle which determined the degrees of eminence and the rewards of service. The most dextrous was the best man, and his profits were assigned accordingly. Verily, a censor was needed; a terrible censor, dreadful in rebuke, armed with a flail of thunder, for the work of retribution. It was not in the power of an ordinary satirist to do this work. Long impunity, and constantly increasing numbers, had made the criminals bold and reckless. They laughed at ordinary reproof, they mocked at wisdom, and despised censure. Mr. Cooper would have written in vain, as others did, but that providence works out the good of man by laws, which, however natural, are not so obvious to him in the blindness of his passion, or the greedy hurry of his avarice. A terrible punishment was preparing for the excesses of our people, — unhappily, a fate which has made the innocent pay the debts of the guilty, — which has swept all with a common besom. The laws of industry, common sense and common honesty, are not to be long outraged with impunity; and the recoil came and the retribution, — and we are — what need not be said — what we are now, and — so far as mere social prosperity is concerned — what, it is feared, we must very long remain.[18] In morals, we trust there is improvement. God works out his purposes to this end, and he does not often work in vain. We are pleased to think, and somewhat proud to say, that, touched by adversity, scourged by the just judgments of Heaven, we are an improving people. Vice is less audacious, — pride less boastful, — labour more honourable, — truth better esteemed, if not yet wholly triumphant.

Mr. Cooper committed two errors when he wrote his satires — the one much more decided than the other. He wrote them at the wrong time, and he wrote them in the wrong spirit. Vanity listens to no homily in the full sunshine of its day. Pride hears no warning, when the homage of vulgar admiration fills its ears. Trade hearkens to no admonitions of prudence, or of principle, in the full tide of a seemingly successful speculation. Mr. Cooper wrote the books which proved so offensive to the American people, at a time when an angel from heaven would have spoken to them in vain, — when, besotted with the boldest dreams of fortune that ever diseased the imagination of avarice, they seemed to have lost the usual faculties of thought, prudence and observation — when, they appeared to think they had but to will, and *presto*, they won — to lift a finger, and, as at the wand of a magician, the waters flowed with sparkling treasures, and the sands glittered with the precious metal. The Spaniards in Peru or Mexico were never half so bedevilled with their own imaginings, as were the people of our trading cities within our recent remem-

[18] A reference to the financial Panic of 1837, which continued until 1842–1843 and whose effects persisted until 1848.

brance. Our merchants assumed the port of princes, and the Merchant-Princes of the Adriatic never loomed out with a more dazzling and determined ostentation.

Was it likely, that, swollen with pride, gloating over their imaginary treasures, and swaggering with the affectations of fashion, borrowed from the old fools — and young ones — of older countries, they should listen to any censor, receive any counsel, tolerate with patience any rebuke? The attempt of Mr. Cooper was unseasonable, and only vexed them. They wished praise only, — nothing more, — praise from any quarter, — they had stomachs for no stronger aliment. They had flattered the foreigner to secure this praise. They had run with headlong speed to hail the advent of English Lord and English Lady, — had spread their dinner cloths, and thrown wide their saloons and ball-rooms and theatres — asking only for praise. That their own countrymen should withold the precious condiment — should, like the foreigner, find fault only — was an offence not to be forgiven. Nay, there was some reason for their anger. The censure of Mr. Cooper was not expressed in the right spirit. The tone of "Homeward Bound," and "Home as Found," was bad. It expressed the language of querulousness and distaste, if not disgust. It was written less in sorrow than in anger, as if the writer took a malicious delight in singling out the sore spots, which it had been the better purpose of the patriot to hide if he could not heal. He showed himself more disposed to revenge his own hurts and injuries than to amend the faults of his countrymen. Besides, as we have already said, he was unjust because too sweeping in his condemnation. This was the consequence of writing in his anger. Passion has no powers of discrimination, and the wilful mind will exercise none. But if Mr. Cooper's censure had been just in all respects, and in its entire application, it must have failed of any good result at the time of its utterance. It was unseasonable, and therefore impolitic and unwise.

We give Mr. Cooper credit for good motives in spite of this imprudence. We regard the promptings as patriotic which drove him to his task. These, no doubt, were farther stimulated by his personal feelings. But this does not alter the case. In the instance of the sanguine temperament, the personal man always enters actively into the principles. The heart co-operates with the head, the blood impels the intellect, and hence the rare energy with which such persons commence and carry on their works. The patriotism of Mr. Cooper has always been a striking trait in this character and writings. It is conspicuous in all his performances. How fondly he dwells, even in his foreign books, while discussing their institutions, on the superiority of our own. How ready he is to do battle in their behalf. This very readiness was one of the first occasions of offence whch he gave to those cold-blooded Americans, who were content to truckle abroad for their porridge, silent when their nation was openly scorned, and snatching their miserable pittance of bread and society from the very hands that were lifted in reprobation of their country. As we have already said, the Americanism of Mr. Cooper would move us to forgive him all his faults, were they twice as many. That he should come home to censure ours, was equally the proof, though an unwise one, of his honest and fearless patriotism.

Of this patriotism he has given a noble instance in his hearty and well-told history of our navy.[19] In this book he has shown himself an equally good critic and historian. We commend him to the similar duty of preparing a select biography of our noblest naval commanders. The subject is worthy of his pen, and can no where find a better biographer. Our limits do not suffer us to remark upon his several works of foreign travel, and those tales which have succeeded them. The former laboured under the misfortune of being published long after

[19] *The History of the Navy of the United States of America*, published 1839.

the period when they were written, — thus, losing in their freshness, and being necessarily imperfect with regard to the existing facts, — speaking for a past and not a present time. Of the novels, "Mercedes of Castile" and the "Path-Finder," [20] we need only say that our general remarks on the structure of Mr. Cooper's former stories, will equally apply to them. Of the "Two Admirals," we have already expressed all the opinion necessary for the reader's judgment. Neither of these works do we regard as comparable to his "Spy," "Pilot," "Mohicans," and "Pioneers." Still they are all interesting, — full of the picturesque, full of sense, and containing matters for reflection, which deserve, and will reward, the attention of any reader. We see with satisfaction that we are soon to have another story from his pen. [21] We are glad of this for two reasons. We always read his books with great pleasure; and we rejoice at this annunciation, as it affords another proof that the terms of relation between this favourite author and his countrymen, are becoming every day more and more grateful to the amenities, equally of patriotism and letters.

[20] *Mercedes of Castile*, published 1840; *The Pathfinder*, 1840.

[21] Probably *The Deerslayer*, which had been published in 1841 but which Simms apparently had not seen, although the reference could be to *Wyandotté* or *Ned Myers*, both published in 1843.

THE JOHN HARVARD LIBRARY

*The intent of
Waldron Phoenix Belknap, Jr.,
as expressed in an early will, was for
Harvard College to use the income from a
permanent trust fund he set up, for "editing and
publishing rare, inaccessible, or hitherto unpublished
source material of interest in connection with the
history, literature, art (including minor and useful
art), commerce, customs, and manners or way of
life of the Colonial and Federal Periods of the United
States . . . In all cases the emphasis shall be on the
presentation of the basic material." A later testament
broadened this statement, but Mr. Belknap's interests remained constant until his death.*

*In linking the name of the first benefactor of
Harvard College with the purpose of this later,
generous-minded believer in American culture the
John Harvard Library seeks to emphasize the importance of Mr. Belknap's purpose. The John Harvard
Library of the Belknap Press of Harvard University
Press exists to make books and documents
about the American past more readily
available to scholars and the
general reader.*